Kunal Books Publishers & Distributors
4596/1A, First Floor,
11, Daryaganj, Delhi-110 002
Ph. 011-30125412
Email: kunalbooks@gmail.com
Email: kunalbooks@yahoo.co.in

Gandhi-Aurobindo and Radhakrishnan on Bhagavadgita

Edition 2009
ISBN : 978-81-907129-0-3

Printed At

Deepak Offset Press, New Delhi

DEDICATED TO OUR PARENTS

Raghunath & Jyotirmayee Pani
Kailash Chandra & Umadevi Mishra
Basudev & Naliniprava Satpathy

Authors

FOREWORD

Working without attachment to any gainful results and to surrender our actions to the Almighty Divine seems to be the main essence of 'Bhagavadgita' and our Hindu philosophy. It has inspired many including great saints and scholars to draw an effective sustenance from this both in India and abroad. Indeed the 'Bhagavadgita' emits the nectar of all Upanishads and Vedic literature. May I describe 'Bhagavadgita' as the most refined poetic representation of the facts and meaning of Hindu view and way of life.

This book to my mind is a humble refreshing addition to the vast literature already in store on the sacred book of 'Bhagavadgita'. Attempt has been made to analyse the observations, interpretations, conclusion and applicability of 'Bhagavadgita' to the life as a whole as realized by Gandhi ji, Sri Aurobindo and Dr. Radhakrishnan. All three of them though belonging to philosophy and thinking of 20th century, sharing a common milieu yet with different upbringing and thought process had pursued diverse careers. The study has been made from an intellectual point of view free from hagiographic bias. The work is comparative in nature and explains to a great extent why these three great thinkers drew different conclusions from 'Bhagavadgita'.

Metaphysical diversions in interpretation by all these three great men converge in the unit of one practical message. The authors have followed a common format of analysing their observations and conclusions. I hope the book shall be very interesting to go through and may prove as a must reading to all those interested to know about 20th century Indian thinking, the Hindu view of life and Bhagavadgita's interpretation by Gandhi ji, Sri Aurobindo and Dr. Radhakrishnan.

The main author–Prof. Susmit Pani has been a Professor of History at Utkal University. His Ph.D research thesis was on Shri Aurobindo's thoughts as his main interest. So far he has produced many Ph.Ds / D.Lits and another 10 are presently working under his supervision. Prof. Pani has already produced other reference books on Gandhi and Aurobindo. I complement Professor Pani and the other two joint authors of this book which I believe shall be an important addition to the classical literature.

August 14, 2008

Dr. HARI GAUTAM
MS FRCS (EDIN) FRCS (ENG) FAMS
FACS FICS FIACS DSc (HON CAUSA)
CHANCELLOR
KIIT University, Bhubaneswar
Former - Chairman, University Grants Commission
Former - Vice Chancellor, Banaras Hindu University
Former - Vice Chancellor, King George's Medical University
Former - President, National Academy of Medical Sciences
Former - Chairman, Board of Governors, National Institute of Technology
Former – Principal/Dean/Professor of Medical Colleges, Agra/Kanpur
Recipient – Dr. B. C. Roy National Award as an - Eminent Medical Man

09937080615
0674-2725615

PREFACE

Thought ought to be an important aspect of historical study as is material culture. Students of history need not always leave out the history of thought to the students of philosophy for, indeed, in the hands of the former history of thought, can take a more synthetic shape. Keeping this in view, an humble attempt is made in the foregoing pages to study the treatment of the *Bhagavadgita* (commonly known as the *Gita*) in its historical perspective with special reference to Sri Aurobindo, Mahatma Gandhi and Radhakrishnan.

The *Bhagavadgita* is easily the best representative of Indian philosophic and religious textual heritage. It is a part of the *Mahabharata*, one of the two great epics of India and is more a *smrti* if not a *srti*. It analyses the six systems of Indian philosophy and is simultaneously considered to be the most practical guide for any one who is interested in leading a spiritual life. In volume, in style and in presentation, it is definitely more acceptable and intelligible to a vast range of readers than the *Vedas* and the *Upanishads*. As such it has caught the attention and imagination of a number of Indian thinkers through her long cultural history spread over centuries. The *Bhagavadgita* asserts in its own words to be the nectar of all the essentials of the *Upanishads*, that is sweetly presented by Krishna, the milker, to Arjuna, the calf. It is poetical in form and is of the nature of a dialogue, which possibly is the best combination for the presentation of the best metaphysics. Of the numerous commentaries on the *Bhagavadgita*, those of Vrittikara, Samkara, Ramanuja, Madhva, Nimbarka, Vallabha, Jnaneswar and the like, stand in bright prominence. All these belong to ancient and medieval period. In modern times great thinkers like Swami Vivekananda, Tilak, Gandhi, Sri Aurobindo, Radhakrishnan and others took it as a sacred duty to give their commentaries on the *Bhagavadgita*. Besides these stalwarts, numerous translations and commentaries in different regional languages have been successfully attempted upon with the growth and development of vernacular literature in the country. In the era of the post-independent India the *Bhagavadgita* still continues to attract the zeal of versatile commentators like Swami Sivananda, Swami Chidabhavananda, Bhakti Vedanta Prabhupada and others, to shower on the masses its nectar like instructions to help them to lead a pious and healthy life. In view of this overbearing importance of the text an attempt is here made to study its interpretation in the first half of the twentieth century through representative thinkers like Sri Aurobindo, Mahatma Gandhi and Sarvepalli Radhakrishnan.

The first half of the twentieth century not only witnessed the birth pangs of a free India but also her flowery out pouring on the eve of the renaissance. Sri Aurobindo, Gandhi and Radhakrishnan immensely contributed towards the enrichment of Indian thinking, each playing an equally vital role in her political history and nationalistic upheaval. Though they have not exhausted the Indian scenario, and may not be the only best representatives of the age, yet they are the true stalwarts in their own rights and spheres of thought. In other words they have been chosen as representative thinkers for the present work. Sri Aurobindo, who in early phase of national movement associated himself with the extreme wing of Indian nationalism, is considered to be the most gifted Indian writer in English language. Both as a poet and an essayist he is credited to have penned a very comprehensive metaphysical treatise titled the *Life Divine*. Radhakrishnan was a scholar par excellence who attempted an encyclopedic history of Indian philosophy. He was equally well conversant with the metaphysics of the East and the West. He served as the Indian ambassador in the Soviet Union during a period when relationship between India and the Soviet Union with Nehru and Stalin respectively at their helm of affairs, stood critical. He rose to the office of the Vice-president and eventually to that of the President of India during a period equally critical marked by the Sino-Indian war and the transition of India from Nehruvian to Indira years. Mahatma Gandhi dominated the Indian political scenario for nearly four decades. Gandhi, a prolific writer, was essentially a politician and a public figure par-excellence. He led and shaped the destiny of the millions of Indians. His overwhelming role in India's freedom struggle rightly qualifies his inclusion in any study relating to the period.

As a background to the study of the representative thinkers, a general sketch of Indian philosophy and religion and a general introduction to the *Bhagavadgita* have been included in the study in its first two chapters. A conclusion on each thinker has also been attempted at the end of the chapter devoted to each. Thus, at the end only a general conclusion is being attempted. The work necessarily does not intend to be comparative in nature. The three thinkers were contemporaries to one another. They had different upbringing, different mental make-up, and had gone through different experiences. Even though they had independent standings as thinkers, yet they were not absolutely without meeting grounds. What is attempted here is a synthetic analysis of the treatment of the *Gita* by these three thinkers as representatives of the first half of the twentieth century.

While analysing the treatment of the *Gita* by these thinkers, the scholars have generally stuck to their respective English version inevitably used to sustain and substantiate their views and interpretations. The principal source of the present work is of course, books, texts, articles and the collection of speeches of the thinkers concerned.

Authors

ACKNOWLEDGEMENT

The authors would love to place on record their sincere thanks to all those whose help have shaped the work. Long discussion with Prof. J.K. Dash, Prof. K.C. Mishra and Sri Basudev Satpathy were enriching. The Sri Aurobindo Ashram Library, Pondichery provided rich sources and an excellent ambience. Shri B.K. Ray, Librarian, Aeronautics College, Sunabeda was extremely helpful for documentation. Mrs Kamala Devi and Mrs Rashmita Nayak of DDCE Library, Utkal University were equally helpful. Ms Mamata Singh and Mrs Laxmipriya Pani provided excellent secretarial assistance. Dr. Sarita Mishra and Sri Dhananjaya Rout have lovingly prepared the index. The proprietors and editorial team of Kunal Books have enthusiastically worked to bring out this book. All of them deserve our thanks and those whom we have not mentioned deserve even greater thanks.

Puja, Akash and Julu our children have lent their play hours when the work was in formative stage. We only hope that as young collegianers they find their sacrifice worthy and share their parent's love for the eternal India.

Authors

CONTENTS

CHAPTER – I

INDIAN PHILOSOPHY AND RELIGION – A GENERAL INTRODUCTION

A general introduction on Indian philosophy and religion forms an inevitable part of the background for the study of the *Bhagavadgita*. The spiritual, philosophical and religious heritage of India is considered to be the most important contribution of India to mankind and the world civilisation at large. It has attracted men of myriad hues including dispassionate, erudite and discerning scholars, traditional Sanskrit *pundits* and antiquarians, iconoclastic religious believers and astute academicians of numerous disciplines among others. What is attempted here is not an assimilation of all these, but is an endeavour in presenting the glimpses from the essentials of the spirit of India's philosophical and religious heritage. This would provide a larger canvas for placing the treatment of the *Bhagavadgita* by Sri Aurobindo, Gandhi and Radhakrishnan in a historical and metaphysical perspective.

Indian Philosophy :

The Indian word for philosophy is *darsana* meaning vision. A philosopher for the Indians is always a *drasta* or one with vision and realisation. Though Indian philosophy is as logical as the western traditions, yet the emphasis has been always laid on spirituality. Spiritualism has meant for the Indians a deeper understanding of the innermost essence of human life, Nature and cosmos. *Atmanam viddhih*, know thyself-sums up the law and the prophets of India. The spirit within is held to heism.

Indian philosophy has evolved very systematic theories of knowledge. It proceeds on the facts of experience as in the West. Logical reflection is also a necessary element of it. However, the Indian theories of knowledge go beyond physical and mental experiences and explore the regions beyond these. Psychological coherence has been emphasised over logical inconsistencies. The empirical and the reflective, the physical and the metaphysical are all synthesised in the Indian systems. The Indian philosophy places the intuition as its master and uses both proof and logic to propagate itself. The philosopher reveals the truth of life which is not a mere intellectual understanding but also a living vision. In this vision experience is reconciled with metaphysics. A philosopher is thus a seeker of truth.

Samkaracharya lays out four conditions for the students of philosophy; i) knowledge of the distinction between the eternal of action either in the present life or a future one , ii) subjugation of the desire for the fruits of action either in the present life or a future one, iii) a necessary change of heart with tranquility, self-restraint, renunciation, patience, peace of mind and faith as the ruling principles of life and iv) the desire for *mokshya* (release) from the cycles of ignorance.[1] Indian philosophy is also a series of continuous revelations. It is essentially esoteric, poetic, reflective and visionary.

Any survey of Indian philosophical system is bogged down with the problems of chronology and historicity of the various schools of thought. Radhkrishnan writes :

"No where is the difficulty of getting reliable historical evidence so extreme as in the case of Indian thought. The problem of determining the exact dates of early Indian systems is as fascinating as it is insoluble, and it has furnished a field for the wildest hypotheses, wonderful reconstruction, and bold romance. The fragmentary condition of the material from out of which history has to be reconstructed is another obstacle."[2]

Thus, it is very difficult to present a summary of the Indian philosophical systems in a historical order. A thematic arrangement of the Indian philosophical systems seems to be a better alternative.

Marx comes to a similar conclusion with a different explanation. He felt that the socio-economic conditions of India have remained unaltered since its ancient past and thus historical development of Indian philosophy is not discernable. "However changing the political aspect of India's past may appear, its social condition has remained unaltered since its remotest antiquity, until the first decennium of the 19th century."[3] "The structure of the economical elements of the society remains untouched by the storm clouds of the political sky."[4] It is very difficult to agree with the presupposition of Marx that the Indian economy and society remained static for so long a period in view of the ocean of historical research and literature which have appeared in the last century. The difficulty in tracing historical development of philosophy lies else where. The synthetic continuity of Indian philosophical thinking and system; and the overlapping of myth, history and philosophy in India appears to be a more rational explanation. There is a unity of essential questions and essential answers that the Indian philosophers have echoed over the centuries. This does not negate the innovativeness of interpretation, presentation and thinking of Indian philosophers. The present study of the *Bhagavadgita*, an ancient scripture as interpreted by the modern Indian thinkers focuses the innovativeness of contemporary interpretations. The appearance of a great variety of views and systems right from the ancient period makes India a country seething with philosophic speculations and this makes introduction of an absolutely new and original system almost impossible. This is also the root of tremendous reverence Indian philosophers have for the past. Another facet of Indian philosophical writing is the emergence of nationalistic trend in the last century. India rediscovered her past partly through the growth of western education. The western understanding of Indian philosophical heritage has a wide spectrum from unsympathetic external views to deep reverence for everything Indian and from Christian missionaries to the academicians. In reaction and response to the unsympathetic western understanding and in view of the nationalistic awakening, many not only strongly defended Indian philosophy but also held out its philosophical superiority as a compensation for their material and scientific backwardness. Some even created the pet theme of India's spiritual mission to counteract the 'white man's burden'.

There are two major views concerning the development of Indian philosophical system. One holds that the Indian philosophical system evolved through contradictions. The other holds that the changing times necessitated the evolutions of the same essentials with new emphasis, interpretation and styles of presentation. According to the former, the *Vedas* are essentially ritualistic with strong philosophical pronouncements and are essentially Brahminic in orientation. The Vedantic, Jaina and Buddhist philosophies arose in opposition to the Brahminic and ritualistic vedic system. They are reflective and logical, rather than symbolic and esoteric. The traditional six systems of Indian philosophy are extensions of vedantic repository. Samkara's revival of vedantic philosophy is explained as an opposition to the subsequent developments in Buddhism which had degenerated. The medieval *bhakti-cult* was an anti-philosophical and anti-ritual reaction. The *bhakti-cult* was also inspired partly by its contact with Islam. The 19th century renaissance and reformation is similarly explained as a product of the response to western contact. It is also an attempt to rid the Indian philosophical tradition of obnoxious faiths and practices, which do not stand upto the modern tests of the scientific age. They seem to seek new sanctifications from scientific explanations for their continuing ancient practices. The other view in contrast, holds that the essential Indian philosophy has evolved through these. The esoteric and poetic symbols of the Vedic age were expressed in logical statements in the *Upanishads*. In other words *Upanishads* are scholastic representations of the Vedic realisations. Buddhism and Jainism are not opposed to the early Vedic philosophies. They are only opposed to the ritualistic part of the Vedic culture, as much as the *Upanishads* were. The Epics and the *Puranas* represent the same truth through myths as necessary for the common folk. The *bhakti cult* caters to the need of a vast majority who need to identify themselves with particular deities and can attain *moksha* through devotion to a personal god. The 19th century renaissance and reformation are revival of the ancient essentials of Indian philosophy and involves the presentation of similar spiritual experiences in the western language and format. These two views, one of contradiction and the other of evolution are not mutually exclusive, for the Indian philosophy has a unique unity not withstanding various expressions. Before attempting to highlight the unique unity of Indian philosophical heritage, the various systems may briefly be introduced. As noted earlier instead of a historical analysis a thematic classification is adopted.

Traditionally Indian philosophy is classified into nine schools of thought. The conventional classification of these nine systems is made under two broader heads : (I) The Orthodox (*asthika*) and (II) The Heterodox (*nasthika*). Though Panini defined a *nasthika* as one who did not believe in the existence of the other world, hence the orthodox or the *asthika* for him was one who believed in the other world. At a later time *asthika* meant a believer in the *Veda* and a *nastika*, a vilifier of the *Veda*. Manu popularised the second concept.[5] However, philosophers have preferred the earlier meaning as described by Panini. At popular level today an *asthika* is considered to be a theist and the *nasthika* is an atheist. The three heterodox systems of Indian Philosophical heritage are : the materialistic concept called *Charvaka Lokayata,* and *Barhasaptya;* Buddhism and Jainism. Basic systems of the *asthika* group are the *purvamimansa, uttaramimansa, samkhya, yoga, nyaya* and *vaisheshika.*

The word *Charvaka* means a materialist. *Charvakas* hold that perception is only the valid source of knowledge. Thus, they accept only the knowledge of four *bhutas* (elements) like air, fire, water and earth. The individual is identified with the body and consciousness is considered to be a quality of a living body and a product of matter. The survival of man in any form after death is not acceptable to them. The existence of God is also a myth for them and the world is explained as an automatic condition of material elements but not as a creation of God. In view of this they advocated hedonism, and pleaded for the greatest enjoyment of the pleasures of life, *"Yavad jivet sukham jivet, rinam kritva ghritam pivet"*, (as long as you live, live happily you may borrow and eat purified butter) the popular and oft-quoted statement of *Charvakas* summarises their philosophy. *Lokayatikas* denied past and future births as there is no reality existing before birth or after death excepting four primary elements, and the mind is the product. Mind at death does not pass on to another body. Minds at different bodies are different. Consciousness of a body, the *Lokayatikas* believed, which has already perished can not be related to a new body which comes into being. Consciousness emerges from sensation and from knowledge, derived from and experiences. While for the Vedists consciousness is identical with the soul and is eternal, for the *Lokayatikas* the chain of consciousness is not an entity. *Lokayatikas* maintain that there is no soul apart from the body. They deny the theory of *Karma* and the existence of any mysterious universal agency like *deiva, adrstha or bhagya.* Religious rituals at best are a means to livelihood for men devoid of intellect.

The school of Brihaspati originally aimed at *vitanda* (destructive criticism). It simply tried to refute the views of the other schools without suggesting any positive theory to propound. Most of their views are derived from the *Vedas* only. Subsequently, it developed a more complete theory. They developed the doctrine of *syabhava* and maintained that effects are self existent and are produced neither by different things and causes nor by themselves. Further, they held that if something could not be found, it definitely did not exist. Similarly for them, pleasure and pain have no cause because they appear only at times. Many draw a parallel between the western concepts of materialism, skepticism and agnosticism with the *Charvaka, Lokayata* and *Barhasaptyas* schools of thought.

The Jaina faith developed from the prehistoric times through twenty-four *thirthamkaras* of whom Mahavira was the last and the most important. They reject the *Charvakas* view that perception is the only valid source of knowledge and do not rule out the possibility of obtaining correct knowledge through inference and testimony. The Jains admit inference and testimony in addition to perception, as valid sources of knowledge. Perception reveals the reality of material substance composed of four elements like air, water, fire and earth. They include also *kala* or time and *akasha* or space. They term these two as *dharma* and *adharma*. But these *bhutas* along with space and time are not all, for they admit the presence of soul in all living and non-living things. By removing *karma,* they hold that the soul can be freed from bondage and regain its natural perfection. They advocate *panchabrata* and *triratna* for removal of the bondage. *Panchabrata* includes abstinence from injury, falsehood, stealing and sensuality. The *triratna* includes right conduct, right knowledge and right faith. In its practical aspect Jainsm demands greater discipline and freedom from material world. Mahavira did not believe in any personal god nor in the God as the Creator, Protector and Destroyer of the cosmos. For him, the cosmos moves automatically without a *Brahman* or *atman* or God. The universe is governed by the universal law, self generating and mechanical. The universe for him is eternal and is divided into a number of cycles or periods of improvement and decline. He does not accept the catabolism of a universal disintegration. The universal law through which the world functions is explained as one of the interactions between the *jives* and the *ajivas* or the souls and the non-living elements. The *ajivas* include ether or space, time, matter and conditions of rest and movement. Thus, non-living existence have also a soul but the soul is never spiritual for him, but merely the principle of life. The accumulation of *karma,* he believed, leads to transmigration of the soul. In its practical aspect Jainism is moralising.

The Buddhist position is too well known. Buddha sought and achieved *nirvana,* the state of perfect bliss, transcending both being and non-being and the eternal state of rest in an important and an uncontrolled world. Through *dharma chakra pravartana* (the turning of the wheel of religion), he taught an apparently paradoxical metaphysics of the futility of man's selfhood in a soul-less transitory cosmos and the final release from worldly sorrow through self knowledge and self-denial. Buddhism is not a singular development. Yet *chaturaryasatya* (the four noble truths) and *aryasthangikamarga* (the noble eight-fold path) are central to its thought. The non-eternal world of continuous flux is in constant sorrow. The sorrow is caused by desire. The desire and sorrow have a cause and effect relationship. The removal of the cause leads to the removal of the effect. Adherence to *aryasthangikamarga,* a moral code of conduct, marked by the path of moderation leads to removal of desire, the cause and ultimately to the removal of sorrow, the effect. Ignorance is considered to be the source of all evil and knowledge to be the ultimate key. Ignorance leads to attachment with fruits of action leading to action and sorrow. Soul for Buddha is a flow of desire and experience and leads to the transmigration of the self. Buddha evolved a non-spiritual metaphysics with a base for causation and a strong moral code of conduct as a practical guide for life. Buddhism developed into various schools of thought. The *madhyamika* holds both mental and non-mental phenomena to be unreal. The *yogachara* admits the mind but denies the physical while the *sautrantika* holds both the mental and the non-mental as real. As a whole, Buddha has a negative approach to life. There are numerous other schools of Buddhist thought spread over several countries.

The *samkhya* and *yoga*, the two schools of ancient Indian thought, had become one in due course of time. The *samkhya* and *yoga* systems were expounded by Kapila and Patanjali respectively. The *samkhya* signifies realising the Ultimate through knowledge and experience. The *yoga* signifies realisation through steady, consistent and persistent meditation. The *samkhya-yoga* system revolves around the pluralistic realism of *purusha* and *prakriti*. It recognises that objects exist independent of mind which perceives them. The *purusha* and *prakriti* are two co-present and co-equal realities. The *purusha* is neither the cause, nor the effect. The *prakriti* is uncaused, eternal, all-pervading; the producer of the world held by the *trigunas* : *sattva, raja* and *tama*. The *gunas* are constituents of the nature, distinct yet interdependent. *Sattva* is the principle of bliss, pleasure, buoyancy and brightness. *Rajas* is the principle of motion, activities and the effective side of pain. *Tamas* is the principle of positivity and negativity. *Tamas* produces the state of apathy and indifference. *Prakriti* admits the principle of *mahat* or intellect and mind. This in turn creates the principles of *ahamkara* or ego. Thus, the *trigunas*, the mind, the five senses and motion all are admitted. In contrast, *purusha* is the principle of pure consciousness, spirit, self and soul. It is the subject and the knower. It is uncaused, eternal and omnipresent. It is the sentient principle and the principle of self perfection. As it is self perfect, it is not bound by the *gunas*. Without *prakriti* it cannot account for the plurality. Without the union of *purusha* and *prakriti* there cannot be creation and without equilibrium of the *trigunas* there cannot be perfection. The *samkhya* advocates the cyclic view of evolution and holds that the manifestation of the physical world is the manifestation of the implicit and the involved. In its practical message, it teaches the futility of secular values and advocates spiritual freedom.

Like *samkhya-yoga, nyaya-vaishesika* systems were closely related and in course of time they came to be treated as a single system. Atomism is the most important aspect of *nyaya-vaishesika* school. The argument put forward by the *nyaya-vaishesikas* runs like this :

The minutest particle visible in the sun's rays coming through the small window hole is made up of parts, because it is a substance perceived visually, as is a jar. Again, the component part of the particle in question is also made up of parts, because it goes to compose substance .[6]

In other words there are two steps in the argument. Every thing that has a perceptible size is made of parts and the parts that go to compose are themselves made of parts. The *nyaya-vaishesikas* understood the production of an effect only in terms of the combination of parts. Anything that is produced has an end, but as the fundamental part or the *paramanu* are not produced, they have no end. Though early *nyaya-vaishesika* atomism did not admit God, it could not keep away the concept for long as fundamental unity was admitted right from the beginning. It assumed that the omnipotent God in conjunction with the inevitable vestiges of the works done by embodied souls, causes concretive activities of various kinds in various atoms' and as a result of such activities, they come into contact with each other and complete products in the shape of dyads, triades, and so on, arise. Thus, creation takes place. And as these have a beginning it is natural that these have to have an end. Thus, the concept of God, creation and destruction were all admitted.[7] Kanda, one of the most important exponents of the system classified all knowables or *padarthas* into six broad categories. Viz : I. Substance (*dravya*) II. Quality (*guna*) III. Activity (*karma*) IV. Universal (*samanya*) V. Ultimate particularity (*vishesha*) and VI. The relation of inherence (*samavaya*). Later, non-existence (*abhava*) was added as the other category of *padartha*. Of the *dravyas* or substances nine were conceived as fundamentals. Earth, water, fire, air and sky; the *panchabhutas*, and time, space, self and mind; were the other four fundamentals added to it. Unlike the Jainas the *nyaya-vaishesikas* argued that the atoms of these fundamental substances were qualitatively different from each other. The *nyaya-vaishesikas* tried to explain the Nature, the everyday experience including the material world by integrating these concepts with the concept of reality.

The *purvamimansa* and *uttaramimansa*, the two other schools of thought, are also called as the *advaita-vedantists* as they are derived from the principles of *Vedantas or Upanishads*. They are regarded as the earliest of Indian philosophical systems. Samkara was the greatest exponent of this theory at a later time. For him *Brahman* alone is real and the cosmos is false, being only an appearance and the individual soul is non-different from the *Brahman*. Thus, *Brahman* and *Atman* are synonymous terms. The world is a creation of *maya* or illusion. The individual self on account of its ignorance (*avidya*) distinguishes himself from the *Brahman* and mistakes the world of plurality to be the *Brahman*. *Maya* to Samkara is not pure illusion. It is not non-existent, yet as *Brahman* alone is real, *maya* is not real, for that would contradict the principle that *Brahman* alone is real. By the dawn of right knowledge, the essential unity of the individual and the *Brahman* is realised and with that the *avidya* (ignorance) and *maya* vanish. The *Brahman* can only be understood as "*Neti ! Neti* !" or "This is not ! This is not ! ." This denial is not to be confused as the non-existence of the material world but as the imperfection of the material world. The *Brahman* is the Supreme self and stands self-revealed as the background of all affirmations and denial. *Brahman* conditioned by *maya* is *Isvara* or god. *Isvara* is the personal facet of the impersonal *Brahma*. *Isvara* is described as *Apara Brahma* and the conditioned *Brahma* as the *Parambrahma*. *Isvara* is also *Saccidananda*, the perfect personality of Truth, Existence and Bliss; world of *maya*, the immanent inner ruler, the transcendent, the creator, destroyer and sustainer of the cosmos. *Isvara* is only *Isvara* to the *jiva* or one who labours under *avidya* or *maya*; *Brahman* never feels Himself distinctly as *Isvara*. He enjoys the *maya* as bliss while the *jiva* is trampled and tortured by *maya*. In its practical message Samkara advocated an ethical code of conduct as much as Buddha and Mahavira Jaina did. This *advaita* philosophy of Samkara was later amended as qualified monism or *visistha advaitavada* by Ramanuja.

Ramanuja conceived the absolute as an organic unity which is qualified by diversity. The Absolute is concrete or *visistha*, while the multiplicity is inter-dependent, interrelated and subordinate, which are known as *visheshanas* (adjectives), under the direct control of the spirit or the *vishesha*. The Supreme *Brahman* holds together the unity of the dependent matter and the individual soul. Thus for Ramanuja, matter, soul and God are the three realities though the former two are subordinate to the later. God is considered as both the material and the instrumental cause of the world. He also accepts the concept of *Saccidananda*. *Saccidananda* is the *Brahman*, is the qualified unity and also both the cause and effect. He is the immanent controller, the very substance and the changeless changer and the immovable mover of the finites. Ramanuja and Samkara are the best representatives of *visistha advaita* and *advaita* theories. The essential features of the Indian philosophy include the attempt to explain the Reality and Cosmos through a single underlying principle. The unity of interdependence of Nature is conceded by both the material and spiritual arguments. The whole Cosmos is considered to be an exercise in bliss and the principle of multiplicity is conceded and is conceived as beautiful. Nearly all these schools of thought advocate a similar ethical social code. Though numerous personal gods are conceived and worshipped by the Indians, the ultimate God remains for them Impersonal and they have no difficulty in admitting the numerous personal gods, even not excluding the conceptions of personal gods of other regions or religions.

To the summarize the Indian philosophical heritage, few representative cantos from the *Vedas* and the *Vedantas* may be appended here justifiably. The *Purusasukta* is considered to be the kernel of vedic literature. It runs thus:

Thousand headed, is the Supreme Being, thousand eyed, thousand footed, embracing the earth all around. He yet exceeds it by a span.

The Supreme Being is beyond this all, That which was and which shall be. He is the Lord of Immorality and of what grows by food.

Such is his grandeur; and yet greater than that is the Supreme Being.

A fourth of Him is all beings, the three fourths is the Immortal in Heaven.

With His three-fourths above rose the Supreme Person; one fourth of Him was again here.

Thence on all sides, he spread out as that which eats and that which eats not.

From Him was born the cosmic egg, and from that the person.

Born, He reached beyond the earth, behind as well as before.

With sacrifice, the gods worshipped the Supreme.

Coming out of the sap of the earth, He was above the creator.

Twashtr, the celestial architect comes designing His form, of that Supreme Person, was the Universe first born.

I know the great Being of the hue of the Sun, beyond the reach of Darkness. He who knows Him thus becomes immortal here; there is no way else for release .... beauty and opulence are Thy wives; Day and Night Thy sights; the constellation Thy form; the Ashwains are Thy mouth. Grant this our desire here, Grant that Yonder; grant us All.[8]

The same thought is also reflected in the Rg.-Veda-1. 164-46 : aum *Indram Mitram, Varunamayanimahuratho sa suvarno gurutman. Ekam sadvipra bahudha vadanti agnim yaman matariswan mahuh."* Which means *"Indra, Mitra, Varuna, Agni,* they call him and he is also the heavenly Garutman of lovely plumage. The one Existent the illumined ones call it variously, call it *Agni, Yama, Matariswan.*

Further in the Rg. Veda. 10.1.298 it is said, *ani davatam svadhaya tadekam tasmaddhanyanna parah kincasa,* which means; "that one lived without breath by his self law, there was nothing else nor ought beyond it."

The *Atharvaveda* (13.5.20) contains; *tamidam nigatam sah esa 'ekabrdeka eva* which means, "This power certainly abides in the God. Such a God is one. He alone exists. He alone is." The *Yajur Veda* (32.1) propounds, *tadevagnistad, adityastad abayustadu chandramah; tadeva sukram tadu brahma ta apah asa Prajapatih,* which means, "He alone is *Agni.* He the *Surya,* he the *Vayu* and He alone is the Moon. He is *Shukra* and he is *Brahman,* the waters are He and He the Creator Lord."

Of all the *Upanishads* one may choose few phrases like *nityonityanam* or the one eternal in many transient, the Absolute and transcendental of all, even of Time, Space and Causality; *cetanscetananam,* the one Consciousness in many consciousness, the one Godhead secret in all beings, all pervading, the inner Self of all; *soaham* and *ahambrahmosmi* or 'He am I' and 'I am the *Brahman*', in order to reflect the essential spiritual nature of Indian philosophical heritage.[9]

Religion in India :

Dharma for the Hindus is a way of life rather than a set system of faith and worship. There is no word, which can substitute *Dharma* in English, and there is no word which can substitute religion in Sanskrit. *Dharma* for the Hindus is also the expected social norm and behaviour in relation to place, time and personality. Though *darsana* may have an independent standing in India and is essentially spiritual, *dharma* can never be diverted from *darsana* in India. While *darsana* is the repository of the *drasta*, the *rshi*, the *visionary*, the poet and the seeker of the Ultimate Truth, religion concerns every one, the highly placed, the elite, and the low of the lowly. Even though we have presented the philosophical heritage independently, many with justification hold that the religio-philosophic tradition of India is one. Most of the philosophical schools of thought and tradition did take shape of religious schools and practices, if not sects. The religion may be traced with an overlapping of historical and thematic approach.

The practice of religion in India can be traced from the remnants of the Indus Valley civilisation. Without the reading of the script and basing exclusively on material remnants, a skeletal picture of the religion of the Indus valley can only be reconstructed. The traces left in their icons include the Mother Goddesses, the Phallus, a male god, sitting in yogic posture, who has been regarded as *Siva*. These factors point out to some fundamental ideas of Hinduism like the primitive beliefs and observances still current in India, the worship of *Siva* and *Sakti*, the belief in female energy as the source of all creation, yoga, etc.[10]

The Vedic age simultaneously sustained monistic, pantheistic and even polytheistic religious practices. Sri Auruobindo writes :

The monotheism of the *Veda* includes in itself also the monistic, the pantheistic and even the polytheistic views of cosmos and is by no means the trenchant and simple creed of modern theism. It is only by a violent struggle with the text that we can force on it a less complex aspect.[11]

In other words, most of the Indian religious practices and ideas can be traced in some form or the other, to the *Vedas*. This is not to suggest revivalism, or the infallibility of the *Vedas* or the lack of creativity of the Indians in the post-Vedic era, but to emphasise the innumerable and multiple facets of the Vedic literature. Though the concept of the omnipotent, and omnipresent God as the final causation and the concept of *Brahman, Vishnu* and *Maheswara* the Hindu trinity along with the concept of *Saccidananda* evolved in the course of Vedic and Vedantic era, the emphasis on the worship of nature gods remained in the earlier phases. Various Gods were propitiated by various means of worship, but principally through *Yajna* or sacrifice. While the philosophical ideas were refined and developed by the *Upanishads*, the *Brahmanas* developed elaborate ritualistic and mechanical details of the *Yajnas*. Myth and supernaturalism played a very important role in the religious thinking and speculation of the Vedic period. A sense of dependence on the powers of Nature for human welfare and the supernatural, mysterious, unexplained characters of gods evolved. In course of time gods were classified and few among them like *Agni, Varuna, Rudra, Aditi, Indra* and others gained preponderant importance. Many gods were conceived as celestial beings, some as atmospheric and still others as terrestrial gods. Most of the gods were associated with various animals as their *vahnas* (vehicles), yet no totemism evolved. The *yajnas* and the rituals varied from very simplistic *grihakarmani* to elaborate sacrifices like *Asvamedha* and *Rajasuya*. *Soma* rituals were also a part of early vedic practices.[12]

In sixth century B.C. many hetrodox schools of thought appeared, out of which Buddhism and Jainism survived for a long period. Buddha in his life time had established the *Samgha* and his followers had gained a distinction in

India. A canonical literature viz, the *Tripitaka* appeared around the first Christian century and Buddhism had almost become a distinct religion. It also received royal patronage from the dynasties like the Mauryas and had spread into many parts of Asia. Later on two schools of thought evolved – *Hinayana* and *Mahayana*. Buddhism also admitted pantheism and at popular level numerous gods were admitted. Buddha himself was raised to the status of Supreme God without the usage of the epithet. Elaborate rituals, methods of yoga, meditation and even physical control slowly became a part of Buddhism. However, predominantly the ethical character was retained. At a later time *Vajrayana*, a new school of thought, appeared which was akin to *tantra* and *saktism*.[13] In course of time at religious level, not withstanding the metaphysical distinctions Buddhism was synthesised in the kaleidoscopic mosaic of Indian religious scenario.

Jainism like Buddhism was a heterodox religio-philosophic tradition. Its antiquity was far beyond the 6th century B.C, the life time of Mahavira Jaina, the last of the twenty four *Tirthamkaras*. Rsabhanath, Neminatha, Parsva and Mahavira were the great *Tirthamkaras* (leaders) of the school. Of them, at least Parsvanatha was definitely a historical character. Unlike Buddhism which had spread far and wide, Jaina church showed quite a modest yet steady progress. It received patronage from great kings like Bimbisara, Chandragupta Maurya and Kharavela. Eminent teachers like Gautma, Jambu and Bhadrabahu contributed to the spread of the religion. Since Jainism admitted the concept of God, as already discussed, it found greater acceptance but could not retain its distinct identity. Like Buddhism it developed into two distinct sects like *Digambara* and *Svetambara*. The basic religious and philosophical doctrines remained same for both the sects, yet they differed on minor dogmas, mythological details and ascetic practices.[14] The Jainas also built great temples and introduced elaborate rituals. The *Tirthankaras* at practical level can be equated with gods. In fact, many of the old Jaina images are presently worshipped in Hindu temples. Jainism in its practical aspect was not only moralising or ethical but also it greatly emphasised the principle of *Ahimsa* (non-violence).

Bhagavatism also developed during the later part of the vedic age. *Krishnavasudeva* the principal deity of *Bhagavatism* appears in *Chandogya Upanishad* (III.17.6). Steadily from 6th century B.C. *Krishna* or *Narayana* emerged as the preserver of the cosmos and became a part of the Hindu Trinity. The epic literature added the cult of Rama, the other *avatara* of *Narayana*. *Harivamsa* further deified and eulogised *Krishna*. The emergence of *Narayana* led to a new mode of worship different from the previous Yajnic and Yogic austerities. *Bhakti* or devotion became the most important aspect of this worship. Metaphysical and abstract knowledge was replaced with mythical and epical ballads. What was true of *Krishna* or *Narayana* was true of the other *Avataras* and the host of other personal gods that the Hindus had conceived. By the 4th century A.D. numerous *Puranas* were written. *Bhagavatism* as a religious school of thought centered around *Narayana* the preserver.

Another sect emerged centering *Siva* in India. *Saivism* was expounded by the *Vayu, Linga* and *Kurma Puranas* and the numerous *Agamas*. Samkara's *Advaita* philosophy had its impact on *Saivism* and in Kashmir a new school of *Saivism* evolved out of this. *Nayanmamrs* or the *Saiva* saints of Tamilnadu composed numerous devotional poems in the honour of *Siva*. Periyapuranam, a Tamil *Purana* devoted to *Siva* was composed. Numerous temples devoted to *Siva*, and his subordinate gods appeared in different parts of India. *Bhagavatism* was regenerated as *Vaishnavism* at a latter time and at a still latter age it was revived under Sri Chaitanya.

Besides these two important religious sects, the *Shakti* cult was another important aspect of India's religious heritage.

Shaktism evolved in India through fertility rites of pre-historic times, mother goddess of the Indus Valley, *Ila, Mahi, Puramdhi, Raka, Kuhu, Lakshmi, Alakshmi, Apeya, Yosa,* etc. of the Vedic pantheon, *Shakambari* of the *Puranic* periods, *Kali, Parvati* and *Durga* symbolising energy, *Sri, Saraswati* and *Lakshmi* symbolising other aspects of mother goddesses; *Uma, Lakshmi* and other consorts of various Gods and so on. The Jaina and Buddhist pantheon also admitted various mother goddesses. Shaktism carried forward the *Tantrik* and Yogic traditions. Many of the primitive practices survived through the *Shakti* cult. Large number of goddesses were conceived by the Indians and systems of worship revolving around them appeared.

Hindus till date follow their ancient practices with a great deal of modifications. Yet *Siva* and *Vishnu* and their numerous subordinate gods and goddesses remained the *summum bonum* of their religious practices. Besides these cults, the *bhakti* cult during the medieval period and the social reformers of late 19th and early 20th centuries contributed immensely to the religious life of the Hindus. In essence they were reformative, humane and they attempted to rid Hinduism of evils which were not acceptable in the changed circumstances. It was an attempt to purify Hinduism from within.[15]

Having surveyed the religio-philosophic heritage of India, few essentials may be re-stated. Hinduism without a single text like the Bible or the *Quoran* as a scriptural authority, is still a unity. It is essentially tolerant, prompted by its own variedness and its inherent subordination of the personal god to the impersonal *Brahman*. It is spiritual for it accepts matter to be a manifestation of spirit and makes god both the efficient cause of the creation and the static uninvolved omnipotent Reality. It is not anti-worldly though it is moral in its ethical guidelines, yet morality for the Hindus is only social and can never be the means of god-realisation. God-realisation remains a goal of everyone attainable through meditation, knowledge or self effacing devotion. Hinduism does not rule out the terrestrial goals of life, of *dharma*, of *artha* and *kama* without losing sight of the ultimate goal of *Moksha*. A Hindu without a sense of guilt prays and seeks the bounties of material world, accepts the ethical order with all its limitations and vices and the best among them and the best in each craves for the Self within. He holds that he is born in bliss, he lives in bliss and departs for bliss and prays – "lead me from Untruth to Truth , from Darkness to Light and from Mortality to Immortality." (*asadoma sadgamaya, tamasoma yotirgamaya, mrityor ma' mritamgamaya*).

REFERENCES

1. Radhakrishnan, *Indian philosophy* – Vol-I; (Centenary Edition): Delhi, 1989, p.28.
2. Ibid., pp.8-9.
3. Karl Marx and Fredrick Angels, *On Britain*; Moscow, 1953, p.380.
4. Kar Karx, *The Capital*, Vol-I; Moscow, 1954, p.358.
5. Debiprasad Chattopadhaya, *Indian Philosophy, A Popular Introduction*; New Delhi, 1986, pp.30-31.
6. Ibid., p.169
7. Ibid., p.173.
8. S.P. Pani, *SriAurobindo- A study of His Thought In A Historical Perspective*, (Unpublished Thesis for Doctoral Degree), Utkal University, Bhubaneswar, 1985, pp.250-52.
9. Binita Pani, *The Indian Scriptures and the Life Divine*; New Delhi, 1993, pp.196-97.
10. Haridas Bhattacharya, *The Cultural Heritage of India*, Vol-IV; Calcutta, 1983, p.32.

11. Sri Aurobindo, *The Secret of the Veda*, Sri Aurobindo Birth Centenary Library (henceforth S.A.B.C.L.), Vol-X; Pondichery, 1972, p.226.
12. R.C. Majumdar (Ed.), *History and Culture of the Indian People*, Vol-I; Bombay, 1988, pp.363-387 and also pp.442-452.
13. A.L. Basham (Ed.) *Cultural History of India*; London, 1975, pp.85-94.
14. Ibid., p.102.
15. Susmita Pande, *Medieval Bhakti Movement*; Meerut, 1989, p.XIII.

CHATPER – II
THE BHAGAVADGITA AN INTRODUCTION

The Importance of the Gita :

The *Bhagavadgita.* is the most translated and commented upon book of Hindu religion. It is also most synthetic in nature of its exposition. Consisting of seven hundred verses in lucid Sanskrit, the *Bhagavadgita* is at once a guide book for every man and woman; transcending the barriers of time, space and personality. It is capable of lending itself to multifaceted interpretations and understanding. All Indian schools of philosophical thought and religious practices can and do interpret the *Bhagavadgita* in their own lines of thought and seek sanctification from it. Large number of Hindus who have not cared to read the *Vedas* and the *Vedantas*; for the esoteric, symbolic and poetic metaphysics eludes them, yet they are at home with the *Bhagavadgita*. They seek solace and glimpse intuitively the truth from it. In his preface to the first English translation of the *Bhagavadgita* by Sir Charles Wilkins, Warren Hastings, the first British Governor General of India, ascertaining the importance of the *Gita* wrote : "The writers of the Indian Philosophies will survive, when the British dominion in India shall have long ceased to exist and the sources which it yielded of wealth and power are lost to remembrance."[1]

The early Europeans who translated the *Bhagavadgita* found the reflections of their own religiosity in it and hence believed that it was a copy of the Bible.[2] Great scholars attempted to prove it. Reserving the issue for a historical and academic analysis it can easily be held that the versatility of the *Bhagavadgita's* inherent meaning and interpretation led them to the conclusion that these two are strikingly similar and hence one could be a copy of the other.

The *Gita* is universally acclaimed for its intense practical nature in addition to the philosophical expounding of the Indian or Hindu Philosophical heritage. "The *Bhagavadgita* is a metrical interpretation of the instructions of the *Upanisads* in their bearing on social life." " It holds that ;" however high a man may soar, to whatsoever higher perspective of things as he may open his eyes, he is ultimately bound in ties of social duties to his fellow beings on earth in every station of life. A high and transcendent philosophy, which can only open itself through the attainment of the highest moral perfection and which leads one through the region beyond good and evil, again draws him down to the sharing of common duties with the other members of society.[3]

The *Bhagavadgita* almost seems to justify all shades of opinion and there is such a wide difference of emphasis in its interpretations that one tends to conclude that either its central message has been confused or people use it purposefully to seek justification from it for their points of view or actions. This is very true of the late 19th century and early 20th century Indian milieu. *Gita* assumed a special significance during the freedom struggle. Cantos from it were trumpeted to urge people into positive action from a state of inertia, apathy and inaction. It was used to justify violence and non-violence equally. "The *Bhagavadgita* still remains powerful in forming the consciousness of upper class Hindus by furnishing the ideological sphere where they fight out their conflict." [4] Translations and commentaries in various Indian languages poured in. Not withstanding the possibility of adding to the confusion or the flood of literature, it is humbly felt that an attempt should be made to analyse the genesis of varied interpretations and to rescue its central message. It is also important to explore the impact of the *Bhagavadgita* on the leaders and others, during the first half of the twentieth century; though only representative personalities, their interpretations and the influence the scripture exerted on their thought and action are being analysed here.

The *Bhagavadgita* was certainly composed after the *Vedas* and the *Upanisads*. As such it carried over synthetically the intuitive thought, the spiritual experiences and realisation; the epistemology and philosophy of the Indians. Along with the *Vedas* and the *Vedantas*, it has been the substratum and the foundation of Indian philosophical out-put right up to the present. Consequently the *Gita* needs to be studied in depth, in relation with the thinkers of the recent past like Gandhi, Sri Aurobindo and Radhakrishnan. It must not be lost sight that other great Indians like Samkaracharya, Ramanuja, Vallabha, Madhva, Madhusudana, Ramakrishna, Vivekananda, Tilak and a host of others, have also responded to the *Bhagavadgita*.

The *Bhagavadgita* systematically provides an enunciation of various paths leading to realisation. It is a great book of *Yoga*. No other text expounds as many various schools of Indian philosophical thought as the *Bhagavadgita* does. Its being interwoven either originally or subsequently with the epic *Mahabharata*, makes the *Gita* more accessible and less complex than pure reflections and symbolisms of the *Upanisads*. Though the problems of shifting myth, reality and history from the ancient Indian scriptures remains, the essence of the *Bhagavadgita* does not elude on above counts.

The Historical Foundation of the *Gita* :

It is almost impossible to fix the date and authorship of the *Bhagavadgita*, as common with most other ancient Indian scriptures. None of the early Indian writings is available in the form of original texts. All have undergone the corruption of numerous copying. All have undergone numerous interpolations under different authors who have used one name. At times, the authors have not at all used their names nor have left any clue to that effect. More than one author have also contributed to many of the works, further adding to the confusion. The historical chronology of India can only be fixed from 6th century B.C though the historical knowledge is also quite rich for the earlier period. The problem of the authorship and historical foundation of the *Bhagavadgita* is limited with all these factors. However, it is possible to fairly place it in the chronology of Indian history. The present work is not a work of comparative philosophy or history of literature. Attempts are being made to broadly summarise the views of some scholars only.

Since the *Bhagavadgita* forms a part of the *Mahabharata*, the problem of its date is linked with it. *Mahabharata* has to be placed before 6th century B.C. in its earliest form, in view of the known chronology of Indian history from 6th century B.C. To treat the whole of the *Mahabharata* as historical is against all common sense. To treat every story of the *Mahabharata* to be real at any point of time defies logic and understanding. The *Mahabharata* remains an epic, a master piece of literature, full of myths, metaphors, allegory and mystic symbolism. Some historical characters may have been represented there, but not without undergoing a dramatic metamorphosis. In view of the internal references to the *Bhagavadgita* in the *Mahabharata*, it has been looked upon as a genuine part of it. Reference is made to the *Adiparvan* and the *Shantiparvan* of the *Mahabharata* to uphold this view.[5] Bal Gangadhar Tilak, on grounds of philosophy and religion argues that the *Bhagavadgita* definitely formed a part of the *Mahabharata*.[6] Radhakrishnan summarises the various opinions expressed by historians, philologists and scholar of Sanskrit literature and the same may be excerpted:

Even when we assign the *Bhagavadgita* to the *Mahabharata* as a genuine part of it, we cannot be sure of its date, since there are products of different periods included in it. Telang in a learned introduction to his *Bhagavadgita* deals with the general character of its teaching, its archaic style, its versification and its internal references, and argues that the work belongs to a period earlier than the third century B.C. Sir R.G. Bhandarkar thinks that the *Gita* is at least as old as the fourth century B.C. Garbe assigns the original *Gita* to 200 B.C., and the present form of it to A.D.200. Samkara (ninth century A.D.) comments on it and Kalidasa knows it. In his *Raghuvamsa* (10.31.cf. the *Bhagavadgita* 3.22) there is found a passage akin to a *Gita* verse. Bana refers to the *Gita,* and these two authors belong to the fifth and seventh century A.D. The *Puranas* (second century A.D.) contain many *Gitas* composed after the manner of the *Bhagavadgita,* Bhasa in his *Karnabhara* has a passage which reads like an echo (*Hato pi labhate svargam jitva tu labhate yasah;* (cf. the *Bhagavadgita* II.37) of a verse from the *Gita.* Bhasa is sometimes assigned to the second or the fourth century A.D., and sometimes to the second century B.C. Even on the former view, the *Gita* must have been earlier. Bodhayana's *Grhya Sutras* are familiar with *Vasudeva* worship, and contain a statement attributed to the Lord (B*hagavan*), which seems to be a quotation from the *Bhagavadgita* (2.22.9 cf. B.G., IX.26) This is also true of his *Pitrmedha Sutras*. If Apasthamba belongs to the third century B.C. (S.B.E., Vol.II., Introduction, p.xliii, cf. Vol. XIV; p.xliii), then Bodhyayana is earlier by a century or two. We shall not, I believe, be far wrong if we again assign the *Gita* to the fifth century B.C. If the references in the *Dharma Sutras* are regarded as interpolated texts, then the *Gita* may be assigned to the third or second century B.C."[7]

In addition to Radhakrishnan's comprehensive analysis, few more opinions may be attached. It is now fairly admitted that about 80,000 stanzas of the *Mahabharata* excluding *Harivamsa,* have grown from an original *Jaya* of Vyasa through *Bharata* of *Vaisampayana* into Souti's *Mahabharata* with many *akhyanas* (parables) and *upakhyanas* (semiparables). The original character of *Mahabharata* as chronicled history or *Itihasa* is now naturally obscure and almost impossible to restore at the present level of historical knowledge.[8] Bhandarkar's brilliant exercise in ejecting provincial interpolation has not succeeded in settling the dispute, save establishing the certainty of *Mahabharata*, gaining its present status of a static text over centuries together. It can usually be considered that the *Bhagavadgita* did not enjoy its primacy in earlier days. However, the progressive elaboration and fragmentary character of the *Mahabharata* may seem to have been justifiably conceded. But to extend the same to the *Bhagavadgita* would call for a debate. Those who argue that the *Bhagavadgita* is a conglomeration or assimilation of different schools of philosophy hold the view of its progressive elaboration. In contrast, others veritably concede the coherence of the *Bhagavadgita* and uphold its unitary character and argue that the *Gita* was composed at an exclusive single period of time. Hopkins views that it was a Krishnite version of an older Vishnuite poem and the poem has different teachings incorporated corresponding to difference in time of their genesis. Any sympathetic reader who judges the *Bhagavadgita* independent of the Bible can find how it is inseparably interlined with all major Indian philosophical questions and the *Mahabharata*.[9] Its unitary feature shall be brought out progressively in the present work. H.C. Ray Choudhury favours the view that the historical *Krishna Vasudeva* and the *Krishna* of the *Chhandogya Upanishad* were not different from the Krishna of *Mahabharata* on the ground that he was known everywhere as *Devakiputra* (son of Devaki). Both worshipped the Sun. Angirasa was the *Guru* (teacher) of *Upanishad's* Krishna and *Sandipani* was only the later *Guru* of Krishna from when Krishna learnt the science of war. This, he justifies for *Sandipani* knew definitely that Krishna was a *Shrutidhara* or well versed with the *Vedas*, which he must have learnt from *Angirasa*.[10]

The *Vrishni Vasudeva*, the *Yadava Vasudeva* and the *Chchandogya Upanisad's Vasudeva*, all may be historic and the historic *Vasudeva* may not satisfy the graphic picture that we get of *Vasudeva* Krishna in the *Mahabharata* or the

Bhagavadgita. The Krishna of the *Bhagavadgita* is definitely greater at least at the level of metaphysical exposition than any known historical Krishna. The composer of the *Mahabharata, Harivamsa* or the *Bhagavadgita* or those who contributed to the composition of these, may be at different times have relied on the historical Krishna. The historical Krishna might have grown as a myth in course of time. It is logical to concede that the Krishna of the *Mahabharata* and the *Gita* definitely transcended the historical Krishna. The historicity of the *Bhagavadgita* is of little consequence in building up of the chronological history. Notwithstanding its historicity, the *Bhagavadgita* is definitely a clue to the minds of the Indians in the hoary past. The problem of dating the *Bhagavadgita* must be judged in this light, at least when its relevance at intellectual or philosophical level is being considered. As it is possible to recite the seven hundred stanzas today in less than two hours, it is not humanly impossible to have rendered the verses or the essence of it is prose form or the conversation having taken place in this light in a battle field where the *Kshatriyas* fought with lot of mutual respect and well defined war-principles where speed was not everything as in modern days. If at all it is a poetic creation using the battle field as a background, the value of the message and the inherent force remains intact irrespective of its historical possibility or poetic formulation.

Significant Themes of the Gita :

The significant themes of the *Bhagavadgita* need to be identified for a systematic study of their treatment by various personalities. This also helps one to identify the points of debate and the grounds of meeting. Besides the problem of its dating and fixing its authorship, with which historians are predominantly concerned, the analysis of the setting of the *Gita* sets the tone of the interpreter or the commentator. At this stage, treatment of major themes are not offered. It is now limited only to their identification.

The questions relating to the setting are like whether it was a historical setting, a battle field, an allegorical scene or merely the conflict of mind or pure poetic imagination. This is important because the relevance of the questions asked and the answers provided in the *Bhagavadgita* depends on the views of the setting. Related with the setting is the question of characters involved. The two principal characters, Krishna and Arjuna are being variously viewed; like the charioteer and the warrior, the *Narayana* and *Nara* or God and the man like two friends, the counsellor and the counselled, the teacher and the taught. Arjuna is taken as a representative character of a *Kshtriya* and some view the whole problem from this angle. The question of the historic nature of the characters is also of great relevance. The problem raised in the *Bhagavadgita* is largely a corollary of the setting and the characters. The apparent problem of the refusal of Arjuna to fight on grounds of morality and the despondence and depression are viewed variously as being a psychological problem, a metaphysical problem, a problem of practical life, a problem of the relationship of the Divinity and man, a crisis of changing social norms and values, the classic problem be of the *Kaliyuga*, a problem of ethical norms; the moral, immoral and amoral questions, a problem of blind attachment to kith and kin, so on and so forth.

Various interpretatiosn of the solutions and the advice rendered by Krishna to Arjuna flows from the understanding of the problem. The solutions are viewed variedly as are the problems. The expounding of various *margas* (paths) like *Jnana* (knowledge), *Karma* (work) and *Bhakti* (devotion) and the illustration of *Samkhyayoga* lead to numerous interpretations and identification of multiple emphases by the commentators.

The *Bhagavadgita* is undoubtedly hailed as a great metaphysical treatise. The *Gita* itself claims to contain the essence of all *Upanishads* and lays claim to its metaphysical value. The fundamental Hindu concepts of Reality; *Dvaita* (dual), *Advaita* (monistic) and *Visistha* (qualified), are all reflected in the *Bhagavadgita*. The concept of evil, the theory of knowledge, the concept of evolution, creation of cosmos, concept of man and *Maya* (illusion) ,etc. are enumerated in the scripture. These key questions of metaphysics have been dealt in the light of the *Bhagavadgita* by many important Indian philosophers right from Samkara to Sri Aurobindo. In view of this, it is vital to study the issues raised, in terms of Indian philosophy in the *Bhagavadgita*.

The *Bhagavadgita* for the commentators and the vast majority of Indians is considered to be a book of practical guidance. The issus raised in the battle field are of practical nature. Besides the problems of despondency, depression and the questions of ethical codes of conduct in changing times find their solution, solace and guidance for the reader in every point of life. People consult the *Bhagavadgita* at times of their every emotional conflict as a practical guide. This necessitates the study of the practical message of the *Gita* in detail.

As the *Gita* offers numerous solutions and discusses various *Margas* (paths) of liberation and God realisation, opinions on the central message of the *Gita* are automatically divided. The central message of the *Gita* is the identified variously as the message of *Anasaktiyoga* or the *yoga* of non-attachment, as the philosophy of moderation in life, as the *yoga* of renunciation, as the path of action without attachment or of *Bhakti* (devotion) and surrender. In view of these multifacets of metaphysics and practical message of the *Bhagavadgita*, the identification of the central message merits discussion.

Issues raised here are representative and all the commentators have not reflected on all of them. Thus, in the following discussion, instead of a fixed format, the themes raised by the thinkers are taken up.

Treatments of the *Gita* :

For a proper understanding of the treatment of the *Bhagavadgita* by Gandhi,Sri Aurobindo and Radhakrishnan it is necessary to summarise the earlier attempts on the same. This would provide the background for analysis and enable the scholar for a comparative study. Of the various commentaries on the *Bhagavadgita* available, Adi Samkaracharya's is the oldest amongst the important ones.[11]

Samkaracharaya (or Samkara) in his interpretations of the *Bhagavadgita* reflects on the Vedantic *Advaita* philosophy. As the metaphysical stand of Samkaracharya has already been discussed in the previous chapter, the scholar limits himself here to few other essentials only. Samkara correlates the verses which he has chosen to comment upon with *Shruti* and *Yukti* (reasoning) and *Anubhava* (experience). He quotes parallel ideas from the *Vedas* and the *Vedantas* to substantiate the validity of his interpretation. Samkara also uses the character of an opponent, probably imaginary, for greater clarity of expression through opposition. Dialogues have always been found to be more logical. Samkara's main argument remains that the world is unreal, not in the sense that it is non-existent but in the sense that it being impermanent can not be equated with ultimate Reality, for the Reality is eternal. The consciousness of the self or the *Atman* is only real for it is indestructible. In this sense, the One alone is real and the multiplicity is only an appearance. Even the *abhava* or the absolute nothing is only a mental construction. The One only whithout a second manifests eternally attached both by *Sat* and *Asat*. The *Brahman* is partless, immutable, all pervasive, indestructible and is free from changes. *Brahman* is unknowable as it is the knower and it is self-revealing. One can only describe its attributes. God who creates the universe, creates it through Its power of *Yoga-maya*. He has the knowledge of the infinity of the finites while the finites, because of *Maya* (illusion) lack this knowledge. This God or *Purusottama* can be identified with individual soul (*atman*). The *Atman* like the *Brahman* is also attributeless, all pervasive and not subject to changes, though it transmigrates from the one to the other. *Prakriti* (nature) is the illusion or the veil controlled by God and this veil transforms itself into body, sense organ and sense objects. It is the *Kshetra* (field) for the *Kshetrajna* (self). However, for Samkara there is no union. It is only an illusory appearance and in that sense *Maya*. In other words *Maya* is the false self identification of the *Kshetrajna* with *Kshetra* or the self with the body. For Samkara, one who does not believe in the existence of self does not perform the sacrificial rites. Similarly the enlightened one who is free from the *Maya* of identification of the *Kshetrajna* with the *Kshetra* is also free from the duties of Vedic rites. The ignorant who has inferred the self as distinct from the body and is desirous of the fruits of Vedic rites may perform them. And in this sense the *Sastras* (scriptures) serve a purpose. Samkara does not advocate abandonment of action for all, for he recognises that as long as that 'I' ness and 'mine'-ness remains, desire and action shall persist. "*Samsara* is described in the *Gita* as the *Aswasttha* tree with its root above. In other words, *Brahman* is the cause of *Samsara* created by *Maya*. This ever changing *Samsara* can be cut only by the sword of knowledge. Realization of *Brahman* puts and to *Samsara*."[12] Samkara has proved the impossibility of *Jnana-karma-samuchaya*, or the possibility of a mixing of the *Jnana* and *Karma margas*, for the realisation.[13] The final liberation, in his opinion, comes only through knowledge. *Karmayoga* also leads to attainment of a pure mind which enables one fit for the path of knowledge. The *Karmayogin* dedicates all his actions to the *Isvara* as the servant to the master and renounces the effects of this action including even the desire for liberation. This freedom from ego and the desire for fruits of action automatically leads to liberation.

Samkaracharya commented "As devotion to knowledge and devotion to action are mutually opposed, it is impossible for one man to resort to both of them at once and the same time."[14] From this, it may follow that each leads to the goal quite independently of the other. But the truth is this : Devotion to action is a means to the end, not directly, but only as leading through devotion to knowledge; where as the latter, which is attained by means of devotion to action, leads to the goal directly, without extraneous help. To show this, the Lord in the *Gita* says : *na karmanam anarambhan naiskarmyam puruso' snute, na ca samnyasanad eva siddhim samadhigacchati* (III.4). Commenting on the twelfth canto of chapter twelve of the *Bhagavadgita* – *sreyo hi jnanam abhyasaj jnanad dhyanam visisyate, dhyanat karmaphalatyagas tyagac chantir anantaram,* (Better indeed is knowledge than practice; than knowledge is meditation more esteemed; than meditation the abandonment of the fruits of actions; on abandonment, peace follows immediately), Samkaracharya draws a parallel from the *Upanishads* and states:

In the *Kathopanisad* (VI.14) it is said that, immortality results from the abandonment of all objects of desire; and this is a truth quite familiar to all and all objects of desire are fruits of actions enjoined in the *Shruti* and the *Smriti*. In the case of the enlightened person who is steadily engaged in contemplation, peace immediately follows the abandonment of desire . . . . . thus, it has been taught that *Karmayoga* accompanied with the abandonment of fruits of action is a means to bliss.[15]

The quoted passages from Samkara are in a way of examples to cite his line of thinking. The above discussion does not exhaust all the ideas of Samkara nor does it summarise the whole of it. What is apparent is contradictory to the popular conception of samkaracharya being anti-terrestrial, his views are fully integrated and are not world-negative. Though Samkara would not take a wife, he is not asking every one to negate life and abandon his society in which he lives.

Ramanuja (11th Century A.D.), the most important exponent of *Visistha-advaita* (qualified monism) school of Indian philosophy also wrote a commentary on the *Bhagavadgita*. He reads into the *Bhagavadgita* the *Visisthadvaita* philosophy. He follows Yamunacharya's *Gitarthasamgraha*. *Brahman* for him is the highest reality, He is Spirit but not without attributes. He has self consciousness with the knowledge of Himself and a conscious will to create the world and bestow salvation on his creature. In contrast Samkara's *Brahma* is attribute-less. The world for Ramanuja is no deception or illusion but is genuine and real, just as the world and god are one as the body and soul are one. They are a whole but unchangeably different.[16] The world is absolutely dependent on the God as the body is absolutely dependent on the soul. In this sense this is *Visisthaadvaitavada* or the philosophy of qualified monism. The God and the soul are one, not because they are identical but the God is the inner-guide, *antaryami* (knower of the heart) who dwells deep with in the soul and as such is the principle of life. Ramanuja develops a type of personal mysticism in his commentary on the *Bhagavadgita*. Accepting the paths of knowledge, devotion and action, he holds out that *Bhakti* (devotion) is the most important of all. "The Supreme is Vishnu, for Ramanuja. He is the only true god who will not share his divine honours with others. Liberation is service of and fellowship with God in *Vaikuntha* or heaven."[17]

In interpreting the principles of relinquishment or abandonment (*tyaga*) of the *Bhagavadgita*, Ramanuja calls for relinquishment of fruit, relinquishment of the idea that the self is the agent and so of attachment also and relinquishment of all idea of agency with the realization that the Lord is the author of all action.[18] Ramanuja's interpretation follows from the following canto of the *Bhagavadgita: tyago hi purusayaghra trividhah samprakirtitah* (XVIII.4). In contrast, Samkara speaks of *Tamasik, Rajasik* and *Sattvik* forms of abandonment.[19]

Besides Samkara and Ramanuja, Vallabha (15th Century A.D.) also wrote a commentary on the *Bhagavadgita*. He develops *Suddha-advaitavada* (Pure Non-dualism) theory. For him, the ego pure and unblended by illusion and the Supeme *Brahman* are one. Souls for him are particles of God like sparks of fire and they cannot acquire the knowledge necessary for obtaining release except by the grace of the Supreme. Devotion to God is the most important means of obtaining release. *Bhakti* is truth associated with love.[20] According to the Vallabha School, a *Bhakta* (devotee) alone attains *Moksha* (liberation). The ideal man for this sect is not essentially a *Samnyasi*. He can be a man of the world who continues to perform works in the world, practices *dhyana* is merged in *Jnana* and he is an instrument of the *Bhagavan* (God). He is filled with a sense of *Bhakti*. Samkara and Vallabha represent two apparently opposite views of the *Bhagavadgita*. Samkara is interpreted as advocating the *Jnanna-marga* and Vallabha, the *Bhakti-marga*.

The modern times is replete with numerous interpretations and commentaries on the *Bhagavadgita*. It seems that the scripture has drawn large number of scholars and saints and attained a prime position among the elite as well as the common folk of India. Vivekananda and Tilak are the two most important thinkers who contributed to the interpretation of the *Bhagavadgita* prior to Gandhi, Sri Aurobindo and Radhakrishnan. It is necessary to generally analyse the Indian milieu of late 19th and early 20th century and the views of Vivekananda and Tilak for a better analysis of the treatment of the *Bhagavadgita* by Gandhi, Sri Aurobido and Radhakrishnan in their historical perspective.

With the discovery of sea route to India, she not only came in contact with the West but also the whole of Indian milieu underwent a metamorphic dynamics. By the last half of the 19th century and the first two decades of the 20th century, the response of India to the West and the *vice-versa* had not only resulted in a conflict between the political and economic interests of the alien ruling class and the elite and the common man of India but also the conflict had pervaded every aspect of life in India. In the 19th century the newly educated elite class was not only moved by the concepts of democracy, liberty, equality, fraternity and scientific developments, but a large section of them also uncritically accepted everything Western. The English had nearly succeeded in creating a class of Indian *saheebs*, English in education, taste and temperament. Simultaneously the educated class rediscovered the past greatness of their country, their own history and cultural heritage, partly through translations in European languages and the scholarship of European Indologists. Not long after, a small section of the Indians along with few Europeans developed more sympathetic studies concerning India, attempted presentation of Indian religious, cultural and spiritual heritage to the Westerners in Western language and format. They counteracted unsympathetic and erroneous treatment of their culture and philosophy. They even advocated their own superiority and even evolved a theory of the spiritual mission of India for the world civilisation to compensate for their own material and scientific backwardness and to carve out a role for themselves in the modern world civilisation. The renaissance and reformation of late 19th century was a manifestation of all these. From Raja Rammohan Ray to Mahatma Gandhi, from Subhas Chandra Bose to M.N. Ray, India produced a host of socio-political thinkers who have contributed to almost every aspect of Indian thinking. They have re-assessed India's past, her history and her culture. They attempted to purify Hindus from within. They provided the much needed political philosophy for their struggle for freedom. They synthesised their own mystic-spiritual ideals with western concepts of democracy and science. They presented India in a new light different from the Europeans. They were not merely men of letters or scholasticism, many of them were men of great action and simultaneously belonged to the select group of most prolific writers of modern times. Most of them wrote in English but quite a number of them were masters of Sanskrit. They created the vision for the future Independent India. Most of them participated directly or indirectly in our freedom struggle. The years of upheaval in India were also the years of Afro-Asian resurgence. The world witnessed momentous events, changes and had almost been re-born during the last decades of the 19th century and first half of the 20th century. In the field of science, man invented the method of inventions and inventions have since boomed. The Industrial revolution had entered new generations of technology. The two wars, the great depression, the formation of U.N.O., the atomic explosion, the socialistic revolutions and the 20th century dictators had tossed the world from one to the other. Upheavals, through periods of despondence, crises of faith, supremacy of science over religion and spirituality, revival of faiths, hopes and dreams : all these are reflected globally in the creative output of man, both in art and literature and in the process of thinking. And India was no exception to it. The reassessment of the *Bhagavadgita* by numerous personalities was a part of this general milieu.

Foremost among the various reassessors of the *Bhagavadgita* in the earlier phases of modern India were Swami Vivekananda and Bal Gangadhar Tilak, in the Indian context. Swami Vivekananda (1863-1902) was the most intense patriot amongst the socio-religious reformers of modern India. A student of metaphysics, a disciple of Ramakrishna Paramhansa, he was the leading Monist interpreter of the Vedantic school of thought. He was the master *Advaita* Vedantist of the modern times. Travelling in the West, he became the torch bearer of Indian spiritual heritage. He defined Hinduism and became an aggressive heroic-spiritual master. He influenced a whole generation of Indian readers right up to Mahatma Gandhi. Though he did not write any full-fledged commentary on the *Bhagavadgita,* he delivered few speeches on various aspects of it.[21]

Vivekananda maintains that the *Bhagavadgita* is the essence of the *Upanishads.* He, in distinction from others, holds, the *Upanishads* to be the notes taken down from the discussions held in royal courts. He traces back the sign of Sanskrit to 5000 B.C. and the *Vedas* and the *Upanishads* to be still older. In one hand, he holds the *Vedas* to be the mother of all religion, the essence of language, the *mantras* being capable of creating every possible effect. On the other hand, he holds that the *Vedas* contain only the elements of Nature worship. Of the *Upanishads,* he emphasises the principle of renunciation. The *Bhagavadgita* for him is historical, so also is Krishna. He almost reads in his own contemporary reflections into the *Bhagavadgita* and thinks that Krishna was born in a time of crisis when India was getting divided. The crisis for him was the crisis between the *Karmakanda* (ceremonial sacrifices) and the path of *Jnana* (knowledge) of the *Upanishads.* He compares Krishna with Jesus Christ and considers Him to be the epitome of non-attachment. Speaking of Him he says :

> You find in Krishna that non-attachment is the central idea . . . . work for work sake, worship for worship sake, do good because it is good to do good, ask no more – that must have been the character of the man . . . . he is the most rounded man I know of, wonderfully developed equally in brain, heart and hand.[22]

For Vivekananda, Krishna was still a man for he believed in *Nirakara Brahma.* Vivekananda also emphasises the background of the battle field of the *Gita*. He finds Krishna to be a great *Yogi,* for he was calm in the midst of intense activities of a battle field. The whole life in the world is a continuous fight and hence, the message of the *Bhagavadgita* is of eternal value. He finds that Arjuna is caught between his heart and his sense of duty, and feels that he should have been self controlled, reasonable and enlightened to perform the duties expected of him. Arjuna should not have felt shy of killing because death is a part of nature and the self is not touched by death. He justifies the need for effort, for without effort mere prayer or devotion shall not achieve anything. Applying it to his own times, Vivekananda says, "the masses of India pray to sixty million gods and still die like dogs, where are these gods ? . . . . . you are infinite, deathless and birthless. Because you are infinite spirit, it does not befit you to be a slave. Arise ! awake ! standup and fight !"[23]

Of all the ideas, Vivekananda emphasises non-attachment to a great extent. Spirituality for him can never be attained unless all material ideas are given up. But work need not be given up. He says, "Go on, work. Only mind that you are not attached."[24] Man must not confuse one self with his body or the consequent miseries. "Let miseries come in millions of rivers and happiness in hundreds! I am no slave to misery! I am no slave to happiness !"[25] Non-attachment to work is justified by him on the ground that work belongs to nature and nature is not the ultimate reality.

The highest religion for Vivekananda is realisation of the Spirit. The *Maya* or delusion seizes man for he identifies himself with nature and says, 'I am doing this'! Vivekananda feels that Arjuna should have acted in the path choosen for him, which was that of a warrior. He is also critical of the weakness of the Indians and says :

All weaknesses, all bondage is imagination. Speak one word to it, it must vanish. Do not weaken! There is no other way out, standup and be strong! No fear. No superstition.

Face the truth as it is! If death comes, that is the worst of our miseries-let it come ! We are determined to die game. That is all the religion I know. I have not attained to it, but I am struggling to do it. I may not, but you may. Go on![26]

These words uttered in connection with the *Bhagavadgita* reflects his urge to use the same for the elevation of the mental strength of the Indians. These words of Vivekananda created a new diversion. These ideas were easily utilised in the political speeches by others.

Lokamanya Bal Gandhar Tilak (1856-1920), an elder contemporary of Vivekananda, wrote the *Gita-rahasya* and published the same in 1911. He was a socio-religious reformer, a defender of Indian culture and heritage, a Vedic and Sanskrit scholar, a great political activist and the chief exponent of the extremism of the Nationalist faction of the early Indian Congress. Identifying the essence of his approach to the *Gita,* he wrote :

About the *Gita* I have finished what I call *Gita rahasya,* an independent and original book investigating the purpose of the *Gita* and showing how our religious philosophy is applied there in to the solution of the ethical problem. For my view of the *Gita* is that it is a work on ethics-neither utilitarian nor intuitional, but transcendental, some what on the lines followed in Green's Prolegiomina to Ethics. I have compared through out the *Gita*-philosophy with Western, both religious and ethical, and have tried to show that our system is, to say the best, not inferior to any of the western methods.[27]

The above words make it amply clear that Tilak was eager to defend Hinduism and to establish its parity with the West, if not superiority over it. He emphasised the need for an unprejudiced and un-prepossessed mind for the study of the *Gita,* otherwise, he saw the possibility of reading one's own philosophical and ethical convictions into it. Summarising the essence of his stand point, Tilak wrote :

I differ from almost all commentators when I say that the *Gita* enjoins action even after the perfection in *Jnana* and *Bhakti* is attained and the Deity is reached through these media. Now there is a fundamental unity undergoing the Logos (*Ishvara*), man, and world. The world is in existence because the Logos has willed it so. It is his will that holds it together. Man strives to gain union with God; and when this union is achieved the individual Will merges in the mighty Universal Will. When this is achieved will the individual say : "I shall do no action, and I shall not help the world" – the world which is because the Will with which he had sought union has willed it to be so ? It does not stand to reason. It is not I who says so, the *Gita* says so. Sri Krishna himself says that there is nothing in all the three worlds that He need acquire, and still He acts. He acts because if He did not, the world will be ruined. If man seeks unity with the Deity, he must necessarily seek unity with the interests of the world also, and work for it. If he does not, then the unity is not perfect, because there is union between two elements out of three (man and Deity) and the third (the world) is left out. I have thus, solved the question for myself and I hold that serving the world, and thus serving His Will, is the surest way of Salvation, and this way can be followed by remaining in the world and not going away from it.[28]

To Tilak, the *Gita* advocates *Jnanakarmasamucaya* (combination of knowledge and *karma*) and does not advocate *Sannyasa*, though it admits of its possibility.[29] His views had great implications on India's political scenario because, they justified action and because he never read the philosophy of abandonment and non-violence into them. His comparison with western philosophy proved his own depth of knowledge about the West, but simultaneously Tilak was a strange mixture at the worst and a synthesizer at the best, of traditional interpretations of the *Bhagavadgita* and the western philosophical approach. Tilak assumes a great importance for the present work because Aurobindo Ghose was a political collaborator of Tilak and the stand of Gandhi was miles apart from his. The interpretation of the *Bhagavadgita* by Tilak in particular and Vivekananda in general contributed immensely to the debate and introduced it to the freedom struggle at best at a theoretical level for the leaders. It was no longer a mere question of defending Hinduism but of sanctification of political methods and actions adopted by the leaders through the precepts of the *Bhagavadgita*.

REFERENCES

1. Swami Ranganathananda, **Eternal Values for a Changing Society** Vol-I; Bombay, 1987, p.62.
2. Urusula King, 'Iconographic Reflections of the Religious and secular importance of the *Bhagavadgita* within the image world of modern Hinduism', **New Essays In the Bhagavad Gita**; Compiled by Arvind Sharma, New Delhi, p.62-63.
3. S.N. Dasgupta, 'Philosophy', **A Cultural History of India**; (Ed.) A.L. Basham, Oxford; 1975, p.122.
4. D.D. Kosambi, **An Introduction to the study of Indian History**; Bombay, 1956, p.121.
5. S. Radhkrishnan, **Indian Philosophy** – Vol.I; Delhi, 1989, p.523.
6. Ibid.
7. Ibid., p.524.
8. S.K. Belvalkar, 'The *Bhagavadgita*, a General Review of its History and Character', **The Cultural History of India**, Vol.II; Calcutta, 1982, p.135-58.
9. Ibid.
10. H.C. Ray Choudhury, **Political History of Ancient India**, Calcutta, 1972, pp.126-27.
11. S. Radhkrishnan, **The Bhagavad Gita**; Delhi, 1989, p.16.

12. G.V. Saroja, **Tilak and Shankara on Bhagavad Gita;** New Delhi, 1985, p.84.
13. A. Mahadev Shastri, (Tr) **Bhagavad Gita with the commentary of Sri Shankaracharya**; Madras, 1947, p.89.
14. Ibid., p.93.
15. Ibid., pp.309-310.
16. S. Radhkrishnan, **The Bhagavad Gita**; op.cit., p.17-18.
17. Ibid., p.19.
18. Ibid., p.352.
19. J.F. Woods, 'The Concept of Abandonment in the System of Ramanuja' in **New Essays in the Bhagavad Gita**; op.cit., p.82.
20. S. Radhkrishnan, **The Bhagavadgita**; op.cit., p.19-20.
21. Swami Vivekananda, **Complete Works**, Vol.I; Calcutta, 1989, pp.446-484. (Vivekananda delivered three lectures on the *Bhagavadgita* in Sanfransisco in May 1900).
22. Ibid., p.457.
23. Ibid., p.461.
24. Ibid., p.465.
25. Ibid., p.466.
26. Ibid., p.480.
27. V.P. Varma, **The Life and philosophy of Lokamanya Tilak**; Agra,

    1978, p.477.
28. G.V. Saroja, **Tilak and Shamkara on Bhagavad Gita**; op.cit., p.131.
29. B.G. Tilak, **Gita-rahasya** (Hindi); Poona, 1950, Preface, as quoted by V.P. Varma, op.cit., p.479.

CHAPTER – III

SRI AUROBINDO'S TREATMENT OF THE *GITA*

Sri Aurobindo – A Brief Life Sketch :

Sri Aurobindo "successively a poet, critic, scholar, thinker, nationalist, humanist,"[1] was most prolific of all modern Indian writers. He appeared like a shining star on the horizon, at the dawn of this century, and casted a spell over the youth of this Nation. He withdrew from the scene of India's struggle for freedom as dramatically as he had appeared, to lead a life of mysticism and spirituality. As a prelude to an analysis of Sri Aurobind's treatment of the *Bhagavadgita,* the scholar intends to shortly sketch the life and writings of Sri Aurobindo, as a key to a better understanding.

Arbind Ackroyd Ghose[2] was born on 15th August 1872, in Calcutta, as the third child of Dr. Krishnadhan Ghose and Swarnalata. Dr. Krishnadhan Ghose was a M.D., from Aberdein University. Swarnalata was the daughter of Rishi Rajnarayan Bose, the great Brahmo leader. Dr. Krishnadhan Ghose, an ardent supporter of the British rule in India in the early part of his career, was an anglicised physician. He was also an aetheist, though he was charitable to the degree of fault. Aurobindo was entrusted to an English nurse right at the birth and was sent to Loretto Convent School at Darjeeling at the age of five. At the age of seven he was sent to England, along with his elder brothers. He was initially taught privately by the Drewetts and later he joined the St. Paul's school in London. In 1889 he was admitted to the King's College of Cambridge University on winning the classical scholarship. He excelled as a student and won many prizes for his academic excellence. He was a keen student of Greek and Latin, in addition to history. He wrote poetry and some of these were also published. He along with his brothers had to suffer from pecuniary hardships. Aurobindo registered himself as a candidate for the Indian Civil Service Examination and secured the 10th position,[3] in the test, in 1890. He was an I.C.S. probationer for almost two years. He was, however, finally rejected from the service, for he could not clear the riding test, inspite of repeated opportunities. Mr. J.S. Cotton, pleaded with the Public Service Commission and the Secretary of State for providing Aurobindo another chance, which was rejected.The Secretary of State, doubted whether Sri Ghose would be a desirable addition to the service.[4] Though Sri Aurobindo did not have any definite plan for the freedom of India during his stay in England, he was a member of the 'Indian Mujlis', the leading forum of the Nationalist students in England and was also a member of 'Lotus and Dagger', a still-born secret society committed to India's freedom. During his long stay in England, Aurobindo developed an apathy, both towards England and Christianity. He nurtured a great love for Greece, particularly Athens and her rich literary and cultural heritage. The Greek philosopher Heraclitus fascinated him most. Sri Aurobindo also evolved a classical style of writing during these formative years of his life. English had almost become his mother tongue. Inspite of his anglicised childhood and youth, he remained Indian in sensibility.[5] While he was still in England, Sri Aurobindo wrote in 1891.

> Mine is not Byron's lightening spear
> Nor Wordsworth's Lucid strain
> Nor Shelley's Lyric pain,
> Nor Keats, the poet with out peer.
> I, by the Indian waters vast
> Did glimpse the magic of the past,
> And on the Oaten – pipe I play
> Wrapped echoes of our earlier day.[6]

Sri Aurobindo returned to India in early 1893 and joined the Baroda state service. His father had died a few days before his arrival, out of shock on getting a wrong information that his son Aurobindo had died of a mishap in the ocean during his journey from England to India. In Baroda Aurobindo served in various departments and was finally appointed as Professor of English literature. To his abiding interest in the classic of the continent, works of Sanskrit, Bengali, Marathi, and Gujrati were added. The scholar Sri Aurobindo slowly emerged. It was in Baroda, Sri Aurobindo wrote a series of articles titled, "New lamps For Old" in *Induprakash*, in 1893, criticising the moderate Congress policy. This was one of the earliest manifesto of the Extremist Nationalist Congress faction. Tilak was naturally drawn by these articles. It was in Baroda that Sri Aurobindo established contacts with the several societies of Bengal, namely the *Anushilan Samiti*.[7] It was also in the Baroda days, Sri Aurobindo began to take interest in Indian yogic systems, even though had not seriously began to practice them. Sri Aurobindo married Mrilalini Bose in April 1901. He had advertised for a bride for himself in a newspaper and had selected her. Mrilalini Devi was younger to him by fifteen years. They lived apart most of the time till 1905. They had the natural barrier of language. Sri Aurobindo couldn't communicate fluently in Bengali and Mrilalini in English. They seemed to have drifted apart gradually and the marriage was not a landmark in the life of Sri Auronindo. Subsequently, he stayed with his wife from 1905 to 1910, when he was in the thick of political activities and had no time for a family life. From the various letters that he wrote to his wife, it is apparent that Sri Aurobindo was not cut out for a family life. Any sign of difference of opinion, however, can not be discerned. Later when Sri Aurobindo left for Pondicherry, Mrilalini Devi wanted to join him. On the advice of Sri Aurobindo she took initiation from Sharada Devi. She died in 1918, on her way to Pondicherry.

In August 14, 1906 Sri Aurobindo was invited to join the National College at Calcutta as the Principal.[8] By that time he had also emerged as the leader of various extremist parties of Bengal. His younger brother Barindra was the leader of the *Yugantara* group. Jatin Mukherjee was his trusted lieutenant. Sri Aurobindo had also a close contact with Brahmabandhabdeb and Sister Nivedita. He had also become the Vice-president of the *Anushilan Samiti,* which co-ordinated the activities of various extremist factions. Aurobindo was a critic of the Congress policy of moderation and representation, and pleaded in place, mass action and movement. Though he was a man who worked mostly behind the scene, he dominated the nationalist *Bande Mataram* movement in the wake of the partition of Bengal. Sri Aurobindo became the editor of the *Bande Mataram,* the fiery journal established by Bipin Chandra Pal. He also dominated through his writings in journals like *Yugantara, Sandhya* and *Navashakti*. Though he failed to get Tilak elected as the President of A.I.C.C. session in Calcutta in 1906, he along with other extremist leaders succeeded in passing the *Swaraj-Swadeshi-Boycott* and *National Education* resolutions, Aurobindo was instrumental in winning over Dadabhai Naoroji's support for these resolutions, without whom they could never have been accepted by the Congress. Through out 1907, Sri Aurobindo was actively devoted to the cause of anti-partition movement in Bengal. He led the Bengal Nationalist faction in the absence of Brahmabandhabdeb and Bipin Chandra Pal at the momentous A.I.C.C. session of 1907 at Surat.[9] While the moderates attempted to rescue the Congress from the 1906 A.I.C.C. resolutions, the extremists not only wanted to maintain the ideological victory, but aspired to capture the organisation. This led to the split. Aurobindo was elected as the president of the Nationalist Congress of the extremist faction. Shortly after his return from the Surat Congress he was arrested for his alleged involvement in the Alipore bomb case and was finally acquitted and released in May, 1909. The Morley Minto reform was already on the anvil and the *Bande Mataram* movement had ended in a whimper. Aurobindo tried in vain to revive the movement when most of the leaders of the extremist faction were behind the bars. Sri Aurobindo articulated the political philosophy and methods of the extremist faction. His thinking was nearly in direct opposition to the moderate line. For him, the faith in British sense of justice was not merely a misplaced one but was against any sane judgement of imperialism. He could never accept social reform as a pre-condition for freedom. The so-called constitutional method was against self-reliance for Sri Aurobindo. India's nationalism was based on the right of every nation to liberty and freedom. Further, the geographical and cultural unity made India, a Nation. His plea for *Swaraj* was not based on the good or bad nature of British rule in India, but on the concept of the right of every nation to self-rule. India's nationalism was the time-spirit; its forces were impersonal; its leaders were divine tools and it was a necessity for the spiritual regeneration of mankind. Sri Aurobindo was not a revivalist and he had a vision of free-India, vibrating with her eternal spirits, scientifically and technologically advanced. It was neither a return to Sanskrit *tols* nor to autonomous self-sufficient villages.[10]

For India's freedom struggle Sri Aurobindo advanced political methods like passive resistance, *swadeshi*, boycott, and national education. He could not accept the constitutional method of petitioning. He had no objection to terrorism. Nevertheless, he did not advocate it. For Sri Aurobindo, British imperialism had not yet reached the level of Russian autocracy, where, save terrorism there was no other way. For practical and tactical reasons he preferred *swadeshi*, boycott, passive resistance and national education, in place of terrorism. Freedom can not be achieved without sacrifices-was the *mantra* of Sri Aurobindo. In a way, Sri

Aurobindo paved the way for the emergence of a generation of leaders, who were prepared to sacrifice everything for the cause of India's freedom.

Sri Aurobindo, along with other militant nationalists, had added a glorious chapter to the history of the Nationalist movement. They had clarified its objectives, taught people self-confidence and self-reliance and prepared the social base of the movement to include the lower middle classes, students, youth and women.[11]

Without the militant Nationalists, Gandhi would not have found courageous and willing tools of sacrifice at a later date. Gandhi himself, recognizing the patriotism of the nationalist-extremist leaders noted, "some of the members of this party are earnest spirits, possessing a high degree of morality, great intellectual ability and lofty self-sacrifice."[12] Further, appreciating the spirit and impact of the *'Bande Mataram'* movement, he added, "an awakening of the national consciousness is unmistakable."[13]

In 1910, Aurobindo retired to Pondicherry at the call of his inner voice. In between his release from jail and departure for Pondicherry, Sri Aurobindo edited two more journals *viz.*, the *Karmayogin* and the *Dharma;* where he attempted an analysis of Indian scriptures, philosophy and her cultural heritage. Sri Aurobindo's departure for Pondicherry was not as sudden as is popularly believed. At the age of seven, Aurobindo experienced a darkness rushing into him and enveloping him, which left him only on his return to India. He had the vacant infinite realisation on a trip to Kashmir shortly after his marriage. While serving in Baroda, Aurobindo experienced the living presence of *Kali* in a shrine on the banks of river Narmada. He had met a *Naga Sanyasi* and Sri Brahmananda during his Baroda days. Sri Bishnu Bhaskar Lele guided him to achieve absolute silence. He had the *Vasudeva Sarvamiti* realisation of seeing God everywhere and in everything, while he was in the Alipore Jail. During his incarceration he realized that India was destined to be free, as she was already free at the 'higher level' and that he was destined for some other role. And Pondicherry, as it seems today, was the venue, destined for Sri Aurobindo, to enact his role. Sri Aurobindo was a mystic from the beginning. In Pondicherry he continued with his yogic practices and to write his experiences in the pages of *The Arya*. In this journal his major works like the *Veda, The Human Cycle, Foundation of Indian Culture and The Upanishads*, etc. were serialised. On 24th November, 1926, Sri Aurobindo and his yogic associate Mirra Richards, The Mother, attained their final over-mental spiritual *Siddhi* (realisation) together. Though he retired to seclusion after this realisation, Sri Aurobindo continued with his spiritual and literary writings. He passed away on 5th December, 1950.

His Philosophical Outlook :

Sri Aurobindo is universally hailed as the greatest philosopher that India produced in this century. However, he considered himself more to be a poet than a philosopher. He wrote:

. . .and philosophy ! let me tell you in confidence, I never, never, never was a philosopher – although I had written philosophy which is another story altogether. I knew precious little about philosophy before I did the *Yoga* and came to Pondicherry. I was a poet and a politician, not a philosopher.[14]

The philosophical system of Sri Aurobindo emerged in the columns of *The Arya*. Paul Richards and Sri Aurobindo jointly launched *The Arya*, with the objective of projecting the Indian philosophy in a Western format for the benefit of the Western readers. However, as Paul Richards died shortly after the launching of the journal, Sri Aurobidno continued to fill the pages of *The Arya*, single handed. His major works noted above, gradually thus took shape.

Sri Aurobindo's metaphysics is a brilliant attempt to synthesise both eastern and western views in articulating the philosophy of integral non-dualism. He asserted that, it was possible to achieve a balanced harmony between the material and the spiritual world. His system is based on a hierarchical and evolutionary premise, that all life and matter constitute material energy and form.[15] He was a teleologist and an idealist. He envisaged the transformation of the present 'mental man' into a spiritually perfect man. As matter for him, is an extension of *Brahman*, it automatically contains the potentiality of the Divine. Self realisation was the first step of *yoga*, for Sri Aurobindo. He aspired that the finites including man shall continue to live with their distinction of finiteness, but with the full knowledge that they are not different from the infinite. Sri Aurobindo asserted that knowledge is characterised by a consciousness of Unity in Diversity. *Avidya* for him is the consciousness of the 'many', without the realisation that the 'one' and the 'many' are not different. Thus ignorance or evil is a result of distorting consciousness.[16]

Sri Aurobindo developed the concept of the 'seven-fold-knot' of 'Being'. For him, the absolute is, *Saccidananda* – 'Truth Conscious-Force Bliss' – which is not a triple but a triune. It creates the 'supermind' as a creative organ, which in turn develops into 'over-mind'. Existence turns into matter, Conscious-Force into life and Bliss or delight into the psychic. Thus Sri Aurobindo conceived a seven-fold-knot of 'Being' with the super-mind, as a link between the world of the Absolute and the finite. While the supermind is conscious of both the infinite nature of the Absolute and the de-limitations of the Absoltue to create the world of finite, the finites forget their origin and their infinite nature. Thus, this ignorance is the root of Evil. For Sri Aurobindo, the principles of matter, life, psychic and mind are introduced one after another and each new principle carries forward the older ones integrating and synthesising them. Thus for Sri Aurobindo, the story of the creation and cosmos is the tale of the *Saccidananda's* involvement in a self-created world and evolution from ignorance to knowledge. In other words, Sri Aurobindo's teleology can only be complete, if men live with full knowledge. He envisaged that either men must be divinised or a new species has to overtake man to complete the course of evolution.[17] It may be noted here that the scholar has attempted to over simplify the metaphysics of Sri Aurobindo. However, in the ensuing discussion on Sri Aurobindo's treatment of the *Bhagavadgita*, efforts shall be made to treat Sri Aurobindo's metaphysics, more justly.

Before the present discussion on Sri Aurobindo's life and philosophical outlook is rounded off, few generalisations may be made to illustrate his mental make-up even at the cost of a few inevitable repetitions. Though Sri Aurobindo was educated in England and had a deep mastery over Western Classics; explained his philosophy through Western format, and even if one concedes that West influenced him greatly, his sensibility remained basically Indian, in all its beauty. He realized that the Creation is but a Divine play. He saw a world deep dark beyond death, yet with sparks of eternal light. There was a passion in him to know the 'Ultimate', but reason or mind was not the instrument with which he was searching. He all along knew that intelligence does not know all , even if it knows a lot. He found that the brain and the body were stumbling-blocks for knowing all, and that it should not be left out in the process of knowing but the body and mind should know as much as the soul and life.

The momentous contemporary world for him was a divine stage, enacting the drama of evolution. He perceived the subjective ignorance of Hitler and the limitations of an expanding science and technology. He was conscious of the struggle of Nature to overcome itself and its own limitations. During most of his days he was within the penumbra of a mightier divine experience. He knew that this body and mind must change their ways so that the new can come. Though he saw the change coming from the outside, he knew that mankind has to change itself from within, so that the change from above can be effectively received. He was essentially a man of feeling and experience; more of a visionary and a prophet than an academic thinker. Though Sri Aurobindo was a voracious reader, it is difficult to concede that books, save the *Vedas, Upanishads,* and the *Gita,* ever influenced him much. Though he was not an indulgent man, he can not be perceived as an ascetic. His life was more in tune with the lives of ancient *Rishis* or seers of India than of the *Sannyasis* or ascetics. Sri Aurobindo himself speaks of his three 'madnesses', *viz.,* to repay the debt to God, to realize and to have a direct vision of God and to make India independent.[18] Spiritual seeking, love for his Motherland and an intense humanism are the hallmarks of Sri Aurobindo.

Treatment of the *Gita* :

Sri Aurobindo's principal work on the *Gita,* was serialized in *The Arya* as *Essays on the Gita,* from August 1916, to July 1918 and the second series from August, 1918 to July, 1920. Sri Aurobindo like Tilak and Gandhi, had a special association with the *Bhagavadgita.* During his stay in England Sri Aurobindo had not taken any keen interest in the *Gita.* He studied the *Bhagavadgita* along with the other scriptures during his stay at Baroda. Sri Aurobindo, like other stalwarts of the freedom struggle, cited examples from the *Gita* to invoke the mass, for participation in the freedom struggle. Echoes of the *Bhagavadgita* can be traced in his early political philosophy as propounded in the columns of the *Bande Mataram* and *Karmayagin.* The most important arguments like the role of spirit of time, the Divine descent for suppression of evil, the concept of leaders being mere instruments for the liberation of India and justification of violence – all came partially from the *Gita*.[19]

As noted above, the *Essays on the Gita,* the principal work of Sri Aurobindo was serialized during 1916 to 1920.[20] Its basic journalistic nature can be conceded, naturally. Each part can stand independently to an extent and being a serial, some amount of repetition was inevitable. When the *Bhagavadgita* was being serialized in the columns of the *Arya,* other principal works of Sri Aurobindo like the *Life Divine, Foundation of Indian Culture,* and *The Human Cycle,* were also serialized. As noted earlier, Sri Aurobindo's principal objective of his writings in the *Arya* was to present Indian philosophy to the Western readers in a Western format, using Western logic. Thus, he did not intend to provide an absolute, original and radically new interpretation of the *Bhagavadgita.* He intended to repair the damage caused by the unsympathetic and inaccurate assessments of the *Gita* provided by the western indologists, philologits, historians and the students of comparative religion. He also endeavoured to rescue the essence of the *Bhagavadgita* from the conflicting hoard of Sanskrit commentaries, where the commentators had overtaken the spirit of the original text. In fact, there were a number of commentaries on the commentaries of the *Gita.* Aurobindo aspired to interpret the *Bhagavadgita* by identifying himself with it, by reliving through the psychological experiences, that had shaped the original *Bhagavadgita.* Without rejecting the contemporary and eternal relevance of the *Bhagavadgita,* Sri Aurobindo attempted to restore it to its original setting and back ground. *The Essays on the Gita* contains the matured reflections of Sri Aurobindo on the subject, when he was already free from the concurrent intersecting forces of the freedom struggle and the subsequent debate on the question of violence, in relation with the *Gita.* In other words, Sri Aurobindo considered the *Bhagavadgita* on a wider canvas than the mere events of the freedom struggle in India. Sri Aurobindo did not deal the *Bhagavadgita* stanza by stanza. He did not attempt a translation, nor even a commentary. Sri Aurobindo himself spells out his objective in writing the *Essays on the Gita* and writes :

Our object then, in studying the *Gita* will not be a scholastic or academical scrutiny of its thought, nor to place its philosophy in the history of metaphysical speculation, nor shall we deal with it in the manner of the analytical dialectician. We approach it for help and light and our aim must be to distinguish its essential and living message; that is in it on which humanity has to seize for its perfection and its highest spiritual welfare.[21]

In other words, Sri Aurobindo took up the writing of the *Essays on the Gita* with the object of providing a guide to the practitioner of his system of *Yoga*.

Essays on the Gita of Sri Aurobindo has to be read along with other principal works which were simultaneously serialized in the *Arya*. Even though Sri Aurobindo identified his objective of the study of the *Gita* otherwise, the scholar in him persisted and his *Essays on the Gita* will withstand academic and scholastic yard-sticks. Sri Aurobindo was cognisant of the multi-faceted nature of the *Bhagavadgita* and attributed numerous interpretations to its readable and poetical nature, in contrast to the *Vedas* and *Upanisads* which are too mystical and much shrouded in the webs of philosophy. Emphasising this aspect of the *Bhagavadgita*, Sri Aurobindo writes, "each finds in the *Gita* its own system of metaphysics and trends of religious thought."[22] To appreciate the various interpretations, the understanding of the setting of the *Bhagavadgita* is a pre-condition. It is important to further highlight Sri Aurobindo's stand and his objectives for the treatment of the *Gita*.

In writing the *Essay on the Gita*, Sri Aurobindo had two distinct objectives, one was to ascertain its importance in relation to the period of its composition, the other was to bring out the eternal message applicable universally, irrespective of its spatial and temporal sequence. He did not consider the *Bhagavadgita* to be a metaphysical text or a treatise presenting Indian philosophical concepts and systems. He emphasised its synthetic nature and its spiritual overtone. "The *Gita* is not a weapon for dialectical warfare, it is a gate opening on the whole world of spiritual truth and experience."[23] For Sri Aurobindo it is a manifestation of a vast synthetic mind and a rich synthetic experience. He writes:

This is one of those great synthesis in which Indian spirituality has been as rich as in its creation of the more intensive, exclusive movement of knowledge and religious realizations that follow out with an absolute concentration-one clue, one path to its extreme issues.[24]

Sri Aurobindo, unlike contemporary indologists, students of comparative religion and Indian history, argued that there was no opposition between the *Vedas* and the *Upanishads;* Buddha and the *Vedas*, and *Gita* and the earlier Indian scriptures. He argued that the latter scriptures always carried forward the experiences of the earlier ones, and the experiences were not necessarily contradictory to each other.[25] Canto 4 of the *Gita Dhyanam* says :

Sarvopanisado gavo
Dogdha gopala nandanah
Partho vatsah sudhir bhokta
Dugdham gitamrtam mahat

Which means, "All the *Upanishads* are the cows, the milker is *Krishna*, the cowehered boy, *Partha* is the calf, men of purified intellect are the drinkers, the milk is the supreme nectar of the *Gita*.[26]

The Setting of the *Bhagavadgita* :

Sri Aurobindo emphasises the practical setting of the *Bhagavadgita*, rather than the metaphysical or the historical. The historicity of the *Mahabharata* war, the plausibility of the *Bhagavadgita* and the feasibility of Lord Krishna's giving such a disicourse on the eve of the *Mahabharata* War; did not tax the mind of Sri Aurobindo. In his opinion, the *Bhagavadgita* is so much interwoven with the *Mahabharata* that it can not be properly understood against any other setting. One may concede that the composer of the *Bhagavadgita,* irrespective of his identity and the time of his compositions; wanted the *Bhagavadgita* to be eternally tagged with the Great Epic. The composer of the *Bhagavadgita* himself has chosen the setting of the *Mahabharata,* for his composition. Thus there is little scope for any doubt or a debate on this.[27] Sri Aurobindo's understanding of the *Bhagavadgita* can be sought in the answers he gave to the following problems :

The relevance of the *Mahabharata* setting.

The nature of the character involved, namely

Sri Krishna and Arjuna.

The problems that they aspired to solve.

The solutions they offered.

Mahabharata is the tale of a war. The situation of the *Bhagavadgita* is the battle field of *Kurukshetra* and the occasion of the discourse is the inner crisis confronted by Arjuna. For Sri Aurobindo war is a necessity of life and an instrument of progress. Struggle and crisis are, according to Sri Aurobindo the necessary preconditions for self progress and self realisation. A warrior can also be an ideal man for him. Man finds himself constantly being tossed by a chaos of battling powers, clash of vast obscure forces, a life which subsists on a constant change, death and renewal; and pain, suffering, evil, destruction; all claiming their due. Man has to accept a struggle or a battle as a part of life and existence. Recognising one among the many utilities of war, Sri Aurobindo pointed out how the French Revolution, the Napoleonic Wars, The First World War and even the second World War had fostered the concept of a single world political organisation.[28] For him

Kurukshetra also symbolises this. *Mahabharata* is not an epic story of the family tree of the *Bharatas*, but is the story of the *Mahabharata* War, that was fought in the battle field of *Kurukshetra*. The conflict and struggle had many aspects including the physical. Sri Aurobindo writes:

The *Gita* proceeds from the acceptance of the necessity in Nature, for such vehement crises and it accepts not only the moral aspect, the struggle between righteousness and the unrighteousness, between the self offering law of good and the forces that oppose its progression, but also the physical aspect, the actual armed war or rather vehement physical strife between the human being who represent the antagonistic powers.[29]

From Hiraclitus, through Hegel, to Nieztsche; there were many thinkers in the history of philosophy who accepted war as an instrument of progress and realisation. War is used by Nature itself as often as love; love and war are not necessarily opposite to each other. Thus Krishna and Arjuna, both the principal characters of the *Bhagavadgita* are entangled in the *Mahabharata* war.

Before we attempt to analyse the conflict of Arjuna and the answers offered by Krishna, one must spell out what they symbolise as characters. The companionship between Arjuna and Sri Krishna for Sri Aurobindo, is a metaphor of companionship between the Human and the Divine soul. Sri Krishna is an incarnation or *Avatar*, the descent of the divine consciousness manifested in the visible human form to intervence and to guide the course of evolution and involution, in the desired direction at a time of crisis, or say the 'Node' of change. Time comes when a thing can not remain what it was previously. At such crucial junctures in the process of eternal change, the role of an *Avatar* becomes vital. The following line from the *Gita* bears out the necessity of the manifestation of an *Avatar* :

Yada-yada hi dharmasya
Glanir bhavti bharata

Abhyutthanam adharmasya
Tada 'tmanam srjamyaham
Paritranaya sadhunam
Vinasaya ca duskrtam
Dharma samsthapanarthaya
Sambhavami yuge yuge IV. 7 and 8.

"Whenever there is decay of *dharma* and rise of *adharma,* then I embody myself, O *Bharata* for the protection of the good, for the destruction of the wicked and for the establishment of *dharma* I am born, age after age."[30] It is important to note that Sri Krishna is the charioteer, one who leads, of the chariot of Arujuna. Parallels of this concept of the joint effort of man and God to fight evil are also seen in other Indian scriptures. In the *Vedas,* we find *Indra* and *Kutsa,* riding together in one chariot, through a great battle. Indra, the master of the world of light and immortality; *Kutsa,* the human soul, both fighting together falsehood and darkness. The relationship between *Nara* and *Narayana,* man in God and God in man, is too well known to be emphasised further. This message is universally delivered through the *Vedas,* the *Upanishads* and the *Gita.*

Krishna is also the teacher in the *Gita,* emphasising this aspect Sri Aurobindo writes :

The Teacher of the *Gita* is, therefore, not only the God in man who unveils himself in the world of knowledge, but the God in man, who moves our humanity exists and struggles and labours, towards whom all human life travels and progresses. He is the secret Master of works and sacrifice and the friend of human people.[31]

Similarly Arjuna is no ordinary human being, "he is the type of the struggling human soul who has not yet received the knowledge, but has grown fit to receive it by action in the world in a close companionship and an inceasing nearness to the higher and divine self in humanity."[32]

When Arjuna urges Him to tell him the details of this *Yoga* and *Vibhuti*, Sri Krishna among other things says that He is Arjuna, (the best) among the *Pandavas.*

> *Vrsninam vasudevo 'smi*
>
> *Pandavanam dhanamjayah.* X. 37.

"Of the *Vrishnis* I am Vasudeva; of the *Pandavas*, Dhananjaya" (Arjuna).[33]

Arjuna was not the best man of his age in any respect, nor was he superior to any among the *Pandavas* or the *Kauravas*. Yudhistira was the greatest in the sense of morality, Bhisma, in the knowledge of state-craft and politics; Vidura in wisdom, Drona in archery, Karna in charity and chivalry, Bhima in strength, Duryodhana in vanity and so on. Yet Arjuna was chosen as the student, for he alone was completely surrendered to Sri Krishna; the Divine Teacher.[34] It is Arjuna alone, who could have said; "Thy word, I will do !", (*karisye vacanam tava* XVIII.73).[35] Arjuna is a *kshtriya*, a man of action, in whom the *rajasik* element of personality is dominant, but he has also a *sattvik* pose. A *kshatriya* has a distinct social and psychological disposition. Sri Aurobindo pointing this out writes, "His real work is the development , the expression in conduct, the power to cast into form and dynamic rhythm of movement, and the law of the active battling royal or warrior spirit."[36]

Arjuna had lived and guided himself by the *shastras*, the moral and social codes of conduct. He is ever eager to obey the laws of *dharma*. He is high-minded, self-governed, chivalrous, a natural warrior and a leader. Arjuna is the man of action, not of knowledge. He is the fighter, never the seer or the thinker.

Having generally spelt out the characteristics of Sri Krishna and Arjuna, the focus must now shift to the crisis itself. The crisis of Arjuna is most appropriately hinted at the title *Arjuna vishada yoga* of the *Bhagavadgita*. The word *vishada* can not be translated exactly into English, as many other

Sanskrit words. However, words like dejection, despondency, gloominess, downheartedness, - all carry the meaning of *vishada* in some way or the other. Arjuna, standing amidst the two equally poised army of the *Kauravas* and the *Pandavas* realizes how men of same race, clan, family and even household stand on opposite sides, to fight against each other; to destroy each other. Death alone seems to be the greatest truth. Arjuna recoils from war and refuses to fight against his own kinsmen.

Tan samiksya sa kaunteyah
Sarvan bandhun avasthitan
Krpaya paraya visto
Visidann idam abravit
Drstve' man savajanam krsna
Yuyutsum samupasthitam
Sidanti mama gatrani
Mukham ca parisusyati
Vepathus ca sarire me
Romaharsas ca jayate
Gandivam sramsate hastat
Rvak cai va paridahyate. 1.27-29.

"Seeing all these kinsmen, thus standing arrayed, *kaunteya*, invaded by great pity uttered this in sadness and dejection. Arjuna said, "seeing these, my own people, O Krishna ! arrayed for battle, my limbs collapse and my mouth is parched, my body shakes and my hair stands on end; *gandiva* (the bow) slips from my hand and all my skin seems to be burning"!.

Na ca sreyo 'nupasyami
Hatva svajanam ahave
Na kankse vijayam krsna
Na ca rajyam sukhani ca. I.3.1

"Nor do I see any good in slaying my own people? in battle, O Krishna! I desire nor victory, nor kingdom, nor pleasures !(Canto 31).

Kim no rajyena govinda
Kim bhogair jivitena va. I.32.
Nihatya dhartarastran nah
Ka pritih syaj janardana
Papameva srayed asman
Ḥatvai' tan atatyinah. I.36.

"What is kingdom to us oh ! Govinda ! what enjoyment, what even life? What pleasure can be ours after killing sons of Dhritarastra, O ! Janardan ! Sin only will take hold of us in slaying them, though they are the aggressors."

Tasman na rha vayam hantum
Dhartarastran svandhavan
Svajanam hi katham hatva
Sukhinah syama madhava. I.37.

"So it is not fit that we kill the sons of Dhritarastra our Kinsmen, indeed ! how may we be happy, O Madhava ! killing our own people"?

aho bata mahat papam
kartum vyavasita vayam
yad rajya sukha lobhena
hantum svajanam udyatah
yadi mam apratikaram
asastram sastrapanayah,
dhartarstra rane hanyuh
tan me ksemataram bhavet. I.45-46.

"Alas ! we were engaged in committing a great sin, we who were endeavouring to kill our own people through greed of the pleasures of kingship. It is for my welfare that the sons of Dharitarastra armed should slay me unarmed and unresisting; (I will not fight !)."[37]

Describing the inner crisis of Arjuna as expressed in the *Arjuna vishada yoga*, Sri Aurobindo writes;

The character of this inner crisis is, therefore, not the questioning of the thinker, it is not a recoil from the appearances of life and a turning of the eye inward. It is the sensational, emotional and moral revolt of the man, hither to satisfied with action and its current standards who finds himself, cast by them into a hideous chaos, where they are in violent conflict with each other and with themselves and there is no sense of moral ground left, nothing to lay hold of and walk by, no *dharma*.[38]

As noted earlier, the crisis of the *Gita* according to Sri Aurobindo is the crisis of *dharma*. The *Mahabharata* war is a *dharma yudha*. Sri Krishna is born to restore *dharma*. *Dharma* means an accepted ethical standard of behaviour which holds the individual and the social life together. That law to Arjuna seemes to be slipping from the ground throwing the whole of the cosmos into a confusion and a chaos. Arjuna finds this *dharma* to be slippery. He is not eager to change one set of *dharma* for another, but is lost and despondent; for he finds that his *dharma* fails to extend support to life and action. Thus, for Sri Aurobindo the essential problem of Arjuna is not ethical. Arjuna is not questioning the 'rightness' or 'wrongness' of the ethics but finds that ethics can not be the true foundation of life and is in search of a more permanent, a more secure foundation of life. The crisis of Arjuna, as seen by Sri Aurobindo is not ethical or spiritual. It is more of a practical situation. With a great sense of humour, Sri Aurobindo says that the *Gita* 'would not have sent Buddha back to his wife'; the question is not of the social duty of Arjuna, but of a situation, where dharma no longer seems to hold the key to the problems of life. The whole tone of Sri Aurobindo is that Arjuna is lifted from the ethics of lower native *Prakriti* and to him the nature of the Divine, *Paraprakriti* is revealed.

Life is a battle and a field of death – that is *kurukshetra*. The vision Arjuna had is of God – the terrible. For Sri Aurobindo, the crisis is also one of evolution. He writes,

> .....the *Gita*, takes for its frame such a period of transition and crisis as humanity periodically experiences in its history, in which great forces clash together for a huge destruction and reconstruction, intellectual, social, moral, religious, political and these, in the actual psychological and social stage of human evolution, culminate usually through a violent physical convulgent strife, war or revolution.[39]

To summarise the setting, it may be noted here that the occasion is the *Kurukshetra*, a battle field, the time is of a crisis in the social, psychological evolution of mankind; Arjuna is the man of action, a soul ready to receive revelation and his crisis is spiritual, rising out of loss of faith in the very validity of ethics and Sri Krishna, the incarnation, is the Divine Teacher, ready to intervene in the process of evolution. The solution and the answers, offered in the *Gita*, as interpreted by Sri Aurobindo, can be best understood from the following analysis of the metaphysics, ethics and the practical message of the *Bhagavadgita*.

The *Gita* being a post *Vedic* and *Upanishadic* work, carries forward the philosophical and spiritual heritage of India from these two scriptures. Though the *Gita* is better known for practical guidance it provides for life, it contains no less brilliant analysis of metaphysical questions that India has eternally posed. The present discussion on metaphysics centres around two issues, namely Sri Aurobindo's understanding of the metaphysical analysis as contained in the *Gita* and the influence of the *Bhgavadgita* on Sri Aurobindo's system of metaphysics developed later.

The Concept of Ultimate Reality :

The concept of God or Reality is the most important component of metaphysics both in the East and the West. As such it automatically occupies a primary position in the present analysis of Sri Aurobindo's understanding of the *Gita's* metaphysics. In the *Bhagavadgita* amongst all other Indian scriptures, the most complete and the most synthetic concept of reality is developed and Sri Aurobindo had the clarity, understanding and vision of recognising the same. In Indian philosophy, basically three positions are offered on the concept of reality *viz.*, monistic, dualistic and either qualified monism or qualified dualism. The *Gita* reconciles absolutely and also logically, the debate on mutability and immutability of the Eternal. The *Purusha, Prakriti* and *Shakti* are all well reconciled in the *Bhagavadgita*. The *Bhagavadgita* has succinctly transcended the apparent logical barrier between theories of reality and recognises every aspect of reality with out any logical or psychological inconsistency. Few quotations from Sri Aurbindo are cited below for an understanding of his interpretation of the concept of reality as expounded in the *Bhagavadgita*. Pointing at the reconciliatory and synthetic aspect of the concept of reality in the *Gita* Sri Aurobindo writes :

To see that we have to look through its silence to the *Purusottama*, and He in his Divine greatness possesses both the *Akshara* and *Kshara*, He is seated in the immobility, but he manifests himself in the movement and in all the actions of the cosmic Nature, to Him, even after liberation, the sacrifice of works in nature continues to be offered.[40]

Sri Aurobindo greatly emphasises the 18th verse of Chapter XV of the *Bhagavadgita* which runs thus :

Yasmat ksaram atito 'ham
Aksarad api co 'ttamah
Ato 'smi loke veda ca
Prathitah purusottamah.

Sri Aurobindo Translates – "Since I am beyond the mutable and am greater and higher even than the immutable in the world and the *Veda*, I am proclaimed as the *Purusottama*." In otherwords, Sri Aurobindo in line with the *Bhagavadgita* considered *Uttama Purusha* or *Purusottama* as the highest status of the Supreme. The *Ksara* and *Aksara* or the mutable and the immutable are two other status of the *Purusottama* alone. *Purusottama* is beyond these two apparent contradictions and yet is both of it. He is infact the non-doer doer, who has no desire to the fruits of action. He is, however, not the combination of both *Ksara* and *Aksara* but He is more or greater than either of these opposites.

Uttamah purusas tv anyah
Parmatme'ty udahrtah
Yo lokarayam avishya
Bibharty avyaya isvarah. XV.17

This verse of the *Purusottamayogah* of the *Bhagavadgita,* is translated by Sri Aurobindo as, "But other than these two is the highest spirit called the supreme is self who enters the three worlds and unbears them, the imperishable lord." Noting its importance Sri Aurobindo adds, "this verse is the key word."[41] *Purusottama* is also *Prakriti,* for *Prakriti* is the power of the "All Soul", the power of the eternal and the infinite self moved to action and creation. *Shakti* (Power), *Maya* (Conscious Nature) and *Prakriti* (Effective force) taken together is called the *Paraprakriti* in the *Bhagavadgita*. The Absolute works through *Paraprakriti* but is not involved in it nor subject to it, nor affected by it or bound by it, even though it is difficult to distinguish Him from *Paraprakriti*. He is the doer, yet the imperishable non-doer. Works donot fix on Him nor has He any desire for the fruits of action.

Absolute is the Eternal, the Infinite, the Impersonal Self, the Spirit, the Supreme Soul, the Master of all, the Omnipotent Originator of all. To Sri Aurobindo :

He is in all and all are in Him. He has become all and yet too He is above all and not limited by his creations. He is the transcendent Divine. He descends as the *Avatara*. He is manifest by His power in the *Bibhuti*. He is the God-head, secret in every human being. All the Gods whom men worship are only personalities and forms and names and mental bodies of the one divine Existence.[42]

Having analysed the concept of Reality of the *Gita* by Sri Aurobindo, we may turn to *Life Divine*, his metaphysical *magnum opus* and point out the striking similarity between the two. In the *Life Divine* the Absolute is named as *Saccidananda* like the *Gita*, and in the *Life Divine*, Reality is described simultaneously as the Creator, the Upholder, the Harmoniser and the Destroyer.[43] The *Life Divine* also admits like the *Gita*, the Absolute to be indefinable and inconceivable by the limited defining mind of man. Both maintain the Reality to be simultaneously immutable, stable, transcendental, supracosmic *Brahman* and also the mutable, dynamic, universal, cosmic and individual existence. However, the *Maya* as described in the *Life Divine* can be equated only to *Paraprakriti* as mentioned in the *Gita*: *Maya* as referred in the *Bhagavadgita* can only correspond *Daivi Maya* of the *Life Divine*. The *Saccidananda* (Supreme existence – Consciousness-Bliss) is also described as the womb of all creation in the *Life Divine*[44] which is similar to the nature of the *Brahman* described in the following cantos of the *Bhagavadgita*.

Mama yonir mahad brahma
Tasmin garbham dadamyaham
Sambhavah sarbabhutanam
Tato bhavati bharata. XIV.3.

Which means, "What ever forms are in the wombs O *Kounteys*! And I the seed giving father !"

Sri Aurobindo in his *Life Divine*, elucidating the concept of Reality and *Maya* refers to the following verse of the *Bhagavadgita*.[45]

Isvara sarvabhutanam
Hrddse 'rjuna tisthati
Brahmayan sarvabhutanam
Yantrarudhani mayaya. XVIII.6.

He translates, "It is seated with every thing as the Lord in the heart of all existence, - he who turns them as an engine by the power of his *Maya.*"

Sri Aurobindo's the *Life Divine* bears out the similarity in the treatment of the concept of the absolute, the creator vis-vis the creation, with that of the *Bhagavadgita.* Sri Aurobindo writes : "The Energy that creates the world can be nothing else than a will and will is only consciousness applying itself to a work and result."[46] Behind our surface self we, "find this becoming, change, succession are only a mode of our being and that there is, that in us which is not involved at all in the becoming."[47]

He also states, "Let us hasten to add the movement, the energy, the becoming are also a fact, also a reality .... To deny one or the other is easy, to recognize the facts of consciousness and find out their relation is the true and fruitful wisdom."[48] Sri Aurobindo emphasises further the need of reconciling the duality of cosmos and says : "We must accept the double fact, admit both *Siva* and *Kali* and to seek to know what is this measurelessness are inapplicable."[49]

The concept of Time Spirit is a valuable one for Sri Aurobindo, in the *Bhagavadgita.* Lord Krishna emphasises the circumstances under which the Godhead intervenes in the form of an *Avatara* (incarnation) in the following verses of the *Gita.*

Yada-yada hi dharmasya
Glanir bhavti bharata
Abhyutthanam adharmasya
Tada 'tmanam srjamyaham. IV.7

Paritranaya sadhunam
Vinasaya ca duskrtam
Dharma samsthapanarthaya
Sambhavami yuge yuge IV. 8.

"When ever there is decay of *dharma* and rise of *adharma*, then I embody Myself O Bharata. For the protection of the good for the destruction of the wicked and for establishment of *dharma* I am born age after age." [50]

Sri Aurobindo also emphasizes this aspect in his *Essays on the Gita*. During freedom struggle, Sri Aurobindo in his speeches, time and again spoke of God intervening in the movement. Hegel's concept of *Zeitgeist* or spirit of time was in popular currency in the first half of the twentieth century.

To Sri Aurobindo the time also manifests as the great destroyer. The *Bhagavadgita* says :

Yadrcchihaya co 'papannam
Svargadvaram apavrtam
Sukhinah ksatriyah partha
Labhante yuddham idrsam. II.32.

"Happy are the Kshatriyas", translates Swami Chidbhavananda, "O Partha!, who obtain such a warfare that comes unsought as an open gateway to heavan."[51]

As pointed out earlier, to Sri Aurobindo, the *Brahman* is simultaneously the Destroyer, and the Creator. He is Lord of peace, love, calm and eternity and also the great destroyer; even the Tyrant and the Oppressor. *Brahman* is also the *Rudra*, the performer of the calm and aweful dance, who is *Kali* with her garland of skulls, trampling naked in battle and flecked with the blood of the slaughtered Titans, who is the cyclone and fire and the earth quake and pain and famine, and revolution and ruin and the swallowing ocean.[52]

Concept of the Cosmos :

Of all the religious scriptures and books the *Bhagavadgita* is more concerned with this world than the world beyond. *Bhagavadgita* is more concerned with the Cosmos. It expounds the being and the becoming equally. The *Gita* describes the cosmic existence in the vedantic image of the *Asvattha* (banyan tree). It has no beginning or end in space and time, is eternal and imperishable. Its original source is above, beyond time and space its branches are stretched below and it extends and plunges in to the other roots, both in the material and in the supra-physical plains. The phenomenal existence is the derivative of the Supreme and is bound down by the *karma* and the *gunas* (nature). By cutting asunder these roots of desire by inaction or by acting without desire, one can attain the Supreme. The *Bhagavadgita* states :

Urdhavamulam adhahsakham
Asvattham prahur avayam
Chandamsi yasya parnani
Yas tam veda sa vedavit
Adhas' co' rdhvam prasrtas tasya
Sakha gunapravrddha visayapravalah
Adhas' ca mulany anusamtatani
Karmanubandhani manusyaloke
Na rupam asye' ha tatho' palabhyate
Na' nto a ca' dir na ca sampratistha
Asvattham enam suvirudhamulam
Asangasastrena drdhena chittva
Tatah padam tat parimargitavyam
Yasmim gatana nivartanti bhuyah
Tam eva ca' dyam purusam prapadye
Yatah pravrttih prasrta purani. XV.1-4.

They mean, "They speak of an imperishable *Asvattha tree* (banyan tree) with its root above and branches below. Its leaves are the *Vedas;* he who knows it is the knower of the *Vedas.*" "Below and above spread its branches, nourished by the *gunas;* sense objects are its buds; and below in the world of men stretch forth the roots, engendering action. Its form is not here perceived as such, neither its end, nor its origin, nor its existence." "Having cut asunder this firm-rooted *Asvattha* with the strong axe of non-attachment. Then that goal should be sought for going whither, they do not return again. I seek refuge in that primeaval *Purusa* whence streamed forth the Eternal Activity."[53]

Explaining this Aspect Sri Aurobindo Writes :

The *Gita* admits the philosophic motive of indifference as a preliminary movement, but the indifference to which it finally arrives, if indeed that inadequate word can be at all applied, has nothing in it of the philosophic aloofness. It is indeed, a position as one is seated above, *Udasinavat* (like an indifferent person), but as the Divine is seated above having no need at all in the world, yet he does work always and is present every where, supporting, helping, guiding the labour of creatures.[54]

The Cosmos/ Nature is nothing but Him. It is but one Divine, the all *Vasudeva,* manifested as variations in the cosmos. It is indeed only a self limitation for the manifesting Godhead.[55] The aim of the whole cosmic manifestation is to return to the unmanifested state of the Supreme Reality at the end of death and destruction. The Real alone is the beginning and the end of all and He is also the middle.

The 28th verse of the second chapter of the *Bhagavadgita* says :

Avyaktadini bhutani
Vyakta madhyani bharata
Avyaktani dhanany eva
Tatra ka paridevana.

It is translated as, "Beings are all, O Bharata, unmanifested in their origin, manifested in their mid-state and unmanifested again in their end. What is the point then for anguish?."[56]

The *Gita* thus speaks of cycles of cosmos, in one cycle all variations, all creation or the whole of the cosmos is thrown out into the world of mutable and in the next cycle all return to the world of immutable. This is according to Sri Aurobindo, same as the Vedic and *Vedantic* ideas of *Brahma's* 'Day' and 'Night'. The *Purusottama* stands beyond this and the *Jiva* (individual soul) which attains this does not return to the world of mutable or immutable. These cycles are of course the workings of the Supreme. At the individual level at the cosmos, the Supreme is the *Jiva* or the *Purusa* at every level. It is the *Purusa* which creates the finite or the limited world with his yogic or *daivi maya*. He creates the same by the *trigunas* of the *prakriti*, a lower form of Nature in every individual. The lower form of Nature is a copy of the higher form of Nature only. The Supreme Creates with the *Panchabhutas* (five elements like earth, fire, water, air and space), the mind, intelligence and ego, all working through the *trigunas* as the limiting agents. The infinite and the unlimited in each being is the *Jiva* which, out of ignorance owing to the limiting agents does not recognise the Self. Even if it recognises Him, he thinks that he works on his behalf and thinks himself to be different from Him. However, in the ultimate analysis He alone acts. He is the field of action, the action, and the enjoyer of the action. He is also the *Vibhuti* or the greater portion of Him or even the *Avatara* or the descent of the time spirit. He is the Sustainer of the creation, the Creation itself and the Destroyer. Sri Aurobindo recognises that the *Gita* does not distinguish between the being and the becoming even at the cosmos level. The difference is at the level of ignorance.

Sri Aurobindo speaks of a twofold understanding of cosmos, one must not only understand that all is one, only one soul pervades everything and the unity of the cosmos with the Supreme, but one must also realize the Supreme itself. True knowledge is also living in knowledge. In other words an intellectual knowledge of the Divine Origin and nature of cosmos without the knowledge of the Absolute itself remains incomplete. Further, Sri Aurobindo upholds that true knowledge of the cosmos and the Absolute must become a living experience. One must know that God is the origin of all, that he is not different from God and he must also live in God.

The cosmos, as Sri Aurobindo understands, is only a replica of the *Purusa* and the *Prakriti* of the higher level. Sri Aurobindo opines that in the *Bhagavadgita* the *Purusa* and the *Prakriti* are totally unified at the *Purusottama* level; while at the cosmos level the *Prakriti* creates a mysterious image of acting without the *Purusa*. Distinguishing the concept of *Purusa, Prakriti* from *Samkhya,* Aurobindo advocates that under the *Samkhya,* the *Purusa* only sanctions the action but not the doer, while in the *Bhagavadgita* the *Purusa* is the non-doer doer. Under the *Samkhya,* the *Purusa* becomes *nirguna* or impersonal, if the *triguna* falls into an equilibrium. This can be achieved by abandoning action. Under the *Bhagavadgita* consecration of the action to the Divine and non-attachment to the fruits of action makes action impersonal. Abandoning the action is not the prescription. To harmonise both being and becoming one must rise above *trigunas* and the limiting factor of ignorance. One must not even distinguish between the individual soul from the Universal Soul, for God's manifestations are also *Sarvabhutani* (all pervading). Explaining this Sri Aurobindo writes :

Nature here is *Ksara,* a constant movement and mutations in time, a constant becoming. But this nature is simply the executive power of the soul itself, only by what he is, can she become.... She works out the becoming of His being..... According to what we are, we act, and by our action we develop. We workout what we are.... Soul is one and many, it is the one Life Being out of which all life is constituted... All the mini *Purusas* are in their original being, the one and the only *Purusa*.[57]

This working of the cosmic becoming is shrouded by ego and mind. One has not only to know the limiting agent, the working of the cosmos but also to know the *Trigunatita Purusa* (the Eternal beyond the attributes) to know the whole of it.

Disseminating the concept of the *gunas* (attributes) of the *Bhagavadgita*, Sri Aurobindo calls them the 'modes of nature', rather the 'modes of the energy of Nature'. For him they are psychological, qualitative and ideative; not physical and quantitative. *Sattva* is equated to the preserving quality of *Vishnu*, *Rajas* to the creative quality of *Brahma* and *Tamas*, to the destructive quality of *Rudra*. At other times Sri Aurobindo describes *Tamas* as inertia or nescience, *Rajas* as kinetic and *Sattava* as the principle of knowledge. In this connection the following two stanzas of the *Gita* are greatly emphasised by Sri Aurobindo.

Sattavam rajs tama iti
Gunah prakritisambhavah
Nibadhnanti mahabaho
Dehedehinam avyayam,
Tatra sattvam nirmalatvat
Prakasakam anamayam
Sukha sangena badhnati
Jnanasangena ca' nagha
Rajo ragatmakam viddhi
Trsnasangasamud bhavam
Tan hibadhnati kaunteya
Karma sangena dehinam.

Tamas tv ajnanajam viddhi
Mohanam sarvadehinam
Pramadalasya nidrabhis
Tannibadhnati bharata. (XIV.5,6,7,&8)

Sri Aurobindo Translates :

The *Trigunas* born of *Prakriti* bind in the body, the imperishable dweller in the body. *Sattva* binds by attachment to knowledge and attachment to happiness, *Rajas* binds the embodied spirit by attachment to works. *Tamas* binds by negligence, indolence and sleep.[58]

As noted earlier Sri Aurobindo emphasises on the need to transform actions into impersonal actions. He agrees with the *Bhagavadgita* that all the three *gunas* are present in everyone.

The discussion on the metaphysics of the *Bhagavadgita* as interpreted by Sri Aurobindo can be rounded off with one or two more illustrations. He indicates at the practical question of Arujuna as to how he is to recognize the *Brahman* setting aside all that has been expounded by Lord Krishna. In other words Sri Aurobindo never lost the emphasis of the *Gita* which is for him not a work of metaphysics but a practical guide to the seeker. He quotes the following from the *Gita* as an answer to Arjuna's querries:

Whatever beautiful and glorious creature thou seest in the world, whatever being is mighty and forceful among men and above men and below him, know to be a very splendour light and energy of Me and born of potent portion and intense power of My existence. But what need is there of a multitude of details for this knowledge? Take it thus, that I am here in this world and every where I am in all and I constitute all, there is nothing else than I, nothing without Me. I support this entire universe with a single degree of my illimitable power and an infinitestimal portion of my fathomless spirit; all these worlds are only sparks, hints, glintings of the I and I am Eternal and immeasurable.[59]

As Arjuna was not wholly satisfied with the explanation, Lord Krishna granted him the vision of His *Visvarupa*. Sri Aurobindo summarises the same as the vision of the one in the many, the many in the one and the knowledge that all are the One. Sri Aurobindo points out to the two facets of the *Purusottama*, the peaceful, calm, benign, kind and the gracious; the other of fierceness, of huge statured distinctiveness and of the *Rudra*. Joy and fear both fill the heart of Arjuna, when he has the *Visavaruppa darsana*. And Krishna makes it abundantly clear that without all those who have arrayed on both the sides of the great battle of *Mahabhrata*, His will alone is acting. From this fundamental understanding of the cosmos and the *Purusottama*, all other questions relating to metaphysics can be derived.

It may be recalled that, though the *Bhagavadgita* offers an excellent metaphysical analysis, it is essentially concerned with few fundamental human problems and is equally an important guide of practical life; offering solutions to the human problems. The original issue of the *Bhagavadgita* for Sri Aurobindo is the refusal of Arjuna, a man of action to fight; on ethical considerations. Arjuna's refusal to fight is not in tune with the *dharma* of a *kshatriya*. Arjuna is infact confused, on one side being a *kshatriya* his calling is for the war; being a brother, a son, a grandson, it is demanded of him not to kill his kith and kin and it seemes futile for him to fight for paltry worldly gain of an empire or of riches. In other words, Arjuna is not sure of his real *dharma*. The whole of the *Bhagavadgita* as expounded by the *Avatara* Lord Krishna, is an answer to this fundamental question. It is infact a guide book for every one to decide what one's *dharma* is at every given point of time. For Sri Aurobindo the *Gita* only provides a general guideline for deciding what is one's *dharma*. It has never described a set of actions only, like *himsa* (violence) or *ahimsa* (non-violence), action or inaction, etc. In other words Sri Aurobindo insists that each individual has to find out his own answer depending on his *Svabhava* (individual nature) or *Svadharma* (individual duty). Sri Aurobindo rightly says, that *Bhagavadgita* would not have send Buddha back to his wife. The *dharma* of Buddha and Arjuna has necessarily to be different. *Gita* presents the best understanding of the concept of *dharma* under Hinduism.

The Practical Message:

The fundamental issue in the *Bhagavadgita* is a practical issue. Arjuna refuses to fight on the grounds of supposed morality. He is overtaken by despondency or *Vishada*, "the ground seems to slip away under his feet." This is a practical crises which Krishna through *Gita* sorts out. Sri Aurobindo never lost sight of this practical aspect. For him the answer of Krishna incidentally includes the exposition of metaphysics, for without it Arjuna's doubts would not have been removed finally. On the otherhand the whole of the *Gita* in fact, is an answer of Krishna to the practical problems of life and the practical message of the *Gita* as gleaned by Sri Aurobindo is to be sought in the whole of his *Essays on the Gita*. The ideas that Sri Aurobindo emphasized in the whole series are summarised below.

There is no such thing as death, for it is the body which dies and the body is not the man.[60]

One must know that every where the Self, only exists and remember that the soul is immortal and the body alone goes back to dust.

A *kshatriya* must know god, know himself, help man, protect the right, must not be shy to destroy, for the world protect the right, must not be shy to destroy, for the world progresses through destruction. He must be calm, strong, equal in spirit, fight and fall nobly and conquer mightly.[61]

The true *yogi* must act abandoning attachment, and becoming equal in failure and success.

One does not attain perfection by renunciation of action or being action-less.

One cannot remain without action. It is action with freedom from attachment which is the duty.[62]

A *yogi* is greater than the doer of sacrifices, greater than the men of knowledge and greater than men of works. One must become a *yogi*. A *yogi* is one who acts without attachment and retains his equanimity in both success and failure.[63]

One must become God-minded, a lover and an adorer of Him, a sacrificer for Him, be unite in himself with Him and attain bliss.

The perfect foundation is equality, desirelessness, and freedom from egoistic nature for true liberation.[64]

One must stick to his *svabhava* or nature and the responsibility corrolary to it. The *brahmana* is one who is calm, self controlled, pure with knowledge and with a seeking for spiritual truth.

A *kshatriya* is heroic, high spirited, resolute, able, not failing from the battle, he is giving and lordship is natural to him.

Agriculture, cattle rearing, trade and craftsmanship are natural to the *Vaishyas* while service is the natural function of the *Sudras*.[65]

The *Svabhava* and *Svadharma* cannot be diverted from the *gunas – sattva, rajas* and *tamas*.

The final message is of course of devotion, and the following lines from the *Gita* are emphasized greatly by Sri Aurobindo.

"By devotion he comes to know Me, who and how much I am in all reality and principles of My being having thus known Me, he entereth into that (*Purusottama*)."[66]

The *mahavakya* (the great sentence or the final verdict) of the *Gita* for Sri Aurobindo is of course the verse which says:

"Further, hear the most secret, the supreme word that I shall speak to thee, beloved art thou intimately of Me, therefore will I speak for thy good. Become My minded, My lover and adorer, a sacrificer to Me, bow thyself to Me, to Me thou shalt come, this is my pledge and promise to thee, for dear art thou to me. Abandon all *dharma* and take refuge in Me alone, I will deliver thee from all sin and evil, do not grieve."[67]

Conclusion :

To conclude, a brief summarisation and critical appreciation of the ideas of Sri Aurobindo may be attempted. Sri Aurobindo's *Essays on the Gita* is the fruition of his general attempt to present Indian scriptures and metaphysics to western readers in English language and in a rational way, distinct from the traditional approach of the Sanskrit *pundits* and *tikakaras* (commentators). It is to be read along with his writings on the *Vedas* and the *Upanisads*. He further believed in reliving the experiences of ancient *Rshis*. Thus his *Essays on the Gita* can be best appreciated in the light of his spiritual experiences. The present work has not exhausted all these aspects, for the work is not a comprehensive work on Sri Aurobindo, but is only devoted to a part of his writings. However, in the introductory part his general spiritual stand has been spelt out and needs no recapitulation. Only the essence of his *Essays on the Gita* is summarised below.

The *Bhagavadgita* has a universal message without spatial and temporal sequence. It is synthetic in nature. It carries forward the Indian metaphysical stand from the *Vedas* and the *Upanisads*. It cannot be understood without a reference to the vast spiritual truth and experiences on which it is founded.

The setting of the *Gita* is a practical setting and its historicity is of little consequences. The *Kurukshetra* symbolises the conflict and struggle, both in mental and physical levels. It symbolises the conflict eternally raging between *dharma* and *adharma* or righteousness and un-righteousness : between forces of good and evil, progress and regression. The setting of the *Bhagavadgita* recounts one of the periods of crises in the progress and evolution of mankind.

The relationship between Krishna and Arjuna is that of *Narayana* and *Nara* and similar to the vedic example of the relationship between *Indra* and *Kutsa*. Sri Krishna is one *Avatara*, a *Vibhuti*, the teacher; and Arjuna, the most receptive amongst the *Pandavas*.

Arjuna is a *Kshatriya* not by mere birth, but also by nature and training, or both in *svabhava* and *svadharma*. He is over taken by *Vishada* or despondency. He has a crisis. His concept of *dharma* is confused. The morality of a *kshatriya* is at war with his morality as a son, a nephew and a disciple and so on.

The transitoriness of Nature also makes him question the necessity to fight, and his strength seems to slip away from him. This confusion is due to the principles of ethics of *prakriti* and the principles of the Divine. In otherways, it is due to the application of the characteristis of the *Prakriti* to the *paraprakriti*.

Krishna, the Divine Teachers is now ready to intervene in the process of evolution and to give a definite direction through his choosen instrument – Arjuna.

The *Bhagavadgita* offers a synthetic concept of Reality into which one may read the monistic, the dualistic or the qualified dualistic and monistic theories of Reality. *Purusa, Prakriti* and *Shakti* are all reconciled in the *Bhagavadgita*. *Purusottama* of the *Bhagavadgita* is beyond the apparent contradiction of *ksara* and *aksara* or the mutable or the immutable and He is still both of it. *Purusottama* is also *Prakriti* which has the power of the Eternal and Infinite Self with all movements in creation.

Maya is two fold, the *daivi maya* and *maya*. For *paraprakriti* the *maya* is *daivi maya* (Divine illusion) or the creation of the multiple with the full knowledge of the Infinite in the finite. The *maya of prakriti* is the confusion of the finites of being separate and distinct from each other, and also form the infinite. The *maya* can only be asundered not with a mere intellectual knowledge of the existence of the Infinite, but with the realisation of a living presence of the Infinite in the finite.

In his *Essays on the Gita*, Sri Aurobindo evolves the concept of *Saccidananda* or of Truth – Conscious force – Bliss, which is also echoed in the *Bhagavadgita*. To him and the *Gita* the cosmos is like a banyan tree whose roots are in the space, eternal, imperishable, beyond time and space and which in its manifestation is bound by work (*karma*) and nature (*guna*).

The practical message of the *Bhagavadgita* to Sri Aurobindo is that of becoming free from the attachment but not of mere renunciation of action or to be actionless. It emphatically advocates one to be equal in mind and spirit, in both victories and defeats, successes and failures and in happiness and sorrow, it is the dire necessity. One must constantly remember that death belongs to nature but not. to the self within. The *Gita*, to Sri Aurobindo insists on the principle that one must uphold his *svabhava* and *svadharma* and decide his duty accordingly.

The *Mahavakya* or the highest revelation of truth and the message of the *Bhagavadgita* is surrender and working out of the Divine injunctions through action without question. Arjuna must fight and completely place himself in body, mind and soul with Krishna.

Sri Aurobindo's *Essays on the Gita*, written during his Pondicherry days, is a matured and reflective contribution to the Indian metaphysical literature. Though the writings are free from references to contemporary political events, either in the Indian or world context, yet they are easily applicable to the analysis of contemporary world. The whole of the years between the Wars, and the half a decade that Sri Aurobindo witnessed beyond the second World War, were for him the years of a turmoil and the crises were nothing but, the birth pangs of a new mankind. It must be remembered that for Sri Aurobindo either man must overcome the limitations imposed on him by the lower nature of the animal world or he must be prepared to be overtaken by yet another race or species as he himself had taken over the nature of the world thousands of years before. Read along with his writings on Supermentalisation of mankind, the present seemed to him to be a crisis as that of the *Mahabharata* and the *Kurukshetra*. In the context of India's freedom struggle freedom of India was not only valid or not only that it was on the side of *dharma* (righteousness), it becomes the responsibility for every one to act for it, for it was divinely ordained, thus Sri Aurobindo was not prepared to find fault with any one who worked towards that goals. Though he himself refrained from violence he saw no theoretical opposition to violence as such.

Considering the object of Sri Aurobindo, that is of presenting the *Bhagavadgita* to the West, he seems to have fairly succeeded. He does not offer a comparative study of the *Gita's* concepts of metaphysics with the West. He finds no need or justification for contrasting it against the *Bible or the Sermon on the Mount* or comparing Krishna with Christ. He seems to be the modern *rishi*, who represents the eternal, mystic and spiritual experiences that the great Indian *rishi* right from the vedic times had experienced. Sri Aurobindo expresses himself in English instead of Sanskrit. He is not a mere *tikakara* (commentator) who falls into the trap of philosophy and grammar. He belongs to the select band of great Indian saints, philosophers, and would share the gallery with men like Adi Samkaracharya and Ramanuja.

REFERENCES

1. S.K. Ghose, "The poetry of Sri Aurobindo", **The Time – Literary Supplement**; 1969, p.26.
2. Sri Aurobindo never wrote an autobiography. However, biographical materials from Sri Aurobindo's writings were collected and published as **On Himself**, Vol-XXVI of Sri Aurobindo Birth Centenary Library (henceforth **S.A.B.C.L.**). A number of biographies have been published on Sri Aurobindo, over the years. K.R.S. Iyengar's **Sri Aurobindo-A History and Biography** is most complete and exhaustive one. A.B. Purani's **Life of Sri Aurobindo** had the benefit of being corrected by Sri Aurobindo himself and is treated as the official biography of Sri Aurobindo. Other standard biographies of Sri Aurobindo include M.P. Pandit's **Sri Aurobindo** and Rishabachand's **Sri Aurobindo.** Nirad Baran's **Evening Talks** provides many biographical details of Sri Aurobindo. Manoj Das's **Sri Aurobindo In The First Decade Of The Century** contains many documents on Sri Aurobindo's role in the freedom struggle of India.
3. By some other accounts, he secured the 11th position.
4. A.B. Purani, **Life of Sri Aurobindo**; Sri Aurobindo Ashram, Pondicherry, 1978. p.335.
5. S.P. Pani, "Sri Aurobindo – as seen from his poems", **Research Bulletin**; P.G. Department of History. Utkal University, 1990, p.74.
6. Sri Aurobindo, "To A Hero Worshipper", ; (1981) **Collected Poems S.A.B.C.L.**, Vol. V; p.8.
7. The most exhaustive account of Sri Aurobindo's association with the secret societies of Bengal is available in A.C. Guha's **Aurobindo and Yugantar**; 1972.

8. S.P. Pani, "National Education – some Early Thoughts of Sri Aurobindo," **The Advent** Vol. XL No. 1; Pondicherry, Feb., 1983, p.45.

9. **Source Materials for Freedom Movement of India** Vol.I; The Government of Bombay, 1958, and S.P. Pani, "Sri Aurobindo and the Surat Congress" **Mother India,** Pondicherry, Feb., 1983, p. 105-109 and March, 1983, p.159 to 163.

10. S.P. Pani, "Nation, Nation states, Nationalism and National Integration : A study of Sri Aurobindo's concepts", **Journal of Historical and Social Analysis,** No.3, Vol.I; Bhubaneswar, 1989, p.19-32.

11. Bipan Chandra and others, **Freedom Struggle**; National Book Trust, New Delhi, 1972, p.94.

12. M.K. Gandhi, "Letter to Lord Ampthill, Dt. 30.10.1909; **Collected Works of Mahatma Gandhi**; Publication Division, Government of India, New Delhi, 1979, p.508-509.

13. Ibid.

14. Sri Aurobindo, "Letter to Dillip Kumar Roy", **On Himself, S.A.B.C.L.**, Vol.XXVI; Introductory.

15. Aleta Yori Mastni, "Sri Aurobindo's Philosophy of Spitirual Transformation", **Journal of Indian Education**, Vol.XI; May, 1985, N.C.E.R.T., New Delhi, Page.1.

16. Sri Aurobindo, **On Himself, S.A.B.C.L.** Vol.XXVI; Pondicherry, p.198.

17. The given summary has been adopted from "The Philosophical Basis of Integral Education', - a talk delivered by Dr. S.P. Pani, in Orientation Course on Integral Education, held at the Regional College of Education, Bhubaneswar, June, 1990.

18. A.B. Purani, op.cit., p.81-82.

19. Amles Tripathy, **The Extremist Challenge**; Orient Longman, New Delhi, 1967.
20. The first series of the **Essays on the Gita** was published in a book form in 1922 and its second series in 1928.
21. Sri Aurobindo, **Essays on the Gita**, Sri Aurobindo International Center of Education Collection (S.A.I.C.E), Vol. VIII; Sri Aurobindo Ashram, Pondicherry, 1959, p.12.
22. Conceding this Sri Aurobindo writes, "each finds in the *Gita* its own system of metaphysics and trend of religious thought" – **'Essays on the Gita' S.A.B.C.L.** Vol.XIII; op.cit., p.3.
23. Sri Aurobindo, **S.A.B.C.L.** Vol.XIII; p.6.
24. Ibid.
25. S.P. Pani, "Sri Aurobindo's Treatment of History – with reference to India's past", **Mother India**, Vol.XXXVI; No.6, June, 1984, p.385-390.
26. Swami Chidbhavananda, **The Bhagavad Gita**; Sri Rama Krishna Topovanam, (Publication Society) Tirupparaitturai, 1982. p.69.
27. Myths have been used by poets both of yesteryears and the contemporary. Certain myths like that of Andormeda and Perseus has been used from the days of Sophocles and Euripides to Long Fellow and Sri Aurobindo.
28. Sri Aurobindo, **The Ideal of Human Unity, (S.A.B.C.L.)**, Vol.XV; Pondicherry, p.331.
29. Sri Aurobindo – **S.A.B.C.L.**, Vol.XIII; op.cit., p.44.
30. Swami Chidbhavananda, **The Bhagavadgita**, op.cit., pp.276-277.
31. Sri Aurobindo. **S.A.B.C.L.** Vol.XIII; op.cit., p.16.
32. Ibid., p.17.

33. Swami Chidbhavananda, **The Bhagavadgita**; op.cit., pp.571-578.
34. Sri Aurobindo, "*Gitar Bhumika*" (Bengali), **Writings in Bengali S.A.B.C.L.**, Vol.IV; op.cit., pp.66-133.
35. Swami Chidbhavananda, op.cit., p.972.
36. Sri Aurobindo, **S.A.B.C.L.** Vol.XIII; op.cit., p.498.
37. Swami Chidbhavananda, op.cit., pp.98-111. The English version of the Sanskrit *slokas* are quoted from **The Message of the Gita** (Ed.) Anilbaran Roy, Sri Aurobindo Ashram, Pondicherry, 1938, Reprinted 1977, pp.7-11.
38. Sri Aurobindo, **Essays on the Gita S.A.B.C.L.**, Vol.XIII; op.cit., p.22.
39. Ibid., p.44.
40. Ibid., p.125.
41. Ibid., p.427.
42. Ibid., pp.558-59.
43. Binita Pani, **The Indian Scriptures and The Life Divine**; New Delhi, 1993, p.284.
44. Ibid.
45. Sri Aurobindo, **The Life Divine, (S.A.I.C.E.)**, Vol.III; Pondicherry, 1960, p.161.
46. Sri Aurobindo, **The Life Divine, (S.A.B.C.L.)**, Vol.XVIII; op.cit., p.14.
47. Ibid., p.77.
48. Ibid., p.78.
49. Ibid.
50. Swami Chidbhavanana, op.cit., pp.276-277.
51. Ibid., p.152.
52. Sri Aurobindo, **Essays on the Gita**; op.cit., p.366.
53. Swami Chidbhavananda, op.cit., pp.749-756.

54. Sri Aurobindo, **Essays on the Gita, (S.A.I.C.E.)**, op. cit., p.281.
55. Ibid., p.432.
56. Swami Chidbhavananda, op.cit., pp.147-148.
57. Sri Aurobindo, **Essays on the Gita, S.A.B.C.L.**, Vol.XIII, op.cit., p.218.
58. Ibid.
59. Sri Aurobindo, **Essays on the Gita**; op.cit., p.351.
60. Ibid., p.57.
61. Ibid., p.61.
62. **The Bhagavadgita**; Chapter III, Cantos 4 to 10.
63. Ibid., Chapter VI, Cantos 46 to 47.
64. Sri Aurobindo, **Essays on the Gita S.A.B.C.L.**, Vol.XIII; op.cit., p.391.
65. **The Bhagavadgita**, Chapter XVIII; Cantos 42 to 44.
66. Ibid., Chapter XVIII; Canto 55.
67. Ibid., Chapter XVIII; Cantos 64 to 66.

CHAPTER – IV

MAHATMA GANDHI'S TREATMENT OF THE GITA

Mahatma Gandhi – A Brief Life-Sketch :

"Gandhi is the greatest Indian since Buddha. Like Buddha he will be worshipped as a god when he dies. Indeed he is literally worshipped by thousands of his people,"[1] remarked John Gunther, when Gandhi was still alive. Gandhi had struck millions of people both in and outsie India with his unique personal traits, sincerity of thought and the magical spell of his personal charm. It is surprising and impressive to find a private citizen without wealth, property, official title, position, scientific achievements, artistic gifts or the power of oratory, to have influenced so many people; people of the lowest rung of the society to men of great achievements, in India and abroad.[2] Gandhi's life, stature and the influence seemed almost to belong to another planet. He defied all expectations. Einstein aptly remarked, "Generations to come, it may be, will scarcely believe that such a one as this (Gandhi) ever in flesh and blood walked up on this earth."[3] A whole era of India's history of her freedom struggle is termed as the 'Gandhian Era'. In the years since his assassination Gandhian ideas have acquired an international appeal and have been shared by individuals and by peace movements through out the world. His role in shaping India's destiny during the intervening period between the two world-wars was gigantic. His care for non-violence in action and thought, his numerous experiments with new political weapons like *Satyagraha* and his voluminous writings, journalistic and personal; made him the most outstanding and dominating figure, from the twenties of this century unto his death. A practical-idealist, an exponent of the *Bhagavadgita,* the gospel of selfless action, and *Satyagraha,* the philosophy of truth and non-violence; Gandhi had many books published, even though he was "neither a prolific writer nor a deliberate author."[4] Nonetheless, Gandhi with his recorded speeches, discourses and writings on various aspects of contemporary India and the world; still remains one of the most distinguished thinker-politicians in the history of mankind. A brief outline of his life and an analysis of his mental make – up would add to the understanding of his ideas and actions, thoughts and writings. In view of the fact that Gandhi's early life and potitical career are too well known, what is attempted here is a presentation of few aspects of his life which throw light on his mental make-up. The biographical sketch is followed by brief on his thought.

Mohandas Karamchand Gandhi was born at Porbandar, of Kathiawar district of Gujarat, on 2nd October, 1869. He was the youngest child of Puttlibai and Karamchand Gandhi, also known as Kaba Gandhi. The Gandhis belonged to the Modh Bania Vaishya caste and were originally traders and grocers by profession. In due course of time they became the royal servants in the court of Rana of Khimji, the ruler of Porbandar. They were known for their integrity and for the courage of their convictions.[5] The teachings of Mahavira and Vallabhacharya; the songs of Mirabai and the poems of Narshi Mehta exerted a great influence on the minds of the people of Gujarat in general and on that of the Gandhis in particular.

Gandhi's relation with his father who remained in sickbed for a pretty long time, vindicated his sincerity of devotion towards his parents, which was earlier germinated in his mind by the *Shravana Pitribhakti Nataka* (A mythological play based on Sharavana Kumar's earnest devotion towards his old and sightless parents). As a child he used to act out the role of Harishchandra[6] to himself for "times without number." The idea of truth as supreme good was thus early implanted in him and appears to have grown naturally in him as a tree or a flower.[7] His love for nursing the sick and his compassionate mind towards the ailing and the down-trodden, might have been the result of Gandhi's long experience of attending to his sick father[8].

Gandhi's nurse Rambha, an old servant of the Gandhi family, had suggested *Ramanama* (the name of *Sri Rama*) to young Gandhi as a remedy for his fear of ghosts and spirits, in his tender age. His faith in *Ramanama* was further strengthened subsequently by the regular reading of the *Ramayana* rendered before ill Kaba Gandhi by a *pundit* called Ladha Maharaj of Bilesvar.

Puttlibai, Gandhi's mother had no formal education. She was deeply religious and orthodox in temperament. In the words of one of the biographers of Gandhi :

Her life was an endless chain of fasts and vows through which her frail frame seemed to be borne only by the strength of her faith. Her abounding love, her endless austerities and her iron will left a permanent impression upon him..... He owed to his mother not only the passion for nursing which made him wash leper's sores in his *ashram* but also an impetus for his technique of appealing to the heart through self suffering.....[9]

Gandhi was married at the age of thirteen to Kasturbai, the daughter of Gokuldas Makanji, a merchant of Porbandar and an old acquaintance and friend of the Gandhis. Being motivated by the vow of life-long fidelity to each other, Gandhi in traditional Indian way always expected Kasturbai to seek his permission for her every movement. Sometimes his restrictions imposed on her were arbitrary and Kasturabi in her own quiet and passive way resisted them. Later Gandhi recollected the situation and felt that the lessons of non-violence and passive resistance were learnt by him from her quiet practice of submission to suffering.[10]

Gandhi in his adolescence had tried meat eating, smoking and petty pilfering like many other children, yet he was made of a different chip. He not only confessed his chicanery before his parents immediately but also resolutely refrained from repeating such practices, having once discovered the pitfalls.

Mohandas matriculated in 1887 and enrolled himself in the University of Ahmedabad, but finally left for England on 12th June, 1888 to study for a degree in law. In London after first few months of embrrassment, uncertainty and deception during which he "wasted a lot of time and money trying to become an English man," he settled down to hard work and led a strictly regulated life.[11] Vegetarianism, practiced out of deference to his parents, though was an inconvenient obligation in London, for Gandhi it became a mission, the starting point of a unique discipline of body and mind, which transformed his life and personality.[12] He became the convener and the Secretary of a vegetarian club in Bayswater and acquired the first and fundamental lessons of establishing and managing an organisation.

During the three years of his stay in England Gandhi witnessed the Anarchist, the Feminist, the Theosophical movements that shook the foundations of the old world. In London, Gandhi who had not read the *Gita*, neither the original nor a translated one; read it for the first time in Sir Edwin Arnold's translation of the *Bhagavadgita* titled the song celestial. The following two verses of the *Bhagavadgita* impressed Gandhi permanently. The text of the two verses runs as follows :

Dhyayato visayan pumsah

Sangas ṭesu' pa jayate

Sangat samjayate kamah
Kamatkrodho bhijayate.II.62.
Krodhat bhavati sammohah
Sammohat smriti vibhramah
Smritibhramsad buddhinaso
Buddhinasat pranasyati.II.63

Sir Edwin Arnold Translated them as :

"If one ponders on objects of the sense, there springs attraction; from attraction grows desire, desire flames to fierce passion, passion breeds, recklessness; then the memory-all betrayed Lets noble purpose go, and saps the mind, till purpose, mind, and man are all undone."[13]

In this regard Gandihi writes in his auto-biography :

(these) verses in the second Chapter made a deep impression on my mind, and they still ring in my ears. The book struck me as one of priceless worth. The impression has ever since been growing on me with the result that I regard it today as the book of par excellence for the knowledge of Truth.[14]

During the same period he read *The Light of Asia*, another book of Sir Edwin Arnold on Buddha and Blavatsky's *Key to Theosophy* and the *Bible*. He was highly impressed by the *Sermon on the Mount* with its message of supreme forgiveness and non-violence. His young mind tried to unify the teachings of the *Gita*, the *Light of Asia* and the *Serman on the Mount*. He later declared, "That renunciation was the highest form of religion appealed to me greatly."[15]

Having completed his examinations in Law in England Gandhi returned to India to practice law and reached Bombay in 1891, to hear the shocking news of the sad demise of his mother. She had expired while Gandhi was still in England. In India Gandhi briefly attempted to practice law, but with little success and finally accepted an offer of appointment as a Legal Counsellor of a big firm in South Africa and left for the same in 1893. For the following twenty one years Gandhi not only remained in South Africa but also began his political career as the protester against the racial discrimination towards the Indian community living in South Africa. He enrolled himself as an advocate in the Natal Courts and sought greater civil rights for the Indians in South Africa. He led numerous passive resistance movements, called them *Satyagraha* and under his leadership large number of Indian indentured labourers and petty traders courted arrest during the agitation. Gandhi carried on several negotiations with their authorities. He published in 1896 the famous Green Pamphlet titled *The Grievances of the British Indians in South Africa*. He continued with his experiments in dietics, health care and education. He established and managed experimental communities of which the *Phoenix* was the most prominent one. He founded a weekly journal *viz.* *Indian Opinion* to propagate his political and non-political ideologies. Civil disobedience movements were led by him against prejudicial laws. Prison and assault were openly courted by the Indians and suffering without retaliation was willingly accepted. The non-violent campaign reached its climax in 1913 and Gandhi and General Smuts finally came to an agreement and the Indian Relief Act was consequently introduced in 1914.

Gandhi had written and published *Hind Swaraj* (Indian Home Rule) in 1908-9 during his return voyage from London to South Africa. A compendious revolutionary political manifesto, the book *Hind Swaraj* expressed Gandhi's theoretical framework for the freedom struggle of India. It was an exposition of his theoretical basis for the future socio-political and economic activities. He outlined his views on society, politics, non-violence, modern civilization and the place of religion in human life. He wrote, "We shall get nothing by asking; we shall have to take what we want, and we need the requisite strength for the effort, and that strength will be available to him only who acts thus."[16] This he followed up with eighteen points of desired change for the Indians and for the country as a whole. If India was to change, each Indian had to change first. The method of change was self-rule, one's ability to rule one self, and non-violence yet Gandhi did not believe that the change would merely come from above or from the British, but from within. Through *Hind Swaraj* he dedicated his life to India's freedom struggle and entered into the scene of National Freedom Struggle as a revolutionary leader.

Gandhi did not question the patriotism of contemporary moderate leaders of India in the first decade of this century. He however, was critical of their non-action, and their petitioning to the British sense of justice for every small change. He shared with the extremist faction of the Congress, their tremendous urge for action and their preparedness for suffering to achieve the goal. He struck a new note on the ongoing debate in India over political methods between the extremists and the moderates. He was moderate in heart and mind but shared the exuberance of agitation of the extremists and had demanded India's independence. He belonged to the moderates but infact became the successor of Tilak.

Gandhi became a political associate of Gokhale, the leading moderate leader and accepted him as his political *Guru* (teacher, guide). Gokhale visited South Africa and acquired a first hand knowledge of Gandhi's sincerity and his hold over the people there in 1912. He had observed that "Gandhi is without doubt made of the stuff of which heroes and martyrs are made. Nay, more, has in him the marvellous spiritual power to turn ordinary men around him into heroes and martyrs."[17]

Gandhi returned to India in 1915 and received a hero's welcome for his achievements in South Africa. He offered his service to British in their war efforts. He travelled far and wide in various parts of India to acquire first hand knowledge of her common folk. Within a year of his return

Gokhale expired. Another foremost moderate leader Firoz Shah Mehta had also died. After Lucknow pact between the Muslim League and the Congress in 1916, Gandhi slowly emerged as an eminent leader of the Party. The dismemberment of the *Khilafat*, the *Jallianwala Bagh* tragedy and such other incidents gradually pushed Gandhi deep into the complexities of India's Nationalist Era. Gandhi led the *Khilafat* movement and subsequently the *Non-cooperation* movement. The death of Tilak in the same year and virtual withdrawal of leaders like Aurobindo Ghose and Bipin Chandra Pal from active political scene made Gandhi the undisputed leader of the Congress party. He was elected president of the All India Home Rule League in 1920. Subsequently through the Civil Disobedience Movemnt of 1930, Quit India Movement of 1942 and several other agitations, *Satyagrahas*, fasts unto death, social works, establishment of *Savarmati Ashram*, *Harijan* upliftment programmes, temple entry movement, experiments on basic education and such other activities Gandhi carried the Freedom Struggle of India. Besides Gandhi, of course there were many Indian leaders and numerous other movements outside the fold of Congress and outside his sphere of influence which immensely contributed to India's Nationalist Movement. As it is too well known it is not recounted here.

The essence of Gandhi cannot be captured in recounting his political chronology or his role in India's freedom struggle. His mental make-up is to be searched for, in other biographical details. Gandhi was essentially an experimental personality. He named his auto-biography as *The Story of My Experiments with Truth*. Vegetarianism, passive resistance, *Satyagraha, Brahmacharya* (celebacy), *Aparigraha* (non-possession), *Ahimsa* (non-violence), *Satya* (Truth), *Anasakti* (non-attachment), Osteopathy, Hydropathy, dietics, fasting, penance were all experiments deliberately and consciously carried out by Gandhi in his life time. In the introduction to his auto-biography he observed, "I simply want to tell the story of my numerous experiments with truth, and as my life consists of nothing but those experiments, it is true that the story will take shape of an autobiography."[18] Gandhi carried on experiments on moral spiritual, religions and existential issues both in his inner life and in outward existence. "And this thought is nothing but a product of the series of experiments that he carried upon."[19]

From his childhood he had an interest in questions pertaining to morality, ethics and religion. But the most formative years of his life had been spent in South Africa, where his political life as well as his personality took shape. And it was only in South Africa that he had an opportunity to study the books of his interest on morality, ethics and religion. Of numerous books that influenced Gandhi the important ones included Tolstoy's *The Kingdom of God is Within You, What is Art ?, The Slavery of Our Times, The First Step, How Shall We Escape, Letters to a Hindoo*; Sherard's *The White Slaves of England*, Carpenter's *Civilization, Its Cause and Cure*; Taylor's *The Fallacy of Speed*, Blount's *A New Crusade*, Ruskin's *Unto This Last, A Joy for Ever*; Naoroji's *Poverty* and *Un-British Rule in India; Dutt's Economic History of India* and Maine's *Village Communities*. Besides these books which Gandhi mentioned in the *Hind Swaraj*,[20] the other books which greatly influenced him included *The Sermon on the Mount* from *The New Testament*, John Ruskin's *Unto This Last*, Emerson's *Essays, Blavatsky's Key to Theosophy*, Cropotkin's *Mutual Aid*, Carlyle's *Heroes and Hero Worship*. "The book which was ultimately to form his strongest bond with Hindusim as well as the greatest influence in his life was the *Bhagavadgita*."[21] The influence of the *Bhagavadgita*, the *Ramayana*, the *Bible*, the *Light of Asia* coupled with the impact of the writers like Tolstoy, Thoreau and Ruskin were taken up and deliberated by Gandhi. He did not take up reading as a pleasant pastime "he never read; he studied."[22]

In South Africa he studied the Original *Gita* with other translations. He was also influenced by the *Krishnacharitra* of Bankim Chandra (a Bengali poet and novelist) which he read at Yeravada prison.

To Gandhi the *Gita* was not merely a book of ethics or metaphysics, but it was his spiritual reference book, a permanent infallible guide of his daily life. Emphasising this aspect he wrote :

When doubts haunt me, when disappointments stare me in the face, and I see not one ray of light on the horizon, I turn to the *Bhagavadgita* and find a verse to comfort me; and I immediately begin to smile in the midst of overwhelming sorrow. My life has been full of external tragedies and if they have not left any visible or invisible effect on me, I owe it to the teaching of the *Bhagavadgita*."[23]

Gandhi was deeply spiritual and moral, though not religious in the traditional sense of the term. In the thick of his political life he had a search for god realisation, though he never experienced any revelations, nor did he ever claim to have realized God. While constantly and critically analysing his activities, experiences and experiments which he consciously conducted at every point of his life time, Gandhi was deeply convinced that morality was the basis of all these and Truth was the basis of all morality. Spelling out his spiritual orientation he wrote in the 'Introduction' to his *Autobiography* :

.....for me, truth is the sovereign principle, which includes numerous other principles. This truth is not only truthfulness in word, but truthfulness in thought also and not only the relative truth of our conception, but the Absolute Truth, the Eternal Principle that is God. There are innumerable definitions of God, because his manifestations are innumerable. They overwhelm me with wonder and awe and for a moment stun me. But I worship God as Truth only. I have not yet found Him, but I am seeking after him. I am prepared to sacrifice the things dearest to me in pursuit of this quest. Even if the sacrifice demanded by my very life, I hope I may be prepared to give it. But as long as I have not realized this Absolute truth, so long must I hold by the relative truth as I have conceived it. That relative truth must, meanwhile, be my beacon, my shield and buckler.[24]

Though Gandhi's realisation of the Absolute was questionable, his seeking was absolute. Conceding this he wrote, "it is an unbroken torture to me that I am still so far from Him, who, as I fully know, governs every breath of my life, and whose offspring I am."[25] His faith in God was firm yet he felt that passion and sin kept him away from God realisation. Thus he added, "I know that it is the evil passions within, that keep me so far from Him, and yet I can not get away from them."[26]

Gandhi remained a politician. He observed, "the politician in me never dominated a single decision of my mind, but politics. The fact is, I am a politician trying my hardest to be a saint."[27] There was a ring of a propohet in Gandhi's personality. Truth, non-violence and morality were the *summum bonum* of Gandhi's life and work.

An Outline of His Thought :

In addition to the foregoing outline of his biography and mental makeup it is necessary to include a sketch of his thought as the background material for a clearer understanding of his treatment of the *Bhagavadgita*. Unlike a study of Sri Aurobindo's philosophical outlook, here an attempt is made to outline Gandhi's thought. Gandhi was not directly concerned with normal questions of philosophy like the concept of reality, cosmos, man, the problem of evil and theories of knowledge. The questions for which he sought answers during his lifetime were of a different content. Thus in place of 'metaphysical outlook', the term 'an out line of his thought' has been preferred for Gandhi.

Gandhi's understanding of Hinduism is of great importance for dwelling on his understanding of the *Bhagavadgita*. Gandhi never studied the *Shastras* of India with a philosophical quest, save reading the Gujarati versions of the *Ramayana* and *Mahabharata* and the *Upanisads*. He did not study the *Vedas* or numerous other philosophical treatise of scholars like Samkaracharya. He had no scholarly knowledge of Sanskrit, not was he a scholar of ancient Indian history, yet he claimed to be a good Hindu and was hailed as such. Most of the Hindus (then and today) have not read the scriptures, not even the translations of the *Upanisads* and the *Bhagavadgita* which Gandhi had read, and yet consider themselves to be good Hindus. Hinduism is a way of life and a basket of attitudes rather than a religion merely confirming to some set rules and regulations, reverence and reading of texts. Yet any exposition of Hinduism requires a deeper understanding of the sacred heritage of India. Students of philosophy and comparative religion would never accept Gandhi as an exponent of Hinduism as they would consider Sri Aurobindo or Radhakrishnan to be. Yet appreciation of Gandhi's views on the *Bhagavadgita* requires a glimpse of his understanding of Hinduism, irrespective of the values it caries for academic scrutiny.

Truth and non-violence were fundamental ingredients of life, the intermediary beacons of light for Gandhi. He judged every aspect of life including the teachings of the *Bhagavadgita* by the tests of truth and non-violence. Truth and non-violence to Gandhi were like the touch stone of a goldsmith and anything that failed to register its absolute purity on either of it was rejected by him. This conviction was fundamental to Gandhi, irrespective of its source – be it Hindu or Christian. Even though most of the Hindus would not accept that sin has placed the Self in the body, Gandhi believed it. He observed, "We are born to sin, enslaved in the body because of our sinful deeds."[28] Thus for Gandhi, morality and ethics assume preponderance. However, Gandhi had to confront the problem of placing violence and war in his thought.

Gandhi considered himself to be a *Hindu* and a *Vaishnava* and outlined his understanding of the same as follows :

According to my belief, a *Hindu* is one who, born in a *Hindu* family in India, accepts the *Vedas*, the *Upanishads* and the *Puranas* as holy books, who has faith in the five *Yamas* of truth, non-violence, etc. and practices them to the best of his ability; who believes in the existence of the *atman* and the *paramatman* and believes, further that the *atman* is never born and never dies but, through incarnation in the body passes from existence to existence and is capable of attaining *Moksha;* who believes that *Moksha* is the supreme end of human striving and believes in *Varnashrama* and cow-protection. Whoever, besides believing in all these, has been born in a family belonging to the *Vaishnava* sect and has not forsaken the *Vaishnava* way, who possesses in some measure the qualities described in *Narasinh* Mehta's devotional song entitled "*Vaishnava – Jana*" and strives to cultivate these qualities in perfection is a *Vaishnava.* It is my firm belief that I possess in a large measure the characteristics described by me and I have been striving to strengthen them. I do not therefore, hesitate to call myself with all firmness, though humbly, a strict *Sanatani Hindu* and a *vaishnava*. I believe the most outward form of Hinduism is cow-protection.[29]

Gandhi respected Islam and Christianity as true religions, as much as Hinduism. He considered Buddhism and Jainism to be a part of Hinduism and adopted their principle of non-violence and accepted it as a general principle of Hinduism.

In addition to believing in the sacredness of the *Vedas* and *Upanisads,* etc. in the need for *panchayama,* (five principles of discipline in the existence of *atman* and *Paramatman,* in *moksha* (liberation) as the ultimate goal of life and in the

Varnashrama dharma, Gandhi considered truth and non-violence as the essence of Hinduism. He wrote :

I believe that the essence of Hinduism is Truth and non-violence.... The active manifestation of non-violence is Love-absence of ill-will..... the central principle of Hinduism is that of *Mokhsya*..... I am certain of the existence of my body and its transience.[30]

Gandhi did not consider the *Shastras* (scriptures) including the *Vedas* to be absolute. He had a simple formula for reading and understanding a *Shastra*. He wrote :

I found the right method for reading – for understanding – the *Shastras*. If any injunction in a *shastra* is opposed to truth, non-violence and *Brahmacharya,* it is unauthentic, which ever the *Shastra* in which it is found. The *Shastras* are not above reason. We can reject any *Shastra* which reason can not follow.[31]

And for Gandhi non-violence and truth were enough reasons. In spite of such limited or unconventional scales of judgement he believed that, "the sum and substance of it all (*Shastras*) is that one should cultivate *Bhakti* (devotion) towards God and attain *Jnana* (Knowledge), and thereby attain *Moksha* (liberation)."[32] His general attitude towards the *Shastras* and the *Bhagavadgita* in particular is discussed more elaborately later in this chapter. Gandhi also revered the Hindu belief in a *Guru* (Guide or spiritual mentor) and his importance in providing true knowledge and spiritual realisation. But he also realised that, it was not easy to find a *Guru,* and that was not be proper to just accept any person as a *Guru,* in the absence of a good one. Gandhi found no *Guru,* either in a person or in a text – his *Guru* was Truth and Non-violence.

However, in part II of his Autobiography, Gandhi has mentioned about a person- Raychandbhai who had left a deep impression on his life and had captivated Gandhi by his living conduct. Raychandbhai was a *Shatavadhani* (One having the faculty of remembering or attending to a hundred things simultaneously). He was just around twenty five years old, a businessman, a connoisseur of pearls and dimonds'. He was a highly spiritual man with a deep aspiration for self-realisation and a strong passion to see God face to face. About him Gandhi wrote :

The thing that did cast its spell over me..... was his wide knowledge of the scriptures, his spotless character, and his burning passion for self-realisation. I saw later that this last was the only thing for which he lived..... and I saw him thus absorbed in godly pursuits in the midst of business, not once or twice but very often. I never saw him lose his state of equipoise. There was no business or other selfish tie that bound him to me, and yet I enjoyed the closest association with him..... when ever I saw him he would engage me in conversation of a seriously religious nature..... I have since met many religious leader or teachers. I have tried to meet the heads of various faiths, and I must say that no one else has ever made on me the impression that Raychandbhai did.... In my moments of spiritual crisis, therefore, he was my refuge. And yet, in spite of this regard for him I could not enthrone him in my heart as my Guru. The throne has remained vacant and my search continues..... though I could not place Raychandbhai on the throne of my heart as Guru, we shall see he was, on many occasions, my guide and helper.[33]

In this connection, Gandhi's biographer B.R. Nanda opines:

While books on Christianity and Islam were easily available in South Africa, Gandhi had to send for books on Hinduism from India. He began to correspond on religious subjects with his friend Raychandbhai, who counselled him to be patient and to seek in Hinduism its unique clarity. Raichandbai's scholarly exposition reinforced Gandhi's sentimental bond with Hinduism and was decisive during the period when his Christian friends believed him to be on the way to baptism.[34]

Gandhi strongly believed *brahmacharya* (abstinence from sex) to be a sure path for the attainment of *Brahman*. "*Brahmacharya* is not mere mechanical celebracy, it needs complete control over all the senses and freedom from lust in thought, word and deed. As such it is the royal road to self realization or attainment of *Brahma*."[35] Procreation for Gandhi was a natural phenomena with limitations. Beyond procreation he believed in a lustless love between husband and wife. He also emphasised *Tapas* (Penance) accompanied by faith, devotion and humility. He accepted the *Varnashrama dharma* (Four-fold caste system of the Hindu *shastras*), but not the contemporary evil of untouchability and the numerous subdivisions of caste. Like many Indian leaders of his time he believed that originally caste system in India was based on the division of labour and distinction in the nature of persons. He also advocated the right of the *Sudras* (untouchables) to enter the Hindu temples.

Politically Gandhi was considered to be a philosophical anarchist. He argued :

True democracy cannot be worked by twenty men sitting at the centre..... it was to be a democracy of autonomous village-republics based on non-violence instead of coercion, on service instead of exploitation, on renunciation instead of acquisitiveness and on local and individual initiative instead of centralisation.[36]

The non-violent democracy of Gandhi implied mass-education and effort. The devices were those of *Satyagraha* expressed through silent self suffering which would result in a change of heart of the opponent or the exploiter. He believed that all society is held together ultimately by the principles of non-violence, love and self-sacrifice inspite of continuance of violence in day-to-day life. By spiritualising politics Gandhi championed the principles of individual liberty and freedom. He always correlated the means with the end and believed that both should be morally justifiable.

"In Gandhian scheme of values, the means and ends are convertible in terms. The two are inseparable and should be equally pure."[37] The concept of *Satyagraha* was a distinctive contribution of Gandhi, as a political theory and weapon. It implied resistance to evil, inculcation of qualities of purity, self-restraint, fearlessness, self-control, non-possession, truthfulness, non-violence, and preparedness for suffering for the sake of love.

Swaraj (self-rule) was the ultimate political ideal of Gandhi for India. *Swaraj* was far more wider than a mere political freedom from foreign rule – according to Gandhi's point of view. Defining the essence of *Hind Swaraj* he wrote :

Real home rule is self-rule or self-control. The way to it is passive resistance; i.e. soul force or love force. In order to exert this force *Swadeshi* in every sense is necessary. What we want to do should be done, not because we object to the English or because we want to retaliate but because it is our duty to do so. Thus supposing that the English remove the salt-tax, restore our money, give the highest posts to Indians; withdraw the English troops, we shall certainly not use their machine-made goods, not use the English language, nor many of their industries. It is worth noting that these things are, in their nature, harmful; hence we do not want them. I bear no enmity towards the English but I do towards their civilisation.[38]

Gandhi also contributed equally to the other aspects of socio-political thought. It is not desirable to stretch the limited discussion on Gandhian thought in view of the fact that the present work is devoted to the study of his interpretation of the *Bhagavadgita* only. This, however, is not to deny the significance of his other ideas which has been excluded from the present discussion nor to claim representative character for the ideas which have been touched upon.

To summarise, the following ideas and principles from the preceding discussion may be recalled :

Gandhi's was an experimental personality. Truth and non-violence were Gandhi's firm convictions and every other idea had to stand the test of these two principles. Morality and ethical principles including abstinence, control of passion and lust and renunciation, purity of ends and means formulated Gandhi – the ethical man. Rama, the great Epic character of the *Ramayana*, who was an ethical character was naturally Gandhi's ideal, Non-violence, love and penance in his opinion, sustained life more than violence and conflict.

He had a tremendous seeking for God. *Moksha* was his highest end, and he hoped to attain it through rational application of the principles of truth and non-violence; abstinence, *Brahmacharya* and service to mankind.

He had a distinct vision for India, free from British control – political and cultural. He wanted to build India full of self-sufficient autonomous republican villages; a democratic India where power did not filter from the center, but ascended from below, an India free from machine and the mad rush for material comforts and consumerism, with dignity of labour. He wanted the righ to hold property and land as a trustee, to be used for the downtrodden.

Above all he wanted every Indian to be fearless, rooted in his own culture, pursuing his spiritual quest and leading a moral life.

Treatment of the *Gita*:

Gandhi read an English rendering of the *Bhagavadgita* by Sir Edwin Arnold titled *The Song Celestial*, for the first time during his stay in England around 1888-89. In his autobiography Gandhi held, "I have read almost all the English translations of it (the *Gita*), and I regard Sir Edwin Arnold's as the best. He has been faithful to the text and yet it does not read like a translation."[39] Gandhi must have been exposed to the *Bhagavadgita* as he was to the epics, during his childhood, even though he did not read it then nor had taken any keen interest in the scripture. It is pertinent to observe that Gandhi read the *Gita* for first time in England and then when he was under the deep influence of the *Bible,* particularly the *Sermon on the Mount,* the Theosophical literature of Blavatsky and the writings of Tolstoy, Ruskin and Thoreau. He read the *Gita* not out of a spiritual quest, initially. Apparently from his writings Gandhi does not seem to have made any deep study of the *Veda* or *Upanisads*. Nor did he read the *Gita* when his mind was virgin. Subsequently Gandhi read other translations of the *Bhagavadgita* including the Gujarati version of Lokmanya Tilak's *Gitarahashya*. He also acquainted himself with the original Sanskrit version, even though in his own admissions his knowledge of Sanskrit remained shallow. He had studied the original along with other translations of the *Gita* in South Africa. He had the whole of the *Gita* by heart, by the regular practice of memorising one verse every morning while going through his morning toilet.[40]

Gandhi was one of the most practical man of his times and his treatment of the *Gita* reflects his practical attitude. He drove every thought of his mind into its personal implications and practical applications. He constantly referred to the verses of the *Bhagavadgita* to sanctify his views and actions. Echoing this Ronald Duncan writes, "All conversations, (with Gandhi) whatever their point of departure returned to the teachings of the *Gita,* the gospel of selfless action."[41] Gandhi cited the verses from the *Gita* to justify even non-violence, which was quite uncommon to the Indians. His co-workers like Swami Anand and others had requested Gandhi to provide a translation of the whole text of the *Bhagavadgita* for a better understanding of his views, actions, political weapons and ideologies. "Just as acted upon by affection of co-workers like Swami Anand and others." Gandhi recollected the event in the introduction to his translation of the *Bhagavadgita* and wrote :

I wrote *My Experiments with Truth,* so has it been regarding my rendering of the *Gita.* 'We shall be able to appreciate your meaning of the message of the *Gita,* only when we are able to study a translation of the whole text by yourself, with the addition of such notes as you may deem necessary. I do not think it is just on your part to deduce *ahimsa,* etc., from stray verses', thus spoke Swami Anand to me during the non-cooperation days. I felt the force of his remarks. I therefore told him that I would adopt his suggestion when I got the time.[42]

Anasaktiyoga (literally, the *yoga* of non-attachment), the Gujarati Version of the *Bhagavadgita* rendered by Gandhi with additions of own commentaries and notes, was completed on June 27, 1929. The book was published by the Navajivan Publishign House, Ahmedabad, on March 12, 1930. The English Translation of Gandhi's *Anasaktiyoga* by Mahadev Desai bore the title *The Gita According to Gandhi,* which appeared first in *Young India* on 6.8.1931. However, Gandhi had translated the Introduction part himself, from Gujarati to English, while he was in the Yeravada prison.[43] Prior to translating the *Gita,* during his sabbatical years in the Satyagraha Ashram, Ahmedabad, Gandhi had daily delivered discourses on the *Gita* (in Gujarati) before the ashramites at the time of their morning prayer. He talked on the *Gita* every morning, from February 24, 1926 to November 27, 1926, regularly for a period of nine months. Notes were taken by Mahadev Desai and Punjabhai, the inmates of the Ashram. These were subsequently edited and published by Narhari Parikh in 1955 under the title *Gandhijinu Gitashikshan,* an English version of which found its place in the *Collected Works of Mahatma Gandhi,* Vol.XXXII; published by the Publication Division of the Government of India, in 1969.[44] These discourses of Gandhi were subsequently published in 1980, under the title *M.K.Gandhi Interprets the Bhagavadgita* by Orient Paperbacks. Earlier to this, Bharatiya Vidya Bhavan published Gandhi's *The Teaching of the Gita.*

Gandhi never claimed any scholarly understanding of the text nor any spiritual or mystic experience being behind his understanding the *Gita*. He did not hope to replace the existing translations and commentaries, nor did he consider them to be inaccurate. Gandhi conceded that he was reading into the *Gita* his own meanings, while commenting upon the verses. He wrote :

This desire (of translating the *Gita*) does not mean any disrespect to other renderings. They have their own place. But I am not aware of the claim made by the translators of enforcing their meaning of the *Gita* in their own lives. At the back of my reading there is the claim of an endeavour to enforce the meaning in my own conduct for an unbroken period of 40 years.[45]

Thus the *Bhagavadgita* for Gandhi was a book not for understanding only, but for enforcing its guidelines into practice in one's life and conduct.

Identifying the objective of the translation he wrote "this rendering is designed for women, the commercial class, the so-called *Sudras* and the like, who have little or no literary equipment, who have neither the time nor the desire to read the *Gita* in the original and yet who stand in need of its support."[46] It seems from this passage that Gandhi was cognisant of the fact that his interpretations translation of the *Gita* would not stand up to its numerous others renderings grounded firmly on earlier brilliant commentaries. He was not writing for the scholarly higher castes or the Brahmins in particular, nor for the men of spiritual merit. He felt probably Tilak's rendering or Samkara's commentary on the *Bhagavadgita* at an earlier time, belonged to a different category. Gandhi thought that he was translating and commenting on the *Gita* for the benefit of common people, particularly the *vaishyas* and the *sudras* and the women folk, and for those who needed the *Gita's* consolation to guide themselves through the mental turbulences in life. On the basis of his sincere endeavour to enforce the teachings of the

Gita in his own life, Gandhi boldly justified his claim of authority to offer an interpretation of the *Gita*, which differed from the traditional views on many important respects. Later in this chapter an analysis of those aspects of the *Gita* shall be made, where Gandhi offered an interpretation which departed from the traditional views. An effort shall be made to examine various factors contemporary and historical, which might have influenced Gandhi to differ from traditional views. At present his basic approach while translating and interpreting the *Bhagavadgita* as a whole may be taken up.

The abundance of references to *the Bible, the Koran, the Pilgrim's Progress,* the works of Rajachandra (Raichand bhai, the Jain Philosopher), Narasingh Mehta and many others in the *Discourses on the Gita* by Gandhi is lacking in his *Anasaktiyoga*. Nevertheless, his readiness and ability to handle the *Gita* not as a sectarian scripture but as a manual of universal religion and pure ethics "which persons belonging to all faiths can read,"[47] can not be denied in either of the two. Gandhi constantly referred to his unerstanding of the *Gita* in his long political career. Reference to the *Bhagavadgita* were spread over in his numerous speeches, letters, articles, journals and conversations. The basic stand and understanding of Gandhi remains unchanged in all these. Thus in the present study most of the references are made to the English translations of the *Anasaktiyoga* and *Gandhijinu Gitashikshan*. Limited attempts shall be made to draw references from other writings of Gandhi to bring out and sustain the general stand.

Gandhi's approach to the treatment of the *Gita* illustrated his attitude to all the *shastras*. Everything written in Sanskrit was not a *shastra* for Gandhi. For understanding the meaning of *shastras* in its true perspective one must have a well cultivated moral sensibility and experience in the practice of these truths. The second rule to be followed in determining the meaning of a text in a *shastra* for Gandhi was that one should not stick to its letter but try to understand its spirit, its meaning in the total context. He argued :

A poet puts a particular truth before the world, it does not necessarily follow that he has known or worked out all its great consequence, or that having done so, he is able always to express them fully in the perhaps lies the greatness of the poem and the poet. A poet's meaning is limitless. Like man, the meaning of great writings suffers evolution. On examining the history of languages, we notice that the meaning of important words has changed or expanded.[48]

Gandhi believed that the *shastras* could be misleading for a reader who did not follow the rules of discipline and religious observances. The following extracts of Gandhi's observations are ample indicators of his understanding of and his attitude towards the *shastras* in general and his approach to the treatment of the *Gita* in particular.

The *shrutis* and *smritis* do not become scriptures merely because they are known by these respectable names. Whatever goes against the eternal principles of truth, etc. cannot be religious. *Manusmriti* and similar treatises put before us seem to be different today from what they were in their original forms as they contain some contradictory statements. In them are found statements that go against morality and reason ...: if we treated every work written in Sanskrit as a *shastra* then virtue could be proved to be sin and sin virtue. This in the language of the *Gita, shastra* can only mean, if the meaning is to be acceptable to reason, the utterances of a *Sthitaprajna* (Man of steadfast intellect). Therefore if the *Pundits* wish to lead the people on the right path along with learning they should also have a steadfast intellect, and they should give up passion and ill-will. Till the *Pundits* strive hard, do *tapas* and become the *Brahma-bhutas* (Those who have become one with the *Brahman*, vide *Bhagavadigita*, 11, 55-72) of the *Gita* an ordinary person like me will have no other altrnative than to serve the people in the light of his experience.[49]

If the reader is not on his guard, he may be misled. The very nature of *dharma* is such that one may easily fall into error, if one is not vigilant. Any one rashly imitating *Prahlad* would do something very wrong. This is the reason for the injunction against the reading of the *shastras* by one without qualification. It is not easy for any person to solve the problems of *dharma* which may face him. He will not successed till he has made himself fit by observing the *Yama-niyamas* (Rules of moral discipline and religious observances) and similar other rules of discipline. To take up a work like the *Gita* without having equipped one self in this manner is the surest way of falling into the slough of Despond. It would be like taking up a study of botany without ever having seen plants.[50]

If any body asks me whether I have made any deep study of the *shastras*, I would say that I have and I have not. I have not studied them from a scholar's point of view .... I have understood the *shastras* from the point of view of *dharma*. I have grasped their real meaning. I know that one can attain *moksha* without reading the *Vedas*.... The *shastras* are not above reason. We can reject any *shastra* which reason can not follow. I have read through only the *Upanishads*. I have also read some among them which my reason could not follow. I did not, therefore, accept them as having any authority. Many poets have told us in their poems that any one who sticks to the letter of the *shastras* is a pedant. Teachers like Shankaracharya have given the essence of the *shastras* in single sentences, and the sum and substance of it all is that one should cultivate *bhakti* towards God and attain *jnana* and thereby attain *moksha*. Akha Bhagat has said : Live as you please. Attain God anyhow, somehow.

That *shastra* which teaches me drinking liquor, eating meat and wicked ways can not be called a *shastra*.

We now have before us the important questions of what, in all the *shastras*, we should regard as interplations, what as acceptable ad what as deserving to be rejected. If there had not been, as I have stated above, a total extinction of the Brahmin spirit, we could have consulted a Brahmin who had purified himself by following the discipline of *Yama niyama* and acquired a good measure of *Jnana*. In the absence of such Brahmins, the path of *bhakti* rules supreme at present.[51]

Shastrasi read and followed, without purity of body and mind of the reader, may be misleading. *Bhakti* alone, which is an embodiment of truth and non-violence for Gandhi can prevent the use of *shastras* in evil ways. He writes :

It is possible to draw any number of evil ideas from *the Bible, the Vedas, the Koran* and other scriptures. I have come across persons who justified even murder on the authority of these works. The *Gita*, however, will serve as a safe guide to anyone who reads it with truth and non-violence as his guiding principles.[52]

Gandhi believes even the author of the *Gita* himself extended the meanings of words like *yajna or sanyasa*. While *yajna* meant offering of animals, prior to the composition of the *Gita*, it attaches a different spirit to these words. Gandhi is convinced by asking Arjuna to fight; Krishna does not intend to prove that violence is in consistence with renunciation of fruits of action. To quote Gandhi :

The author (of the *Gita*) himself extended the meanings of some of the current words. We are able to discover this even on a superficial examination. It is possible that, in the age prior to that of the *Gita*, offering of animals in sacrifice was permissible. But there is not a trace of it in the sacrifice in the *Gita* sense. In the *Gita* continuous concentration on God is the king of sacrifices. The third chapter seems to show that sacrifice, the third and the fourth chapters read together will give us other meanings for sacrifice, but never animal sacrifice. Similarly has the meaning of the word *Sannyasa* undergone, in the *Gita*, a transformation. The *Sannyasa* of the *Gita*, a transformation. The *Sannyasa* of the

Gita will not tolerate complete cessation of all activity.... The *Sannyasa* of the *Gita* is all work and yet no work. Thus the author of the *Gita*, by extending meanings of words, has taught us to imitate him. Let it be granted that according to the letter of the *Gita* it is possible to say that warfare is consistent with renunciation of fruit. But after 40 year of unremitting endeavour fully to enforce the teaching of the *Gita* in my own life, I have, in all humility, felt that perfect renunciation is impossible without perfect observance of *ahimsa* in every shape and form.[53] We shall do no injustice to Vyasa by expanding the meaning of his words. Sons should enrich the legacy of their fathers.[54]

As to the arrangement of the themes of Gandhi's understanding, the earlier format for the treatment of Sri Aurobindo in this thesis is not found to be very suitable. The content and the trend of Gandhi's interpretation and understanding was different – in a way it was unconventional. The format of the present chapter has to necessarily be deduced from Gandhi's writings. Hence, even though there are meeting grounds for Gandhi's treatment and the treatment of the *Gita* by Sri Aurobindo or Radhakrishan, a slightly different arrangement is followed here. Though Gandhi was not interested in the metaphysical subtelities of the *Gita*, his views on its metaphysical aspects are not obscure. In view of this it shall not be impertinent to draw a brief sketch of the metaphysical aspects analysed by Gandhi while he translated and commented upon the *Gita*. Therefore, the present discussion shall touch upon the Gandhian concept on the setting and historicity of the *Bhagavadgita*, and the problem of Arjuna *vis-à-vis* the concept of non-violence. Then an attempt shall be made to bring out a picture of Gandhi's metaphysics on the concepts of Reality, Cosmos, Man, Problems of evil and his philosophy.

Apart from this, effort shall be made to systematically arrange his ethical insights in consonance with the contemporary values for which he derived spiritual sanction from the *Bhagavadgita* and which forms the most significant theme of Gandhi's treatment of the *Gita* as a whole. Gandhi like all other leaders of his time, was "embraced by the snake of polities." For him politics without religion was "like a corpse, only fit to be buried."[55] Consequently he tried to justify his political actions and ideologies by quoting from different religions. Since the *Gita* was his 'infallible guide' and the 'spiritual reference book' for his daily conduct; it shall be interesting to study Gandhi's treatment of the *Gita vis-à-vis* his socio-political ideologies and his concept of *Ahimsa* (non-violence), *Satyagraha* (passive resistance) *Swaraj* (self-rule), *Swadeshi* (the concept of belonging to one's own counry), *Asahayaga* (non-cooperation), *Sarvodaya* (the good of all), Nationalism/patriotism, communal harmony, cow-protection, untouchability, *Varnashrama*, position of women in the society, education, so on and so-forth. These experiments in the political field were of no significance to Gandhi, even though they were highly acclaimed as the panacea for India's regeneration. His sincere striving was aimed at attaining *Moksha* (salvation) and therefore, his personal experiments were spiritual, rather moral.[56] He tried to achieve his personal transformation first. He believed in the *Gita* dictum :

Yad-yad acarati srethas
Tad-tad eve 'taro janah
Sa yat pramanam kurute
Lokas tad-anuvartate. III.21.

Which is translated by the author of the *Song Celestial* as "what the wise choose the unwise people take; what the best men do the multitude will follow."[57] Gandhi's greatness was acquird through a constant personal endeavour. In the words of K.R. Srinivas Iyengar, "The greatness of Gandhi was no sudden overwhelming greatness but rather the greatness of an ordinary man who through a long process of trial and error, aspiration and endeavour, achieved a greatness undoubtedly his own."[58] His contemporaties and close associates like Pt. Jawaharlal Nehru felt that Gandhi conducted himself according to the teachings of the *Gita* "dispassionately without attachment to results, and so results came to him."[59] In view of these it would not be improper to analyse the key concepts of *Bhagavadgita* like *Niskama karma* (desireless action), renunciation of fruits of action, qualities of a true *Bhakta* (devotee), *Brahamacharya* (non-possession), etc. in the way they regulated Gandhi's personal conduct as well as his public action. Before concluding, an attempt shall be made to systematically highlight Gandhi's treatment of the practical message of the *Gita* where he differed from the traditional interpretations in order to justify his actions and political ideologies.

Setting and Historicity of the *Gita* :

Gandhi, while analysing the war-setting of the *Bhagavadgita*, was definitely disturbed. An apostle of non-violence and a foremost leader of Indian politics, Gandhi was not prepared to accept the Mahabharata war in general and the *Gita* episode in particular as historical events. Analysing this one of his critics writes :

His devotion to the *Bhagavadgita* and his commitment to non-violence demanded reconciliation which became more imperative on his emergence as a top most leader in Indian politics on his return from South Africa, for his political opponents challenged him most on this point thinking that this would prove to be his Achiles' heel. But for Gandhi there was no contradition in his devotion to the *Gita* and his commitment to non-violence since, in his opinion, the superiority of non-violence over violence can be easily deduced from the teaching of the *Bhagavadgita*, though he admitted that it was not written to establish *Ahimsa* which was already an accepted norm of Hindu ethics.[60]

Gandhi's conviction in non-violence, more than the challenge of his opponents was responsible for his attitude and the treatment of the war setting of the *Bhagavadgita*. He knew that a battle field has the efficacy of providing a rich experience. In his speech at a public meeting in the Albert Hall of Calcutta on Jan 27, 1902, he spoke :

As a Hindu, I do not believe in war, but if anything can even partially reconcile me to it, it was the rich experience we gained at the front. It was certainly not the thirst for blood that took thousands of men to the battle field. If I may use a most holy name without doing any violence to our feelings, like Arjun, they went to the battle field because it was their duty. And how many proud, rude, savage spirits has it not broken into gentle creatures of God?[61]

Nevertheless, the key concept around which all actions of Gandhi revolved was non-violence. He abhorred the practice of referring to old scriptures like the *Bhagavadgita* to justify war or violence. In *Young India* (26.9.1929) he wrote :

And experience has shown that in every case where there is an appeal to reason, any inference drawn from the writings of a great person, however illustrious he may be, is irrelevant and calculated to confuse the issue at stake..... Have not the skeptics drawn opposite deduction from the identical sayings of Jesus?...... and is not the *Bhagavadgita* today quoted in support of even of assassination? To me it is as plain as a pike staff, that where there is an appeal to reason pure and undefiled, there should be no appeal to authority however great it may be.[62]

Violence in any form, even on the authority and sanction of the *Bhagavadgita* was not acceptable to Gandhi. To him the *Gita* was not an aphoristic work but a great religious poem. As has been pointed out earlier, Gandhi did not believe the *Mahabharata* (of which the *Bhagavadgita* is a part) to be a historical work in the accepted sense. To establish his conviction he referred to the miraculous origin of the principal warriors of the *Mahabharata viz.*, the *Kauravas* and the *Pandavas*. The *Pandavas* consisting of Yudhisthira, Bhima, Arjuna, Nakula and Sahadeva whose fatherhood has been attributed to the five gods *viz., Dharma, Vayu, Indra* and *Asvinikumaras*; respectively were on one side. On the other were the *Kauravas*, "a hundred brothers all born at the same instant," wrote Gandhi and questioned "Have we ever heard of such a thing actually happening?"[63] Thus the story of the *Mahabharata* could not be accepted by Gandhi as historical.

Further Gandhi believed that it was not possible on the part of human being to describe an actual event perfectly. He said, "A man cannot describe even a drop of water seen by him. God having created him so weak, how can he describe an actual event perfectly?"[64] Gandhi believed that Vyasa, the author of the *Mahabharata* had depicted the characters of the epic symbolically. The battle between the *Pandavas* and *Kauravas* represents the conflict "betweent he countless *Kauravas* and *Pandavas* dwelling within us. It is a battle between the innumerable forces of god and devil which became personified in us as virtues and vices."[65] Gandhi raised two fundamental questions :

i. If the physical battle of the *Mahabharata* is nothing but an analogical or allegorical piece of descriptive literature, does the *Gita* then prohibit physical fighting altogether ?

ii. Why did the author of the *Gita* take a war like illustration?

The answers to these questions are provided by Gandhi himself in the following statements :

The battle field described here is primarily the one inside the human body..... fighting there may well be. But here (in the *Gita*) the physical battle is only an occasion for describing the battle field of the human body. In this view the names mentioned here are not of persons but of qualities which they represent. What is described is the conflict within the human body between opposing moral tendencies imagined as distinct figures. A seer such as Vyasa would never concern himself with a description of mere physical fighting. It is the human body that is described as *Kurukshetra*, as *Dharmakshetra*. It does become that when used in the service of God. The epithet may also mean that for a *Kshatriya* a battle field is always a field of *dharma*.[66]

The object of the *Gita* appears to me to be that of showing the most excellent way to self-realisation..... That matchless remedy is renunciation of fruits of action. This is the centre round which the *Gita* is woven. This renunciation is the central sun, round which devotion, knowledge and the rest revolve like plants..... Thinking along these lines, I have felt that in trying to enforce, in one's life the central teaching of the *Gita*, One is found to follow truth and *Ahimsa*. When there is no desire for fruit, there is no temptation for untruth or *himsa*. Take any instance of untruth or violence, and it will be found that at its back was the desire to attain the cherished end. But it may be freely admitted that the *Gita* was not written to establish *ahimsa*. It was an accepted and primary duty even before the *Gita* age. The *Gita* had to deliver the message of renunciation of fruit. This is clearly brought out as early as the second chapter.

But if the *Gita* believed in *ahimsa* or it was included in desirelessness, why did the author take a warlike illustration? When the *Gita* was written, although people believed in *ahimsa*, wars were not only not taboo, but no body observed the contradition between them and *ahimsa*.[67]

The hypotheses that *Mahabharata* is not a historical event, that some of the places, events and persons referred there in might be historical, that wars were not taboo when the *Gita* was written, and that the battle field of *Kurukshetra* was only a symbol of the battle between good and evil which rages in every human heart, etc. are founded on Gandhi's own intuition, logic and experience only. Gandhi did not claim any academic authenticity in favour of his conclusions. Highly learned people like Shyamji Krishnavarma, Vinayak Damodar Savarkar and others refused to accept what Gandhi interpreted. Consequently Gandhi had a wish :

How much better it would have been if the sage Vyasa had not taken this illustration of fighting for inculcating spiritual knowledge. For when highly learned and thoughtful men read this meaning in the *Gita,* what can we expect of ordinary people? If what we discribe as the very quintessence of all *shastras,* as one of the *Upanishads,* can be interpreted to yield such a wrong meaning, it would have been better for the holy Vyasa to have taken another, more effective illustration to teach sacred truths.[68]

To Gandhi, the choice of Vyasa to convey great truths of life through a war setting was an error. Nevertheless, after a deep study of the *Mahabharata* Gandhi realised that the illustration which Vyasa had taken was a beautiful one. Vyasa did not believe that fighting was wrong. "Just as in Aesop's *Fables* and in *Panchatantra,* the authors have created conversations among birds and animals to impart moral teaching, so in the *Mahabharata* virtues and vices are personified and great moral truths conveyed through those figures. The description of the battle serves only as a pretext."[69] Gandhi further emphasised that Vyasa, the author of the *Mahabharata* did not try to establish the necessity of physical warfare but on the other hand he had proved the futility of a war by making the "victors shed tears of sorrow and repentence" and by leaving them with nothing "but a legacy of miseries."[70] Gandhi also justified the war illustration of the *Bhagavadgita* by Vyasa while analysing the problem of despondency of Arjuna which led to the *Gita* discourse delivered by Sri Krishna in the battle field of *Mahabharata.*

The problem of Arjuna was not whether it was necessary that he should fight, but against whom he had to fight.

Gandhi found the cause of Arjuna's despondency in the following verses of the *Bhagavadgita*.

Kairmya saha yoddharyam

Asmin ranasamudyame !! 1.22.

Which means, "With whom I must wage this war."[71]

Tan samikshya sa kaunteyah

Sarvan bandhun avasthitan

Krpaya paraya visto

*Visidannidam abravit.*1.27

"He, the son of Kunti, gazing at those kinsmen posted in position spoke thus in sadness, filled as he was with choking compassion."[72]

drstve' mam svajanam krsna

yuyutsum samupathitam

sidanti mama gatrani

*mukham ca parisusyati.*1.28

"Seeing these my kinsmen, collected here prompted by war my limbs fail me, O Krishna, and my mouth is parched up."[73]

na ca sreyo' nupasyami

*hatva svajanam ahave.*1.30

"I do not foresee any good ensuing from the slaughter of Kinsmen in battle."[74]

tasman no'rha vayam hantum

dharta rastran svabandhavan

svajanam hi katham hatva

*sukhiah syama madhava.*1.31.

"We should not therefore slay the sons of Dhrtarastra, our kinsmen; for how can we, O Madhava, killing our own kinsmen be happy?"[75]

In these verses, the repeated use of the word *svajanam* (Kinsmen), by Arjuna leads Gandhi to believe that Arjuna's problem was due to his bias arising out of the distinction he made between his kinsmen and others. Arjuna had no aversion to fighting. He was ready to fight. In case Arjuna had an aversion to fighting, Gandhi thought that Krishna would have asked Arjuna to got to Duryodhana and win him over. But that was not the case. Arjuna was unhappy, not at the thought of killing but at the thought of killing his kinsmen. By putting the word "kinsmen" repeatedly in the mouth of Arjuna, the author of the *Gita* had tried to show into what darkness of ignorance Arjuna had sunk. In the past Arjuna never hesitated to fight even against his relations. Arjuna was a *kshatriya*. He was known as *gudakesha*, which means one who has conquered his mind, who is always vigilant. Gandhi was also convinced that Arjuna was a seeker who observed the disciplines of *yama-niyama*. He was a *brahmachari* in perfect control of all his senses. As a follower of *shastras*, he was aware of the supreme value of non-violence. But he was also a *kshatriya* for whom fighting to protect the weak and uphold Truth- was the sacrosanct duty. Still he decided to quit the battle field, out of despondency and due to his reason of delusion arising out of his attachment to ego. This was a deliberate imagination of *Vyasa* adopted in order to create a situation for the enunciation of the principles of the *Bhagavadgita*. Accepting this stand Gandhi further advanced his arguments justifying the course of action that was suggested to Arjuna by Krishna. He wrote :

Should it become necessary, to cut off, with a sword, one's father's head, one must do so if one has a sword and is a *kshatriya*, and if one would be ready to cut off any one else's head in similar circumstances. Shri Krishna, therefore, asks Arjuna to free himself from ignorant attachments in this world.... Even if we believe in non-violence, it would not be proper for us to refuse, through cowardice, to protect the weak. If Arjuna had forgotten the difference between kinsmen and others and had been so filled with the spirit of non-violence as to bring about a change of heart in Duryodhana, he would have been another Shri Krishna. Actually, however, he believed Duryodhana to be wicked. I might be ready to embrace a snake, but, if one comes to bite you, I should kill it and protect you. Arjuna has two courses open to him : he should either kill Duryodhana and others, or else convert them. In the circumstances, Arjuna's laying down arms would mean the annihilation of all those on his side. His refusal to fight would bring on disaster thus Vyasa has taken the right illustration. A person who believes in fighting and does not regard it as violence, though it is violence, is here being asked to kill.[76]

Even Gandhi conceded that *ahimsa* (non-violence) is an ideal which it is impossible to realize to perfection. May be it is possible to realize *ahimṣa* in thought but not in action. Samkaracharya believed that one seeking *moksha* (salvation) should have far greater patience than one who would try to empty the sea, drop by drop, with a blade of grass. Gandhi was convinced that one must possess equal patience for realising the ideal of perfect non-violence. It is not possible to follow *ahimsa* fully, in this body violence is inescapable because while the eyes wick and nails have to be pared, violence in one form or another is inevitable. Evil is inherent in action, Arjuna did not raise, therefore, the question of violence and non-violence. Nor Shri Krishna exhorted the *Gita* to support violence. Arjuna simply raised the question of distinction between kinsmen and others, which according to Gandhi was due to Arjuna's reason of delusion arising out of his ignorance and attachment to ego. The cause of all spiritual evil is this ignorant attachment to ego and the central teaching of the *Bhagavadgita* according to Gandhi is the surrender of all attachments to self. Through out his discourses on the *Gita* during the daily prayer meetings at Sabarmati Ashram Gandhi emphasised his stand on the setting of the *Gita* by repeatedly referring to the first chapter of the *Bhagavadgita* while analysing the verses from its other chapters, and explaining the real motive of the author of the *Gita* behind his selecting the war setting of the *Mahabharata*.

To Gandhi, what he propounds on the common sense level is that, once plunged into battle, one should go on fighting. One is not expected to give up the task one has undertaken. Thus, the illustration of war used in the *Gita* is not be pointless or inadequate. But a wise man should not read a wrong meaning in it under any circumstances. The principal aim of the *Mahabharata*, however, "is to represent the most invisible of all invisible wars." It proposes to highlight Arjuna and other *Pandavas* in one's mind who are battling with the evil forces (*Kauravas*) in it. The duel of morality which confront one in this inner war is extremely difficult in comparision to a physical war. Gandhi also believed and that a mistake committed in the sphere of practical action may at the most result in the destruction of this perishable body, but the result of such an error in this inner invisible war will lead to perdition. The *Gita* according to Gandhi shows how one may emerge safe from such inner ongoing invisible wars.[77]

Gandhi's view on the *Gita* denying the historical account of the battle of *Kurukshetra* was in sharp conflict with the traditional view, and the interpretations of eminent scholars like Bal Gangadhar Tilak and Sri Aurobindo. Scholars suspected that Gandhi had given a twist to the *Gita* to fit his doctrine of non-violence, and that his view was effected by the study of the *Bible*. But Vincent Sheen pointed out that :

From this to an assumption that his was a Christian interpretation of the *Gita*, is an unjustifiable step. If you grant him the initial bold leap in which *Kurukshetra* becomes the heart of man all the rest of his interpretation is within the frame work of the *Upanishads* and the text of the *Gita*.

His reasons for making this bold leap were all based upon his perception of self-evident truth (i.e. self-evident to him) as shown by the long study of the *Gita* itself.[78]

Some of the biographers of Gandhi inferred that he had taken a bold leap, away from the traditional view by interpreting the battle field of *Kurukshetras* as the human heart and by denying the incidence of the physical battle of *Mahabharata* altogether. But from the preceding discussion, it is evident that Gandhi's approach while interpreting the setting of the *Gita* was not at all rigid. In spite of his total adherence to the principle of non-violence, Gandhi has not ruled out the occurrence of *Mahabharata* war altogether. He has kept open two avenues for the interpretation of the war setting of the *Gita* : one physical at the common sense level and the other mental, ever raging in the hearts of men. A practical philosopher-saint-politician as he was as claimed to be, he was insistent not to allow justification of any wicked act by citing the example from the *Gita*.

To Gandhi, all that Krishna said in the *Bhagavadgita* were not meant to be followed by all in general. Some of them were meant exclusively for Arjuna, and with respect to the then prevailing conditions only. Others must not try to follow them, until they qualify themselves by attaining the status of *gudakesha* like Arjuna by observing disciplines like *yama-niyama* and *brahmacharya*. However, like Arjuna, every human being is bound to be disturbed in the heart by such problems due to failure of reason as an inevitable result of his ignorant attachment to ego, at some point or the other of one's life time. Gandhi was convinced that the *Gita* provides the clue to the solution of all those problems.

The Concept of Reality :

Having scrutinised Gandhi's interpretation of the setting of the *Bhagavadgita*, it is now proposed to analyse his understainding of the metaphysical concepts like God (Reality), Man, Cosmos, problems of eveil and the concepts of the means and the ends inherent in the *Gita*.

Gandhi was not a philosopher. He was neither trained in philosophey in the academic sense like Radhakrishnan nor did he desire to offer a new understanding of philosophy like Sri Aurobindo. Consequently it becomes extremely difficult to reduce Gandhi's philosophy of God to an accepted philosophical model. The fundamental basis of Gandhi's philosophy is the conception of God or an omnipotent fundamental spiritual reality, 'an all embracing living light' which could be called *Sachchidananda* or *Brahman* or Rama or simply Truth or Law or Love or *Aum*. To Gandhi, God is a self-existent all knowing living force which inheres every other force known to the world. From his very childhood, the *Vaishnava* tradition of his family had implanted in his mind the seed of the idea of a theistic God.

Gandhi was a metaphysical idealist. Like all other *Vaishnavas* Gandhi also had a tremendous regard towards the authorities of the *Vedas* and the *Upanishads*, but he did not believe in the concept of an undifferentiated absolute or *Nirguna Brahman*. The concept of Advaita Vedantists led by Samkara that the world is not real, but an illusion, was also not totally acceptable to Gandhi. He did not accept the way of knowledge propounded by Samkara as the only way for liberation. He believed in a personal God who is to be felt and realised. So the way of devotion was the only way of liberation and realisation for him. He wrote in *Young India*, (31.12.31), "He is no God who merely satisfies the intellect, if He ever does. God to be God, must rule the heart and transform it."[79] God is to be realised not by dialectical skill or conceptual cognition but by spiritual experience and faith. Gandhi states, "Reason is a poor thing in the midst of temptations ..... Faith that transcends reason is our only Rock of Ages."[80]

Nevertheless, Gandhi also relied upon the 'inner voice', or the voice of the *atman* or conscience or intuition to be the carrier of a dependable testimony for God's existence. To

Gandhi, a living faith in God's existence is a necessity. The urge for spiritual satisfaction inherent in every individual is not materialised by all the worldly ways of life. So one has to have faith in some supreme object of love, as a source of strength, peace and happiness. God can be felt only by the experiences of a moral man, a true *Bhakta* or a *Sthitaprajna* as described in the *Bhagavadgita*. In other words for Gandhi the call of conscience is nothing but a representative of a Being, which is the embodiment of Supreme Goodness and He reveals Himself daily to every human being. But he who is a moral man or a *Sthitaprajna,* only can experience the revelation. To Gandhi, God realisation is possible by *anasakti karma* i.e. selfless action. Though Gandhi accepts the *Advaitist's* concept "God is, nothing else is" of the *Gita* he continues to uphold the view that there is something about the world which persists inspite of its constant state of flux. This is reflected in his analysis of the following verses of the *Gita*.[81]

Na' sato vidyate bhavo
Na' bhavo vidyate satah
Ubhayor api drsto' ntas tv
Anayos tattvadarsibhih.II.17

"What is non-Being is never known to have been, and what is Being is never known not to have been. Of both these the secret has been seens by the seer of the Truth."

Avinasi tu tad viddhi
Yena sarvam idam tatam
Vinasam avyayasya 'sha
Na kascit kartumarhati.II.17

"Know that to be imperishable where by all this is pervaded no one can destroy that immutable Being."

Antavantaime deha
Nityasyo 'ktah saririnah

Anasino prameyasya

Tasmad yudhyasva bharata.II.18

"These bodies of the embodied one who is eternal, imperishable and immesurable are Finite. Fight, therefore, O. Bharata."

Analysing these verses, Gandhi writes :

The *Jnanis*, the men of knowledge, have discovered what exists and what doesnot exist. Name and form are brittle as glass. The *Jnanis* know what is implied in the difference between existence and non-existence. We only know one simple thing : God is, nothing else is.

Gandhi accepts the *Gita* concept of Reality which is both *Saguna* and *nirguna* (with and without attributes respectively), *Aprameya* (for which there can be no evidence), *Aja* (which is never born), *Achchedya* (which cannot be pierced with) as desribed in the *Bhagavadgita*. The *atman* in every being is nothing but a reflection of the *Paramatman* who is eternal, imperishable and immeasureable. "The *atman* (the individual self) may be a ray of the *Paramatman* (the universal self); but the ray of the sun is the sun itself'.[82] The supreme objective of the individual self is to realize its identity with the Universal Self or to become like unto God, by surrending oneself to Him, body and soul. The *atman* is eternal, and imperishable and is the driver of the body, the charioteer Krishna."[83]

Commenting on the verse 12 of chapter XIII of the *Bhagavadgita* which says :

Anadimat param brahma

Na sat tan no' sad ucyate.

(it is the supreme *Brahma* which has no beginning, which is called neither Being nor non-Being), raises a question Gandhi writes :

Why does Shri Krishna say this, when they say that the *Brahman* is *Sachchidananda* and that it alone is real ? What he means to say is that *Brahman* does not mean being, the contrary of non-being when we use the word *sat* in connection with the *Brahman* its meaning transcends the two opposites and it signifies neither being nor non-bieng. It is, so to say, a neutral term. God can bot be described as evil, nor as good. He is above either. The reality which is God is beyond the three categories of time.[84]

To Gandhi, the *Brahman* who is the creator, sustainer and destroyer who has no *gunas* (attribute) but at the same time who experiences *gunas*, who is all pervasive still undivided, immovable yet moving who is so far yet so near, who is the doer yet the non-doer seeming to possess the functions of the senses, yet who is devoid of senses without all beings, yet within, is attributed with all these contrary qualities because" we can not free our minds from dualities."

That God is impersonal and hence does not perform any physical activity is not acceptable to Gandhi. "For the unceasing movement of the sun, the moon, the earth, etc." wrote Gandhi, "signifies God in action. This is not mental but physical activity. Though God is without form and impersonal, He acts as though He had form and body. Hence though He is ever in action, He is free from action, unaffected by action."[85] At the same time Gandhi reconciles with the following verse of the *Gita* :

Mama yonir mahad brahma

Tasmin garbham dadhamyaham

Sambhavah sarvabhutanam

Tato bhavati bharata XIV.3

Which is translated as – "The great *prakrti* is for me the womb in which I deposit the germ; from it all beings come to birth, O Bharata."

Commenting on the verse Gandhi draws a simili with the *Bible* and writes :

Among the very first sentenced in the Bible is; God said let there be light, and there was light, [that is] let there be a universe, and a universe came into existence. A potter has to mould clay into a shape on his wheel and then put the things into fire to bake; God does not have to act in that manner. He is a magician, He simply puts the seed in his imagination which is *prakriti* Lakshmi or Mother Goddess of the world – and the universe comes into existence.[86]

Gandhi accepts the concept of *Prakriti* and *Purusa*. For him *Prakriti* is the cause and *Purusa* the witness – the non-doer doer. *Prakriti* is the cause of creation and *Purusa* is the cause of experiences of happiness or misery. *Purusa* is beyond *Maya*, in that sense he is *Para*, he is the master, the *Atman*, the *Jiva* and the unmanifest. The 'Ego', 'I' ness and the individuation is the product of manifestation through *Prakriti*.

As discussed earlier morality to Gandhi is the only basis of realisation while Truth and Non-violence are the principal foundations of all morality. Thus he identifies God with Truth and draws support from the *Bhagavadgita* to re-affirm this conviction. He wrote in his Autobiography; "My uniform experience has convinced me that there is no God other than Truth." And for him the only means for the realisation of Truth is *Ahimsa*. All his labour was directed to substantiate this view. It is apparent that Gandhi had no doubt on the existence of God whatsoever, yet he had no deep spiritual experience of a seer, or a poet or a philosopher. He was equally firm in his conviction in *Ahimsa* and felt that only full realisation of *Ahimsa* in the thought and practice would lead to a final realisation of God. He writes, "But this much I can say with assurance, as a result of all my experiments, that perfect vision of Truth can only follow, a complete realization of *Ahimsa*."[87] He was uncompromising on the concept of truth and non-violence. He equates truth and non-violence with God and says, "I do not care for God if He is anything but Truth."[88]

Referring to the oft quoted 8th verse of chapter IV of the *Bhagavadgita* where Krishna says, "To save the righteous, to destroy the wicked, and to re-establish Right I am born from age to age", Gandhi writes, "here is the comfort for the faithfull and affirmation of the truth that Right ever prevails........ For Right – which is Truth can not perish; .... Wrong has no independent existence."[89] As a whole, notwithstanding the existence of wrong and evil, the world is predominately sustained by Truth, Love and Goodness. For Gandhi, God is Life, Truth, Light and Love. He is also the Supreme Good.[90]

To Gandhi *Avatara* is not the decent of God to man-hood but the ascent of man to God-head. He writes :

In Hinduism incarnation is ascribed to one who has performed some extra-ordinary service of mankind. All embodied life is in reality an incarnation of God, but it is not usual to consider every living being an incarnation. Future generations pay this homage to one who, in his own generation, has been extraordinarily religious in his conduct. I can see nothing wrong in this procedure; it takes nothing from God's greatness, and there is no violence done to Truth. There is an Urdu saying which means : '*Adam* is not God but he is a spark of the Divine'. And therefore, he who is the most religiously behaved has most of the divine spark in him. It is in accordance with this train of thought, that Krishna enjoys, in Hinduism, the status of the most perfect incarnation. This belief in incarnation is a testimony of man's lofty spiritual ambition. Man is not at peace with himself till he has become like upto God. The endeavour to reach this state is the supreme, the only ambition worth having. And this is self-realisation.[91]

For Gandhi *Avatara* is not the descent of God. But Krishna or Rama is God for him, as every other human being is, as a manifestation of the Almighty. For Gandhi any man who has excelled in life, is more God like than the vast majority. He is called an *Avatara;* a word in the language of humanity but no of God.[92] This rise to Godhood for Gandhi, through greater goodness is an ascent rather than a descent.

Nevertheless, Gandhi reconciles with the common faith of the Hindus that Rama and Krishna were incarnations of God, by stating that whomsoever one worships, one should look upon him as *Purna Purusottama* (perfect incarnation of God). There should not be any element of doubt whatsoever.[93] Gandhi's understanding of the concept of the Hindu Trinity of *Brahma, Vishnu* and *Siva,* however, is slightly different from the traditional. He does not look upon them as distinct Beings. He regards them as representations of various aspects and powers of God. To him the concept of *Brahma* as the creator, *Vishnu* as the sustainer and *Siva* as the destroyer is only imagined to teach people *dharma* somehow. "In truth, there is no such being as *Brahma* or *Siva*. The only reality is the neutral *Brahman*. But as God is conceived of as doing nothing, it is imagined that this universe comes into existence out of Brahma."[94]

Gandhi like Rajgopalchari was trying to reconcile many aspects of Hindu faith and practice. To illustrate we may point out that it was then commonly argued that cow slaughter was banned in India to save cattle in a society which depended on it. Even caste was similarly justified on grounds of division of labour. For Gandhi God is also Law. He refers to the *Gita* where the Lord says, "In whatever way men resort to Me, even so do I render to them. In every way, O Partha, the path men follow is Mine" (II.11). Commenting on this verse of the *Bhagavadgita* Gandhi emphasises the principle of 'as you sow, so you reap' concept and says, "This verse merely lays down God's Law." God's Law for Gandhi is the law of *Karma* or action. To Gandhi this Law is immutable. Not a single school of philosophy has questioned the existence of His Law. This law is a living law for Gandhi. "If we equate it with God, recognize that it is God, people will then have no reason for quarrelling. That is the implication of this verse." This interpretation reflects Gandhi's over-bearing political consideration to teach people to respect each other's religion and belief in the equality of all religion. Gandhi like Aristotle recognised the architectonic beauty of the cosmos and conceded God as the Creator and the Law on the argument of self evident order in the nature. He comments, "Since the universe displays some order in its running we may assume that God is the author of that order."[95]

A metaphysical analysis of the concept of God is not Gandhi's cup of tea. Somehow or anyhow God is to be realized. If by some God is worshipped as a personal god Gandhi has no objection to it. But for one there should be only one God, who is to be worshipped for attaining salvation. Worshipping various gods of nature or of heaven for materialisation of different desires of man does not lead to salvation. To him the forces of nature like steam, electricity-,etc. are all gods. "Propitiation of these forces quickly bears fruit, as we well know, but it is short lived. It fails to bring comfort to the soul and it certainly does not take one even a short step towards salvation."[96] Like any other Hindu, Gandhi concedes that the propitiation of natural forces and innumerable god heads can grant material boons. However, *artha, kama* are subsidiary objects of life, which do not lead to *moksha. Moksha* demands higher sacrifies and aspiration than mere propitiationary rituals.

Gandhi does not only explain the aspects of nature as God, he also explains social aspects of God. The concept of thirty three crore Gods in India means for him, the poetic expression of the presence of the divine in all of us. It also follows for him that service to mankind, is service to God for mankind is not different from it. He is advocating the practice of showing sincere respect for the living and the non-living, highly and the lowly, etc. It reflects Gandhi's conviction in the omnipotent manifestation of God and he seeks spiritual sanction for his philosophy of humanism and social welfare. On a similar fashion he draws sustenance for his bread labour theory from the principle of *yajna* or sacrifice. He writes, "the thirty three crores of Gods belong to the world of imagination....... We should serve the whole world."[97] Referring to the twenty third verse of chapters VII of the *Bhagavadgita* where the Lord says : "But limited is the fruit that falls to those short sighted ones; those who worship the gods go to the gods, those who worship Me come unto Me;" Gandhi says: "If there were many independent deities who could act on their own there would be no God."[98] For Gandhi worship of deities or lesser gods without the consciousness of the Eternal Brahman as the final goal is attributed to the ignorance of man.

Commenting on the twenty fourth verse of seventh chapter of the *Bhagavadgita* Gandhiji adds:

These persons of little intelligence do not know My unmanifest state, says Shri Krishna. 'They mistake the manifest universe for the invisible reality behind. They do not know the best part of Me at all (the part beyond the manifest), do not know me as the changeless, supreme *Purusattoma*'. If for instance, we worship the Sun, who gives light and heat, we divide the divine power of God into its several aspects and worship one of them. Instead, we should try to know the highest, the invisible state of God. This visible universe is ever taking new shapes. The gods change their forms but God is ever the same.[99]

To Gandhi, every object or image is a manifestation of the Unmanifest. Since it is difficult to concentrate one's devotion on the formless, one may worship God in various forms. But fruition of such worships in material gains should not prevent one from striving to achieve his higher goal like realisation of God or *Moksha*. He refers to the fifth verse of chapter XII of the *Gita* which says : "Greater is the travail of those whose mind is fixed on the Unmanifest; for it is hard for embodied mortals to gain the Unmanifest-Goal." Emphasising the concept of a Personal god inherent in this verse Gandhi writes :

Mortal man can only imagine the Unmanifest, the Impersonal, and as his language fails him he often negatively describes it as *'Neti'*, *'Neti'*. (Not That, Not That). And so even iconoclasts are at bottom no better than idol worshippers. To worship a book, to go to a Church, or to pray with one's face in a particular direction all these are forms of worshipping the Formless in an image or idol. And yet both the idol breakers and the idol worshippers can not lose sight of the fact that there is something which is beyond all form, Unthinkable, Formless, Impersonal, Changeless. The highest goal for the devotee is to become one with the object of his devotion. The *bhakta* extinguishes himself and merges into, becomes, *Bhagavan*. This state can best be reached by devoting oneself to some form, and so it is said that the short cut to the Unmanifest is really the largest and the most difficult.[100]

Thus to Gandhi though God is formless and unmanifest, the easier way to attain God is through devotion to a personal god with a form. But the consciousness of the Supreme Divine without form and attributes should always prevail in the mind of the devotee. The practice of propitiating various powers of the Supreme inherent in the forces of nature may bestow some material boon, but can not lead to *Moksha* or *Salvation*, which is the highest goal of every individual. He advocates the path of *Bhakti* (devotion) and *Karma* (action) as a better alternative to the path of *Jnana* or knowledge and reason which may lead one to great error. To Gandhi, the question of the gradation of the paths of devotion or whorship should be avoided. All religious sects believe in the worship of a personal god, in some form or the other. But it is better, believes Gandhi, that one remains silent on this issue. He writes :

Neither Christians, nor Muslims, nor certainly Hindus, have risen above the worship of the Personal God...... Even a person who aspires to cultivate devotion exclusively for the Unmanifest worships some visible symbol..... for this reason, Shri Krishna told Arjuna that it would be better for him to take no interest in the problem at all. 'Silence is golden in this matter', he says, 'Don't you see, you dear simpleton, that I Myself have taken on a human body ? And you ask Me, of all persons, whether worship of the Unmanifest is better or that of the Personal God. You had better stop asking such question and do as I tell you. Free yourself from all thoughts of violence and act towards all creatures with equal love and regard'. If we understand this truth, we should escape many problems. We should not mind it, because we worship the Personal God we are called idolaters and criticised for being so.[101]

The Concept of Man:

Gandhi's concept of man is ethical, unlike that of Sri Aurobindo, which is spiritual. From his treatment of the *Bhagavadgita*, one finds Gandhi's man to be a manifestation of the Supreme Being in a partial way. The *atman* is the replica of the Supreme Reality, imprisoned in the body. Everything with a body to Gandhi is imperfect. He compares the human body with the battle field of *Kurukshetra* and concludes that :

The human body is a battle field where the eternal duel between Right and Wrong goes on. Therefore, it is capable of being turned into the gateway to freedom. It is born in sin and becomes the seed-bed of sin. Hence it is also called the field of *Kuru*. The *Kauravas* represent the forces of Evil, the *Pandavas* the forces of Good.[102]

Gandhi generally shared the Jaina popular faith prevalent in Gujarat region that the Divinity (*Jiva*) is bound by the *Ajiva,* freedom from this bondage of *Ajiva* only restores the radiance of *Jiva*. Thus for him the body is automatically less spiritual and is an obstacle to the attainment of *Moksha*. In contrast for Sri Aurobindo, body can be as divine as the soul. The body for Gandhi is not self and the actual self is the *atman*. The body is impermanent and several, where as the *atman* is permanent and one. Liberation of the *atman* from the cycle of getting repeatedly into the bodies, birth after birth, is *Moksha* the final goal for all men. To Gandhi, the *Gita* advocates the path of fulfillment of one's duty in the spirit of selflessness as the true path for attaining *Moksha*.

Gandhi's concept of man proceeds from Head, Heart and Health (Body, Mind and Spirit) – all the aspects in a simultaneous triple; not in a triune like Sri Aurobindo's concept of Matter, Life and Mind coupled with the ultimate State of Bliss. For Sri Aurobindo, these aspects of man are evolved stage wise, in the process of evolution. Gandhi's concept however, does not attribute these to the process of evolution. To Gandhi life is sustained more by a sense of sacrifice than by a sense of violence. Good deeds must always out number bad deeds, though both good and evil must be there simultaneously.

Gandhi not only pre-supposes the imperfection of man but also emphasises on his absolute weakness even "to describe an actual event perfectly." This is due to ignorance or 'by reason of delusion' or *Maya* in the form of senses. The relation between man and God is spontaneous like the reflex action of the eyelids. Man has to be conscious of it and has to shed all attachments to the fruits of action in order to realise himself and his identity with the Supreme Lord. Becoming God is not the object of man. Knowledge is not the *Jnana* to Gandhi. But *Moksha* (liberation from the chain of birth and death) is the last resort. Other things follow after *Moksha*. Emphasising on the need of a determined conscious effort for men to achieve this goal Gandhi writes: "Our only right is to *Purusartha*. We can only strive and work. All human beings and animals too, struggle. The only difference is that we believe that behind our struggle there is an intelligent purpose."[103]

To Gandhi the purpose of this struggle is three fold : To keep alive this body. To know that which has taken on this body. And to raise it to its final goal. For the first objective man works mechanically without even a conscious will. But *Purusurtha* to Gandhi is only that effort aimed at the welfare of the *atman*.

Gandhi's man is not individualistic. He consistently treats man as a social being whose greatest *sadhana* (edneavour and purpose) ideally being maximum good for others at the cost of maximum suffering of the self, even at the risk of one's life. Like Buddha, Gandhi also points out that life is full of suffering. The process of human birth is in itself amounts to unbearable pain. The state of life form birth to death is one of imprisonment only. However, this is the prison through which freedom is won.

To Gandhi attachment with ego is the root of all evil. The absence of it can be achieved by everyone by adopting a life in accordance with the practical message of the *Gita* which shall be discussed later in this chapter. Gandhi has not analysed the concept of man *vis-a-vis* animal, nature, creation or its future.

Commenting on the following verse of the *Bhagavadgita* which says :

Na' date ksyacit papam

Na cai' va sukrutam vibhuh

Ajnanena' vratam jnanam

Tena mokhyanti jantavah. V.15.

"The Lord does not take upon Himself anyone's voice or virtue; it is ignorance that veils knowledge and deludes all creatures."

Gandhi enumerates the real nature of man and writes :

Man's real nature is to serve others and to work for self purification, and so we should not cherish the I in us...... When a man's ignorance, which develops the knowledge in him, has been destroyed by the knowledge, the light of God is revealed to him. God is the witness of all that occurs. The idea that we should live in obedience to Him, act only as prompted by Him – that is knowledge. We can experience its truth directly only when all the twists in the heart have straightened out and the *atman* alone shines there for ever.[104]

Gandhi's man has no extra-terrestrial goal. All he has to do is to eradicate his ignorance by acquiring true knowledge through austerities like *Aparigraha* (non-possession), *Abhaya* (fearlessness), *Brahmacharya* (celibacy), *Ahimsa* (non-violence) and *Seva* (service). Thus Gandhi's basic ethical attitude to life is clearly reflected in his philosophy.

The Concept of Cosmos :

Gandhi lays sole emphasis on the following first two *slokas* (verses) of the chapter XV of the *Bhagavadgita* in order to depict the nature of cosmos :

Urdhvamulam adhahsakham
Asvattham prahur avyayam
Chandamsi yasya parnani
Yas tam veda sa vedavit. XV.1.
Adhas co' rdhvam prasrtas tasya sakha
Gunapravrddha visayapravalah
Adhas ca mulany anusamtatnai
Karmanubandhini manusyaloke. XV.2.

These verses are translated by Gandhi as "With its root above and branches below the *asvattha* tree, they say, is imperishable; it has Vedic hymns for its leaves, he who knows it knows the Vedas."

"Above and below its branches spread, blossoming because of the *gunas* having for their shoots the sense – objects, deep down in the world of men are ramified its roots, in the shape of the consequences of action."

The *Gita* has symbolically represented the creation in the form of a *asvattha* (banyan tree) with its roots above and the branches below. By describing the cosmos having its roots above, the author means to state that the origin of the universe lies with the Supreme reality, the *Brahman*.

To Gandhi, this fact is the reason why the cosmos is described as imperishable. However, he finds *asvattha* to mean (*na svapi sthata*) "that which will not last even until tomorrow." Gandhi reconciles these two contradictions with each other in the line of the *Bhagavadgita*. He interprets that by comparing the cosmos with an inverted banyan tree the *Gita* expresses the nature of constant flux of the universe but not its perishability. The banyan tree is believed to expand by multiplying its roots from its branches, which come down from above and it is believed to be in a constant process of change but not in the process of decay or death. Its leaves are compared with the Vedic hymns. To many, Hindus believed that the universe was sustained by the ritualistic rites of the *Vedas*. But the concept is changed today. To Gandhi, the Vedic hymns described here as the leaves or sustainer of the cosmic tree or the universe is to be understood as *dharma* (religious way of life). He writes :

Shvah means tomorrow, and *asvattha* (*na svapi sthata*) means that which will not last even until tomorrow, is the world of sense which is every moment in a stae of flux. But even though it is perpetually changing, as its root is Brahman or the Supreme, it is imperishable. It has for its protection and support the leaves of the Vedic hymns, i.e. *dharma*. He who knows the world of sense as such and who knows *dharma* is the real *jnani*, that man has really known the *Vedas*.[105]

The second *sloka* (verse) cited above, describes for Gandhi, "the tree of the world of sense as the unenlightened see it. They fail to discover its Root above in *Brahman* and so they are always attached to the object of sense. They water the tree with three *gunas* and remain bound to *karma* in the world of men."[106]

The sixteenth verse of chapter VIII of the *Gita* says :

A brahmabhuvanal lokah
Punaravartino 'arjuna
Mam upetya tu kaunteya
Punarjanma na vidyate.

This means to Gandhi – "From the world of *Brahma* down all the worlds are subject to return, O Arjuna, but on coming to Me there is no rebirth."

Brahma is the creator in the Hindu trinity, different from the absolute impersonal *Brahman*. The visible universe is one of several heavens/worlds. All these including the world of *Brahma* will return to their source, the imperishable Supreme Reality. The sun, the moon, *Brahman, Vishnu* all will perish. 'But' Krishna says, 'Once a human being comes to Me he never perishes'. Referring to the eighteenth verse of chapter VIII of the *Bhagavadgita*, Gandhi further comments that when Brahma's day (A day and a night of Brahma consist of 8,640,000.000 years or 2,000 *mahayugas*), begins the Unmanifest becomes manifest. Then all creatures which had vanished into nothingness comes to existence. When his night begins, the whole cosmos vanishes by merging in to the Unmanifest. Thus all creation appears and vanishes endlessly.

To Gandhi, *yajna* is the source of sustaining energy of the cosmos. *Yajna* to Gandhi can be bodily labour, spinning, non-cooperation, farming or truth, service or anything that is absolutely moral. It is the 'good' that sustains the world. Not the vedic sacrificial rituals but the acts of goodness, anything that is done for the welfare of the society for Gandhi is *yajna* or the *dharma* which act as the leaves of the cosmic banyan tree described by the *Gita*.

Problems of Evil :

The concept of the problems of evil is an important aspect which finds place in Gandhi's treatment of the *Gita*. To Gandhi every object and every state which can be thought of in this universe are God. "This means that God is not merely all that is good. He is also the evil. Nothing exists unless He wills it. It is not true that God is the Lord of light and Satan of darkness. While we live in this body, we may believe in these dualities."[107]

That God has in Him the qualities of both virtue and sin is not acceptable to Gandhi. He evolves a third state in which contraries are reconciled, which is not a mere mixture of the two. God has something else which is above good and evil. "The existence of the two in God is a miracle and He alone knows the mystery." By saying this Gandhi simply avoids the question and does not seem to be reconciled with the idea.

In the *Gita* the Lord says : "Of deceivers I am the diceplay, of the splendid, the splendor; I am victory, I am resolution, I am the goodness of the good."

Gandhi comments, "The author's intention is only to assert that God is omnipotent, God's creation contains both good and evil. By saying this, Shri Krishna gives us some freedom to choose between the two."[108] To Gandhi whether God is evil or good is not the question here. The question is the directing, immanent and all pervasive power of God. All wicked or evil from *Ravana* downwards are destroyed by God. Only goodness prevails and the universe is sustained by good alone. Good must prevail. As already pointed out earlier, to Gandhi the concept of *avatara* propounded in the *Gita* is an ample evidence of the winning power of good over evil, though physically, both the wicked and the virtuous perish. Yet in one sense the good do not die. Their glory remain immortal for the posterity. "Virtues never die," says Gandhi, the contrary seen in the world "is but God's *maya*." He also admits that "virtues are cultivated with effort," where as "vices require no such effort." In any case to Gandhi "ultimately vices perish and virtues prosper."

The most important aspect of Gandhi's understanding of the concept of the problem of evil from the *Gita* is his conviction that it is not evil but goodness which rules the world and that evil can not exist independently. In his own words :

The wicked can prevail only when they number crores, but goodness will rule when embodied to perfection even in one person. Non-violence has been described as so powerful that all forces of violence subsided in its presence. Under its influence, even beasts forget their nature. Even one good person can change the world. Such a one enjoys an empire over people's hearts' we do not, because we follow goodness only as best we may. The type of good man I have mentioned has but to send a message, and people will do what he wants them to do, such is the power of goodness. Where wickedness prevails, there is disorder in every field of life, but where goodness rules, order prevails and people are happy.[109]

Emphasising the dependence of evil on good for its existence, Gandhi refers to the setting of the *Mahabharata* war, during which *Gita* was delivered. While the *kauravas*, are said to be the representatives of the demoniac, they were not exclusively so. They had to take the support of good souls like Bhisma, Drona and many others. Gandhi comments : "Besides Karna, Duryodhana had good men like Bhisma and Drona also on his side. This suggests that evil can not by itself flourish in this world. It can do so only if it is allied with some good."[110]

Applying his interpretation and understanding of this concept Gandhi believes that :

This was the principle underlying non-cooperation, that the evil system which the Governemnt represents, and which has endured only because of the support it receives from good people, can not survive if that support is withdrawn. Just as the Governemnt needs the support of good men in order to exist, so Duryodhana required men like Bhisma and Drona in order to show that there was justice on his side.[111]

To Gandhi evil or good can not be exclusive in themselves. He feels, "Even the best thing has an element of evil in it.

Nothing in the world is wholly good or wholly evil. Where there is action there is some evil."[112]

While Sri Aurobindo and Radhakrishnan explain evil as a manifestation of ignorance and explain logically the tenability of evil under God who is Good, Gandhi is not concerned with this classic debate of metaphysics – reconciling Evil with God. His understanding and interpretation stands on a different footing.

Concept of the Ends and Means ;

Gandhi had two goals in life, one spiritual and the other political. His spiritual goal was to attain *Moksha* or liberation of the soul. His political aspiration was the establishment of *Swaraj* in India – *Swaraj*, concept wider than mere political liberation. In the world context Gandhi aspired for the equality of all races. The establishment of the principle of non-violence and truth globally was his dream. Gandhi resorted to the means of non-violence, truth and morality for attaining these aspirations. His life mirrored the correlation he established between the ends and the means as a whole.

While philosophers are at pain to retain the absolutness of the ultimate Reality in an apparent transitory world full of evil, misery and falsehood, Gandhi had to reconcile Krishna the God of millions of the Indias with the principle of violence, diplomacy and all that goes with a war – which he had held to be wrong. He had to stretch his relativeness to accept the war setting of the *Mahabharata*, which has been already discussed. He almost concedes that at the time of Vyasa – war was not considerd wrong, but to-day there is no need to accept war and no need to find fault either with Krishna or Vyasa. Gandhi even suggest that Arjuna having once chosen to fight was not justified in shrinking from it, having reached the battle field. In his life Gandhi was caught with three wars – Boer war, First World War and the Second World War. He would not fight but he did not criticise those who fought. He was opposed to Indians participation in the Second World War as Indians were not consulted by the English but his sympathy was still with the Allies and their cause. War of *Mahabharata* to Gandhi was symbolic of the war between evil and good. Gandhi firmly believes that untruth and violence, etc. as means can never achieve truth and non-violence – the highest goal for both the individual and the makind. "As you sow, so shall you reap" – was too firmly entrenched in Gandhi's mind. However, Gandhi was not naïve to believe that life can be sustained without violence altogether. What he emphasises is that love and sacrifice sustains life and the world and that they are the predominant factors of life but not violence.

In his preface to *Anasakti Yoga* Gandhi has lucidly put forth his understanding of the concept of the means and the ends. While describing the characters of a devotee he finds that :

To be a real devotee is to realize oneself. Self-realisation is not something apart. One rupee cannot buy us either salvation or bondage. These are not media of exchange. They are themselves the thing we want. In other words, if the means and the end are not identical, they are almost so. The extreme of means is salvation of the *Gita* is perfect peace.[113]

To Gandhi even knowledge and devotion of the *Gita* have to stand the acid test of the renunciation of the fruits of action. Knowledge of right and wrong alone will not give one salvation. To him, even the noble ways and means of knowledge (*jnana*) and devotion (*bhakti)* may falter and fail to achieve the goal of self-realisation without renunciation of the fruits of action. Because without the renunciation the devotee broods over result and is like a man given to objects of senses; he is ever distracted, he says goodby to all scruples, everything is right for him and thus he resorts to means fair and foul to attain his end. To Gandhi all acts performed without the attachment to their fruits of action are taboo. In other words the attachment to end or the goal must not distract one from the right means of achieving it.

To believe that religion has no place in worldly matters is a delusion and Gandhi says "*Gita* has dispelled this delusion. He (the author of the *Gita*) has drawn no line of demarcation between salvation and worldly pursuits." In other words, the means either for salvation or or material good have to be religious and right. Whatever the goal if the means are right, the end shall be inevitably good. A wrong means to achieve even the noblest of all goals is not acceptable to Gandhi.

The religiosity of the means of action is lost if one is attached to the cherished end. Renunciation of the end product ensures the right means of action. And to Gandhi, "the *Gita* had to deliver the message of renunciation of fruit."[114] As matter of fact, Gandhi's interpretation of the *Gita* revolves round this concept. Consequently the practical meassage of the *Gita* according to Gandhi is to take resort to the right means of action and surrender of the end result to the supreme. If some of the means towards attaining the goal of self-realization propounded there in seem to be immoral, then to Gandhi, a new meaning in the *Gita* is to be sought by the seeker. Thus the terms like *Karma* (action), *Sannyas* (renunciation) and *Yajna* (sacrifice) of the *Gita* and the war setting of the *Mahabharata* as its backgound, etc. are subject to modified interpretations. In any case the central teaching of the *Gita* remains unchanged. It must be re-stated that Gandhi never accepted the *Gita* or for that matter any scripture from the east or the west, to be infallible nor did he think that even though they were sacred – all parts need to be accepted in full. Each text, every part of it for him had to pass the acid test of truth, non-violence and morality. It is equally important to re-state that this is not necessarily the Hindu view of life. For the Hindu – God is not subject to one's standards of morality.

Gandhi refers to verse 48 of chapter II of the *Bhagavadgita* where Krishna says to Arjuna, "Act thou, O Dhananjaya, without attachment, fast in *Yoga,* even minded in success and failure – even mindedness is *Yoga.*" Commenting on this Gandhi says :

It means not desiring the fruit of work which is *akarma.* We should do no work with attachment. Attachment to good work, is that too wrong ? yes, it is. If we are attached to our goal of winning *swaraj,* we shall not hesitate to adopt bad means. If a person is particular that he would give up silvers to me personally, one day he might even steal them. Hence, we should not be attached even to a good cause. Only then will our means remain pure and our actions too.[115]

Once the end is decided one should concentrate on the means, "if they are right, the end is as good as attained." If Gandhi had not realized God, in the eyes of others, for him the means he had adopted stood for such realization."[116]

Practical Message of the *Gita* According to Gandhi :

In the words of Gandhi, "The *Gita* is a work intended to be a guide in life and we should be able to find in it support for all our actions in practical life."[117] The *Bhagavadgita* for Gandhi was a constant companion, he looked for answers, solace and sustenance from it in periods of crisis and doubt. It was not a book just for interpretation or for writing a metaphysical treatise for him, but was a practical guide, "a book of home remedies." As such the practical message derived from it was the *summum bonum* of the *Bhagavadgita* for Gandhi. Sri Aurobindo also partly used the *Bhagavadgita* as a practical guide and cited from it extensively in providing spiritual guidance to his disciples. Gandhi constantly used it as a practical guide for himself and advised others to develop a spontaneous devotion for the *Gita* and to derive guidance for their daily conduct. Gandhi finds the *Gita* to be full of ethical insights. Starting from the first chapter of the *Gita* upto its last, Gandhi derives a series of practical ethics from the scripture which are discussed below, in the order of the progress of the teachings in the *Gita* vis-à-vis Gandhi's discourses on the Gita delivered to the ashramites. The practical aspects as emphasised by Gandhi in his discourses on the *Bhagavadgita* has been identified below and each message is followed by a brief explanation.

One Must be Free From the Ignorant Attachments in the World :

Arjun's despondency, according to Gandhi was due to his ignorant attachment towards his kinsmen, which disturbed him from discharging his duties as a *Kshyatriya*. Such discrimination could also be distractive for him, felt Gandhi. Ignorant attachment to body, society, self or action, etc. are an impediment to the discharging of one's duty to God and inner-self. Gandhi felt that every individual should discard such attachments in life.

Surrender of Ego is the Central Message of the *Gita* :

All arguments advanced by Krishna in the *Bhagavadgita* to Gandhi are meant to deliver the central teaching of the *Gita* which is surrender of the attachment to ego. One can follow truth only in the measure that he sheds his attachment to ego. Surrender of ego is possible by the renunciation of fruits of one's action to God, with faith, right knowledge and unreserved devotion. To Gandhi at the back of every instance of violence or to untruth the desire of and attachment to a cherished end are bound to be there.

To be a True Devotee is to Realize Oneself :

In order to realize one's self, one has to have the qualities of a *sthitaprajna* (a man of steadfast wisdom). A true devotee is jealous of none is a fount of mercy, selfless and without egotism; ever forgiving and contented. His mind and soul are dedicated to God. He causes no dread nor is he afraid of others. He is free from exultation, sorrow and fear. He is pure and versed in action, yet he remains unaffected by it, by renouncing all action, good or bad. He treats friends and foes alike and is beyond respect and disrespect, praise and condemnation. He loves silence and solitude and is in possession of a disciplined reason. "Such devotion," to Gandhi, "is inconsistence with the existence, at the same time of strong attachments."[118] Hence renunciation of fruits of action is obligatory. Renunciation means not inaction, but action without hankering after the fruits of action.

One Must Not Give up a Task Once Undertaken :

To Gandhi, Arjuna's aversion to duty already undertaken is due to his ignorance. One must do his duty in a detached way with a fixed aim. Gandhi writes : "The actions of a man whose intellect is not fixed on one aim, who is not single minded in his devotion will branch out in many directions."[119] Gandhi felt that the want of single minded devotion to spinning was the cause of all evil in the politics of his times.

Gandhi had to emphasise the single mindedness to a great extent for he was probably afraid that the great mass of his followers may lose hope and spirit along with the tide and web of various political movements that Gandhi launched in the course of the India's freedom struggle. *Gita*'s plea for non attachment to the fruits of action was capable of eroding the consistent perusal of goal through action. In his political career Gandhi was remarkable as a chaser of goals set by him.

God Makes us Dance, Like the Master in a Puppet Show:

The Master of all creation, the God to Gandhi is also the Master of all actions. He is believed to be the *atman* in the body, the charioteer. A true *yogi* offers everything he does to God and looks upon Him as the sole author of everyting. Notwithstanding Gandhi's rational yardstick or the tests of truth and non-violence he had a firm faith in his personal God – Rama. He was literally in the innermost recess of his heart constantly and on his lips even in the last moment of his life on earth. He genuinely believed that the whole world is controlled by God – even a personal God. Radhakrishnan observing this facet of Gandhi's life remarked "Gandhi's death was a classical ending to his life. He died in the name of God on his lips and love in his heart...... He lived upto what he preached."[120]

One Must Not Grieve at Some One's Death :

The *atman* is subtler than air. The *Gita* says that the weapons can not cleave he *atman,* nor fire can burn it. The *atman* is eternal, all-pervading, stable, immovable and everlasting. Only the body dies. Death of the body is certain of the born. He who dies is born again. "We outght not grieve over what is inescapable, what can not be helped. Birth and death are God's concern."[121] One must fight the weakness of his heart and rely on the mercy of Rama, the God, according to Gandhi.

All Actions Must be Righteous Actions :

One must constantly remain vigilant of his actions. One has to decide whether a particular action serves the *atman* or the body. All actions, to Gandhi which are meant for the satisfaction of the body are tainted with sin. All righteous actions provide peace to the *atman* and enables it to grow towards perfection. Even a little of the righteous course delivers one from great fear. An action is righteous or not can be decided by the voice of the *atman* and one must always remain intent at listening to the inner voice of the *atman* or the conscience. The *atman* advances through action that is natural to it and falls back through action that is contrary to its action.

A follower of righteous action or *Niskama karma* must be above the pairs opposites, should give up all claim of holding or defending possessions.

To Gandhi, Arjuna in the *Gita* is asked to rise above the pairs of opposites, which means to be indifferent to joy and sorrow. This is applicable to all men of true action.

Gandhi writes," He should be *nityasattvastha* which means that his mind should always remain steadfast. He should be *niryogakshema,* that is to give up all thought of acquiring, holding and defending possessions. One should learn to implement the principle of *aparigraha* (non-possession) and must learn to be content in himself.

In order to attain perfection the senses must be controlled.

Actually man is a slave of his senses. From this slavery he must win 'Swaraj for the *atman*'. The *atman* should dwell in the body as its master. Referring to the 64 verse of chapter II of the *Bhagavadgita* Gandhi comments, "The person who is ruled by his *atman* will have the gift of inner senses and will not need the outer ones."[122]

Fasting is the most effective way of controlling senses and self purification .

Emphasising the need of control of senses for every spiritual aspirant Gandhi writes :

Three things are essential for control of the senses (i) faith, (ii) a conviction of the necessity of subjugating the senses, so strong that we would persist even if we were all alone in this belief; (iii) food is body's nourishment, a means of keeping it alive, but it is also the cause of the senses becoming turbulent and therefore, when it ceases to serve the purpose of nourishing the body, eating should cease........ if feeding the body results in senses becoming turbulent, we should stop eating.[123]

It may be mentioned here that fasting was Gandhi's choicest weapon for a *Satyagrahi*. Gandhi felt that the banishment of all sensual desires should come naturally but not as a matter of compulsion. Fasting is an effective aid to observe *brahmacharya* or abstinence in one's life. One must non-cooperate with the evil impulses of his senses. Fasting is an effective means for *sattva suddhi* or purity of the self. "*Brahmacharya* leads to immortality;" feels Gandhi and "sexual indulgence necessarily leads to death."[124]

No one can cease from *Karma* or action even for a moment.

Verses 5 and 6 of chapter III of the *Bhagavadgita* say, "For none ever remains inactive even for a moment. For all are compelled to action by the *gunas* inherent in *Prakriti.* "He who curbs the organs of action but allows the mind to dwell on the sense-objects – such a one, wholly deluded, is called a hypocrite-."

To Gandhi one can never experience the state of *naishkarmya* (freedom from experiencing results of action) or attaint to *moksha* by simply refusing to work. To Gandhi *karma* means any action, any bodily activity or motion. *Karma* includes even thought. The decision to stop breathing entails *karma*. "Even the refraining from *karma* is *karma*."[125] Signifying the importance of the *gunas* (*sattava, rajas* and *tamas*) Gandhi believes that one is always driven to work by one or the other of those three forces or modes of *prakriti* or by a combination of them. Control over one's *prakriti* by conscious effort and true devotion to God can enable one to avoid the contradition between his thought and action. Gandhi accepted the general notion that everyone must transcend all the three *gunas* – as God is beyond the *gunas*, so also for liberation an individual has to be beyond the *gunas*.

One must always act out of a sense of duty.

One should do the work assigned to him. Action is superior to inaction. To Gandhi, Krishna asks Arjuna to act only as an instrument of the God's Will. All action to Gandhi is tainted by some violence or sin. But action performed with a sense of duty without attachment and a sense of surrender to God is not tainted. *Swadharma*, of the *Gita* to Gandhi is one's allotted duty or the duty prescribed by one's *atman* through conscience, at a particular point of time.

By serving the humblest beings one serves the whole world.

Referring to the verse of the *Gita* which says, "with this may you cherish the gods and may gods cherish you; thus cherishing one another may you attain the highest good." (III.11.). Gandhi believes that living aside the world of gods, one should try to serve the humblest of human beings, known or unknown with utmost honour and respect. By this attitude the sphere of our service will enlarge itself to embrance the whole world. Gandhi worked incessantly for the lowly, untouchables, disadvantaged, diseased and aspired for equality for all including women. He had to draw religious sanction for his humanism and philosophy of social upliftment of people fromt the lower rungs of the society.

We should undertake bodily labour to do service.

To Gandhi man can not thrive without physical work. He equates physical labour, labour in the agricultural fields, with *yajna*. To him evil desires will never disturb one who is engaged in physical work through out the day. He writes, "if we do our bodily *yajna* properly, all will be well with us, we shall advance the good of our *atman* and of the world, our mind and body will be ruled by our *atman* and we shall be filled with serene peace."[126] The bread labour theory may not necessarily follow from the *Gita*. Gandhi even before writing on the *Bhagavadgita* or discussing on it, had talked of bread labour theory. He read the meaning to the *Bhagavadgita* also. No other commentator looks at this aspect of the *Gita* from Gandhi's angle of view.

Something done to serve others' good, but without causing suffering to any creature is true *Yajna*.

Gandhi believes that simply burning a few sticks in fire is not *Yajna* of the *Gita* where Krishna says : "This world of men suffers bondage from all action, save that which is done for the sake of sacrifice, to this end, O Kaunteya perform action without attachment." III.9 Burning wood was probably a necessity in ancient times to clear the forests as a social requirement. Gandhi believes that had the *Rshis* lived in Sahara desert, "they would have conceived the *Yajna* as refraining from cutting a single twig, as planting of trees or drawing a certain quantity of water."[127] But today *Yajna* assumes a different meaning. *Yajna* for Gandhi is not labour as a means of livelihood. By defining spinning as a true *Yajna* Gandhi believes that the true meaning of the *Yajna* in the *Gita* is not inconsistent with it. To Gandhi bodily labour, service to the needy and all other work dedicated for the welfare of mankind and the spirit of maximum comfort for others with all the suffering for the self – can be called a *Yajna*. The *Gita* says that he who eats without performing a *Yajna* is a thief. Gandhi attributes a new meaning and holds that he who eats without work is a thief. He further writes : Man does not live by bread alone, where as the lower creatures need only food to live......Whereas man lives by performing *Yajna*.... The spinning wheel is one type of yajna. Prayers, too are a *yajna* for us. They represent a mode of spiritual cleansing.[128]

Not action, but the spirit behind it may cause bondage.

In the third verse of the chapter III of the *Bhagavadgita* Krishna tells Arjuna that :

Dedicating every action to Him, having purified his mind, fixed it on his atman and emptied it of all desires, and without entertaining any thought of gain, he should go on doing *karma* as a matter of duty and irrespective of whether or not he was likely to benefit...... Freedom from attachment and aversion is the first step towards understanding one's duty.[129]

To Gandhi one's duty can be discovered by reflection. When an operation on a patient is conducted by a doctor to save the life of the patient as a matter of the latter's duty, it is not an act of violence. To quote Gandhi, "violence does not consist in the act of cutting off some one's head, it consists in the motive behind the act."[130]

When one acts as an instrument of God, his actions do not accure sin. Such action does not bind. Of many political implications that Gandhi derived from the *Bhagavadgita*, the concept of *Yajna* and that of equating the spinning with it was most important. Some historians have also suggested that Gandhi's adoration of the spinning wheel as a part of national flag was an attempt to identify the same with *Sudarsana chakra*. Even though Gandhi might not have desired or aspired to be hailed as godhead – the average Indian believed that he was divinely sent to India for the deliverance of the country from English rule. Gandhi's constant reference to religion particularly the *Bhagavadgita* contributed to the religious aura that was associated with him.

We can offer Satyagraha only against a person who has some love in his heart.

Analysinig the work *nigraha* of verse 33 of Chapter III of the *Gita* Gandhi points out that control can only be exercised on one who is willing to be controlled. He writes :

We can offer *Satyagraha* only against a person who has some love in his heart. We can control another only if there is mutual love between us, where there is no such love the only course for us is non-cooperation with the other party. Tulsidas advised non-cooperation with the wicked.[131]

Gandhi believes that since God is in every heart so love in varying degree is bound to be present in every body. Thus, if used efficiently *Satyagraha* as a means of changing one self as well as others has an universal applicability. Violence or war has not. Gandhi believes that god resides in every one's heart including in the hearts of opponents. The oppression they (including the English) inflicted is due to ignorance. If we can appeal to the good, the God or even the better sense in them, there is bound to be a change in their hearts. Thus it is not necessary to fight, to inflict injury but to touch the heart of our opponent and transform him. *Satyagraha* was based on this firm conviction.

Action is not different from *Sannyasa*.

Gandhi feels that he who surrenders all his works to God does his duty without looking for a reward is both a *Sannyasi* as well as a *Yogi*. He explains : "But that person who never lights the fire for *Yajna* – originally it was an act of public service to keep a fire burning in the home for performing a *Yajna* – or never works is neither a *Sannyasi* nor a *Yogi*. Such a person would in fact be a prince of idlers."[132]

To Gandhi *Sannyasa* for Arjuna in the *Gita* lies in fighting the battle. Gandhi also adds, "*Sannyasa* is not something which can be demonstrated outwardly; it is a matter of the spirit within. The restless play of desires and fancies should cease; only then can one be a *Sannyasi*."

If we wish to give up sin, we should transcend virtue too.

Attachment either to sin or to virtue is a taboo according to the *Gita*. Gandhi feels for the evil God is evil. God has both evil and good in Him. The true surrender is possible when one offers both the good and the evil to God. "There is possessiveness in clinging even to virtue."[133]

The first thing to realize God is the observance of the rules of *Yama-niyama*.

As has been seen, Gandhi lays maximum stress on self-discipline thtough *Yama-niyama*. Any body who has not followed the principle of purifying one self by observing *Yama-niyama* (rules for moral discipline and religious observances). He refers to Patanjali's five *Yamas* (cardinal vows) like non-violence, truth, non-stealing, celibacy and non-possession, and five *niyamas* (casual vows) like bodily purity, contentment, the study of the scriptures, austerity and meditation of God.[134] These practices to Gandhi help the *Yogi* to keep his body in condition and his senses in subjugation.

Though Gandhi says that the *Gita* is not a book of do's and do not's his faith in the supremacy of ethical values in the scripture is clearly visible in his attitude of drawing practical message from almost all verses of all the chapters of the *Bhagavadgita*. He found sustenance from the *Gita* for his political ideologies like non-cooperation, *Swadeshi, Satyagraha, Swaraj* or even for a motion in the congress party. To illustrate this aspect a few statements of Gandhi are appeanded below.

One sould go on working without attachment to the fruits of work. I deduce the principle of *Satyagraha* from this........ As far back as 1889 when I had my first contact with the *Gita*, it gave me a hint to *Satyagraha* and, when I read it more and more, the hint developed into a full revelation of *Satyagraha*.[135]

Surely the *Bhagavadgita* does not say that we should dress ourselves in delicate Japanese fabrics. Every *shastra* says that only our own *dharma* can save us and it is our *dharma*, in our country, to wear cloth made by our workers in their homes singing hymns as they work.[136]

I venture to submit that the *Bhagavadgita* is a gospel of non-cooperation between forces of darkness and those of light.[137]

I again appeal to Tilak Maharaj and I appeal to Mr. Das and to everyone of you, not on the strength of my service – it counts for nothing, not on the strength of my experience – but on the strength of inexorable logic. If you accept your own civilisation, I ask the author of the commentaries on *Bhagavadgita* (*Gita Rahasya* which Tilak wrote during his incarceration at Mandalay), if he accepts the teachings of the *Bhagavadgita*, then let him extend the hand of fellowship to Mr. Montagu.[138]

The above extracts from various writings of Gandhi do not exhaust all the occasions where he sought sustenance from the *Gita* for his actions. They are only representative examples of Gandhi's steady faith in the scripture, as the unfailing source of guidance for all his actions – political, social or personal.

Conclusion:

In modern times Gadhi is the first gift of India to the domain of world history. In the Indian context his importance is reflected from that of "Gandhian Era" used for the years from 1920 to 1947 in modern Indian context. He remained the greatest apostle of peace and non-violence during the years marked by the two great world wars. As a personality no one's life is as open a book as was his. Yet no none's life and ideas were as complicated as that of Gandhi. To many-, not without justification, he was one of the most baffling characters.

There is no need to recall the essence of his early life or his political career. What may be reiterated is the essential character of Gandhi. Though Gandhi was not influenced by the Indian scriptures in early life, he was exposed to the Christian literature and was simultaneously steeped in the essential moral character of Hidnu faiths and practices. Sri Aurobindo was deep in the woods of classic Greek literature and the Sanskrit heritage from the vedic period. Radhakrishnan was well conversant with the western philosophers and the philosophers of India from the Upanisadic days to modern times. But Gandhi was not a voracious reader in comparison to these two, yet he had a simple heart to imbibe the essence of the Christian and the Hindu thought. In contrast he was a man of greater involvment in action though he reflected on many of the fundamental issues of religion and philosophy he did not meditate on them. While Sri Aurobindo was a seer and a poet and was incidentally in politics for some time; while Radhakrishnan was an academician and thinker essentially and got into politics in the fag-end of his life, holding an ornamental office only, Gandhi was a public figure and a politician with an interest in religion, metaphysics and spiritualism in his own way. The *Bhagavadgita* was his spiritual reference book, an infallible guide for daily life to which Gandhi turned constantly for comfort and sustenance. As a whole Gandhi was a rational and moral idealist. This is amply reflected in his approach to and the treatment of the *Bhagavadgita*.

For Gandhi Truth is the sovereign principle equal to the concept of God and this is a matter of realization. As he had no God realisation he held that until such realisation it was necessary for him to hold the relative truth as he had conceived it. In this scheme of Gandhi truth and non-violence were the central nerves. His adherence to these two principles was neither foolish nor an unbending sticking to a position devoid of rationality nor was it the sign of weakness or lack of courage. He described himself as a *sanatani* (oththodox) Hindu *vaishnava* and described the characteristics of such a person as having an acceptance to the *Vedas*, the *Upanisads* and the *Puranas*, faith in the practice of *Yama-niyam*, aspiring for *moksha* the freedom from the chain of birth and death and joining the *paramatman*, belief in *varnashrama dharma*, etc. He respected Islam and Christiantiy as true religions. However, all texts of religion for him were subject to tests of reason. He did not entirely accept all that is contained in these texts. By any imagination, Gandhi was not a revivalist though he might have romantically idealised the past at times. He was an experimental personality. Rama, the *Maryada Purusa* (supreme ethical personaltiy), was his ideal. He had a tremendous seeking for God, *Moksha* was his highest end. He had a distinct vision of a *Ramarajya*, an ideal Independent India.

Gandhi was initiated to the *Gita* partly-through regular exposure to it in the religious atmosphere of his childhood and through Sir Edwin Arnold's translation, during his stay in England. Gandhi's ideas as a whole was built on his own faith and understanding and the deep influence, of the *Sermon on the Mount*, the theosophical literature and the writings of Thoreau, Ruskin, Tolstoy and others, in addition to those of many Indian authors. By his own admission Gandhi's commentary on the *Bhagavadgita* was not meant for the scholars, the English educated Indians, or the Sanskrit *pundits*. It was basically for the simple hearted followers of him, the women and the people in the lower rungs of the society. He never claimed to have a deep understanding of the *Shastras* including the *Gita*. But he claimed that he had tried to live upto the principles of the *shastras*, specially the *Gita*, as understood by him.

Gandhi does not accept the war setting of the *Bhagavadgita* completely. As a whole he does not take the allegorical and extra-natural descriptions of the epic as a whole to be historical. Thus the war theme and the setting of the *Gita* for him is more symbolic than historical. He is aware that the vast majority of the Hindus at that time generally believed the epics to be the gospels of truth. Gandhi is not a rationalist, criticising these elements. He is still a spiritualist and a moralist prepared to accept the essence of the *Gita*. Gandhi advocates a rather unconventional reason to reject the historicity of the *Mahabharata* and the *Bhagavadgita*. He argues that no event can be faithfully described from the past, as God's work is unfathomable and man in his opinion is too weak and small for such a task.

Even though Gandhi partly accepts the war background of the *Gita* as being justified on the grounds that Vyasa and his contemporary ethics did not view war and violence there in to be untenable as in the case of the present. It is for him a conflict in the human heart between opposing moral tendencies and values. It represents the confrontation between the righteous and the unrighteous. The battle is only a pretext for the presentation of a far more important and greater principles of truth; like renunciation of the attachment to the fruits of action, total surrender to God, desireless action, etc. Arjuna's problem for Gandhi is not a choice between war and peace, nor the answer is choice of war over peace for Gandhi. Arjuna's problem is that even though he has chosen to fight and accepted violence, he is not prepared to kill his kinsmen, although he knows them to be on the wrong side. Arjuna's problem for Gandhi is his ignorant attachment to ego and unnecessary distinction between his kinsman and others.

From the *Bhagavadgita* Gandhi illustrats his understanding of the concept of Reality or God. As noted earlier, he was not a trained metaphysician nor was he concerned with the standard questions of metaphysics. His concepts on metaphysical questions must be read along with this limitation of Gandhi in mind. Even though he respected the authorities of the *Vadas*, the *Upanisads* and great commentators like Samkara he did not share the ideas of *nirguna Brahman* and the concept of illusion (*maya*) advocated by the *advaita* vedantists. He believs in a personal god and argued that devotion to a personal god is the only way of liberation and realization. The personal god for him is *Vishnu* and his numerous *avataras*, more so that of Rama. A faith in God's existence transcending reason for him is essential. Gandhi cites several stanzas of the *Bhagavadgita* to describe various aspects of God the Supreme. The *Gita* concept of the Supreme is both *Saguna* and *Nirguna* for him. He is *aprameya, aja, avyaya* and *achchedya*. He believes that the Supreme Self is present in everything as the *atman*. Gandhi argues that the ultimate is beyond the *trigunas*, and as such beyond the categories of good and evil and the temporal and spatial limitations. He accepts the concepts of *Prakriti* and *Purusa*, yet the all transcending principle of Gandhi's concept of reality is Truth and Non-violence. He always claims that evil has no independent standing and for him the overbearing principle that sustains the world is love and sacrifice, not withstanding the existence of evil and violence. He conceded the possibility of an *avatara* but an *avatara* for Gandhi is the ascent of man to greater goodness rather than the descent of God. He considers the Hindu trinity of *Brahma, Vishnu* and *Siva,* not to be a triple but a triane. He accepts the propitiation of natural forces and also accepts the social aspects of religious life. Service to mankind is service to God for him. His spiritualism is eternally wedded to the philosophy of social upliftment and humanism. The whole world is spiritual for him. The practical way to God realisation for Gandhi is devotion and work without attachment to fruits. He does not grade the *Bhakti, Jnana* and *Karma margas,* for each is involved in the other paths.

Gandhi's concept of man is ethical. Man is a manifestation of the God. Yet Gandhi believes that the soul is caught in the bondage of the body and has lost its radiance due to the limitations of the human body. The body for him is eternally imperfect and *Moksha* is indeed release from the imperfect body and this release comes by complete freedom from the desire to be born again. The practical methods to achieve *moksha* for Gandhi are the practice of *Yama-niyama, brahmacharya,* etc. Even though Gandhi points out the limitations of the body he simultaneously advocates physical education to a great extent. As he is an ardent advocate of the bread-labour theory, he feels the necessity of maintaining a healthy body. For others like Sri Aurobindo the body can transcend the limitations imposed by ignorance and can become divinely radiant with the growth of consciousness in it. Sri Aurobindo in partiular aspired for transformation of human body in its march for the conquest of death. Sri Aurobindo had no dislike for the body. He did not consider the body to be an obstacle or to be spiritually less important. Gandhi insists on the avoidance of indulgences and purification fo the body through good habits. Man's greatest problem for Gandhi is the ignorant attachment with ego. Freedom from this attachment is of supreme importance for him. In his views on the cosmos Gandhi emphasises the world as an order, divine in origin, and controlled by the God. He emphasises the social aspects of the cosmos. He reads into this concept the principles of racial equality, democracy, freedom, etc.

As to the problem of the evil, he feels that God is both above good and bad, and all dualities. He is omnipotent and for Gandhi the omnipotent rules the world through good. He believes in the change of heart of others. The means are as important as the ends and the acid test for all means for Gandhi is morality and renunciation of the fruits of action. He never compromises the necessity of concentration and single mindedness. In his practical message he emphasises freedom from attachment to ego and the necessity to develop qualities like devotion, concentration, equanimity, fearlessness, adhering to righteous action and involvement in *Niskamakarma*. For all these he feels that one must act with a sense of duty, with humility and with a love to serve others with the object of changing the heart of one self as well as the others, all through, by acts of self purification and control of senses. He applies these principles to draw political parallels. One may even argue that he drew his political mileage out of these.

As a whole, Gandhi's is a distinct example of a different understanding of the *Bhagavadgita*. Though elements of traditional interpretation may be traced in his writings and discourses, it is refreshingly original and innovative. One may criticise him for misrepresentation of the ideas in the *Gita*, for differing from the standard meaning set froth and derived from the *Gita* since the long past years, yet it is difficult to ascribe negative motives for Gandhi's newer interpretations. It can be conceded that Gandhi's ideas and philosophy of life were fairly well settled before he began to interpret the *Bhagavadgita* for the public. In other words it is humbly suggested that Gandhi interpreted the *Bhagavadgita* in the light of his firm convictions in the principles of Truth and Non-violence as understood by him. Not withstanding the innovative interpretation, Gandhi has not missed the essentials of the *Gita* like devotion, faith in

God as the all pervasive, all controlling omnipotent Reality above all dualities. He also argues that evil has no independent existence. He agrees with the general Hindu precept that ignorance is the source of evil and he has no difficulty in admitting evil as a secondary reality. Gandhi lived in an age where rationality was the presiding principle and as such his spiritualism and moralism was subject to the same. Gandhi largely succeeded in drawing sustenance from the *Gita* for his political activities and methodology which he carried out during his long career. Gandhi's understanding of the *Bhagavadgita* remains an important component of his mental make-up, particularly during his political career from the South Africa days. Without getting into the debate whether Gandhi gave a true or right interpretation of the *Bhagavadgita*, it may be fairly admitted that Gandhi interpreted the *Bhagavadgita* within the frame work of his total thinking.

Gandhi represented the conscience of the future man. He presented to this unbelieving world all that is noblest in the spirit of man. He belonged to the type that redeems the human race. He stands out as a great prophet of a moral and spiritual revolution without which the world will not find peace. Gandhi laid the paths of reconciliation and sympathetic adjustment of all differences. His religion was an intensely practical one. His spirit was invincible. Gandhi learnt from the *Gita* to be truthful, to be simple, to be pure and of gentle heart, to remain cheerful and contented in sorrow and danger, to love life and not to fear death, to serve the spirit and not to be haunted by the spirits of the dead. He lived, totally guided by his convictions in morality, supported by the gospels from the *Gita*. None lived as he did.[139]

REFERENCES

1 John Gunther, "Mr. Gandhi". **Profiles of Gandhi**; Ed. Norman Cousins, Delhi, 1970-47.

2 Louis Fischer, **The Life of Mahatma Gandhi**; London, 1982, p.19.

3 B.R. Nanda, **Mahatma Gandhi, A Biography**; New Delhi, 1982, p.8.

4 Ronald Duncan, (Ed.). **The Writings of Gandhi** ; Oxford, 1983,p.30

5 B.R. Nanda, op.cit., pp.15-16.

6 The episode of king Harish Chandra, who lost his kingdom, wife and son to keep up to his commitments for truth.

7 Vincent Sheen, **Mahatma Gandhi, A Great Life in Brief**; Publication Division, New Delhi, 1982, p.5.

8 Ibid, pp.81-82.

9 B.R. Nanda, op.cit., pp.19-20.

10 Ibid, p.21.

11 Romain Rolland, **Mahatma Gandhi**; Publications Division, New Delhi, 1976, p.4.

12 Ibid, p.27.

13 M.K. Gandhi, **The Collected Works of Mahatma Gandhi**. (henceforth, **Collected Works**), Vol.XXXIX; Publication Division, New Delhi, 1972, p.60.

14 Ibid.

15 Ibid, p.61.

16 M.K. Gandhi, **Collected Works**, Vol.X; op.cit., 1963, p.63.

17 B.R. Nanda, op.cit., p.129.

18 M.K. Gandhi, **Collected Works**, Vol.XXXIX; op.cit., pp.2-3.

19 B.K. Lal, **Contemporary Indian Philosophy**; Delhi, 1978, p.93.

20 M.K. Gandhi, **Collected Works**, Vol.X; op.cit., p.65.

21 B.R. Nanda, op.cit., p.98

22 Ibid, p.123.

23 M.K. Gandhi, **Young India**, (6.8.25), Quoted by Louis Fisher, op.cit., p.44.

24 M.K. Gandhi, **Collected Works**, Vol.XXXIX; op.cit., p.4.

25 Ibid, p.5.

26 Ibid.

27 William Cenkner. **The Hindu Personality in Education**; New Delhi, 1976, p.87.

28 M.K. Gandhi, **Collected Woks**, Vol.XII; op.cit., p.375.

29 M.K. Gandhi, **Hindu Dharma**; Delhi, 1993, p.41.

30 Ibid, p.42.

31 Ibid, p.43.

32 Ibid.

33 M.K. Gandhi, **An Autobiography**; Ahmedabad, 1994, pp.73-75.

34 B.R. Nanda, **Mahatma Gandhi – A Biography**; op.cit., p.68.

35 M.K. Gandhi, **Hindu Dharma**; op.cit., p.66.

36 G.N. Dhawan, **Political philosophy of Mahatma Gandhi**; Ahmedabad, 1946, p.5, as quoted by B.C. Das in **Gandhi in Today's India**., New Delhi, 1979, p.4.

37 B.C. Das, **Gandhi in Today's India**; op.cit., p.64.

38 M.K. Gandhi, **Collected Works**, Vol.X; op.cit., p.64.

39 M.K. Gandhi, **Collected Works**, Vol.XXXIX; op.cit., p.60.

40 B.R. Nanda, op.cit., p.68.

41 Ronald Duncan, **The Writings of Gandhi**; op.cit., 1983, p.24.

42 M.K. Gandhi, **Collected Works**, Vol.XLI; op.cit., 1970, pp.90-91.

43 Ibid, p.90.

44 M.K. Gandhi, **Collected Works**, Vol.XXXII; op.cit., 1969, pp.94-376.

45 M.K. Gandhi, **Collected Works**, Vol.XLI; op.cit., p.92.

46 Ibid.

47 M.K. Gandhi, **Collected Works**, Vol.XXXII; op.cit., pp.VI and 350.

48 M.K. Gandhi, **Collected Works**, Vol.XLI; op.cit., p.92.

49 Ibid., pp.177-78.

50 M.K. Gandhi, **Collected Works**, Vol.XXXII; op.cit pp.102-103.

51 M.K. Gandhi, **Hindu Dharma**; op.cit., pp.42-44.

52 M.K. Gandhi, **Collected Works**, Vol.XXXII; op.cit., p.314.

53 M.K. Gandhi, **Collected Works**, Vol.XLI; op.cit., pp.99-100.

54 M.K. Gandhi, **Collected Works**, Vol.XXXII; op.cit., p154.

55 M.K. Gandhi, **Collected Works**, Vol.III; op.cit., p.221.

56 M.K. Gandhi, **The Story of My Experiments with Truth** (Tr.Mahadev Desai); Ahmedabad, 1927, pp.4-5.

57 M.K. Gandhi, **Collected Works**, Vol.I; op.cit., p171. Also vide **Collected Works** Vol.XLI; p.418.

58 K.R. Srinivas Iyengar, **Indian Writing in English**; New Delhi, 1985, p.249.

59 Jawaharlal Nehru, **Mahatma Gandhi : Reflections On His Personality and Teachings**; (Ed. T.K.Madhavan), Bharatiya Vidya Bhavan, Bombay, 1989, p.5.

60 S.L. Malhotra, "Gandhi and the Problem of Violence And Non-violence in the Gita"; **Studies On Gandhi**; (Ed.) V.T. Patil, New Delhi, 1983, p.19.

61 M.K. Gandhi, **Collected Works**, Vol.III; op.cit., 1979, pp.264-265.

62 M.K. Gandhi, **Collected Works**, Vol.XLI; op.cit., p.469.

63 M.K. Gandhi, **Collected Works**, Vol.XXXII; op.cit., pp.95.97.

64 Ibid.

65 Ibid.

66 Ibid.

67 M.K. Gandhi, **Collected Works**, Vol.XLI; op.cit., pp.94.99.

68 M.K. Gandhi, **Collected Works**, Vol.XXXII; op.cit., p.102.

69 Ibid.

70 M.K. Gandhi, **Collected Works**, Vol.XLI; op.cit., p.93.

71 Swami Chidbhavananda, **The Bhagavad Gita**; Sri Ramakrishna Tapovanam, Tirupparaitturai, 1982, p.94.

72 Ibid., p.98.

73 Ibid., p.99.

74 Ibid., p.102.

75 Ibid., p.106.

76 M.K. Gandhi, **Collected Works**, Vol.XXXII; op.cit., pp.100-104.

77 Ibid., pp. 108-9.

78 B.R. Nanda, op.cit., p.69.

79 B.K. Lal, op.cit., p.94.

80 V.P. Verma, op.cit., p.344.

81 M.K. Gandhi, **Collected Works**, Vol.XXXII; op.cit., p.109-110.

82 Ibid., p.129.

83 Ibid., p.109.

84 Ibid., p.308.

85 M.K. Gandhi, **Collected Works**, Vol.XLI; op.cit., p.107.

86 M.K. Gandhi, **Collected Works**, Vol.XXXII; op.cit., p.314.

87 M.K. Gandhi, **An Autobiography**; Ahmedabad, 1994, pp.419-20.

88 B.K. Lal, op.cit., pp.96-97.

89 M.K. Gandhi, **Collected Works**, Vol.XLI; op.cit., p.109.

90 Rajmohan Gandhi, **The Good Boatman**; New Delhi, 1995, pp.166-67.

91 M.K. Gandhi, **Collected Works**, Vol.XLI; op.cit., p.94.

92 M.K. Gandhi, **Collected Works**, Vol.XXXII; op.cit., p.188-189.

93 Ibid., p.310.

94 Ibid., p.162.

95 Ibid., p.196-200.

96 M.K. Gandhi, **Collected Works**, Vol.XLI; op.cit., p.110.

97 M.K. Gandhi, **Collected Works**, Vol.XXXII; op.cit., pp.154-56,160.

98 Ibid., p.260.

99 Ibid., p.261.

100 M.K. Gandhi, **Collected Works**, Vol.XLI; op.cit., p.125-26.

101 M.K. Gandhi, **Collected Works**, Vol.XXXII; op.cit., p.125-126.

102 M.K. Gandhi, **Collected Works**, Vol.XLI; op.cit., p.101.

103 M.K. Gandhi, **Collected Works**, Vol.XXXII; op.cit., p.350.

104 Ibid., p.230.

105 M.K. Gandhi, **Collected Works**, Vol.XLI; op.cit., p.130.

106 Ibid.

107 M.K. Gandhi, **Collected Works**, Vol.XXXII; op.cit., p.282.

108 Ibid., p.291.

109 Ibid., p.193.

110 Ibid., p.97.

111 Ibid.

112 Ibid., p.117.

113 M.K. Gandhi, **Collected Works**, Vol.XLI; op.cit., p.96.

114 Ibid., pp.98-99.

115 M.K. Gandhi, **Collected Works**, Vol.XXXII; op.cit., p.125.

116 Ibid., p.122.

117 M.K. Gandhi, **Collected Works**, Vol.XLI; op.cit., p.95-96.

118 Ibid.

119 M.K. Gandhi, **Collected Works**, Vol.XXXII; op.cit., p.120-121.

120 S.Radhakrishnan, **Radhakrishnan Reader, An Anthology**; Bombay, 1990, p.585.

121 M.K. Gandhi, **Collected Works**, Vol.XXXII; op.cit., p.119.

122 Ibid., p.139.

123 Ibid., pp.133-135.

124 Ibid., pp.327-328.

125 Ibid., p.148.

126 Ibid., p.157.

127 Ibid.

128 Ibid., p.219.

129 Ibid., pp.176-78.

130 Ibid., p.179.

131 Ibid., p.182.

132 Ibid., p.236.

133 Ibid., p.258.

134 M.K. Gandhi, **Collected Works**, Vol.XLI; op.cit., p.117.

135 M.K. Gandhi, **Collected Works**, Vol.XV; op.cit., p.332-313.

136 M.K. Gandhi, **Collected Works**, Vol.XVI; op.cit., p.112.

137 M.K. Gandhi, **Collected Works**, Vol.XVIII; op.cit., p.115.

138 M.K. Gandhi, **Collected Works**, Vol.XV; op.cit., p.367.

139 S. Radhakrishnan, **Radhakrishnan Reader, An Anthology**; op.cit., pp.553-585.

CHAPTER – V

TREATMENT OF THE GITA BY SARVEPALLI RADHAKRISHNAN

Sarvepalli Radhakrishnan : A brief life Sketch :

Sarvepalli Radhakrishnan, won global reputation as a great intellectual, and academician of India. He immensely contributed through his writings to the domain of Indian thought in the modern world. Indira Gandhi in her tribute to his erudite scholarship wrote :

Radhakrishnan's scholarship, was phenomenal in its range and it was not of the ivory tower variety.... He was one of the most brilliant exponents of our philosophy, striving untiringly to explain that India's message was a positive one-not flight from life but action, action unattached to its fruits. His inspiring eloquence made people aware of the human heritage and enabled us to reaffirm our faith in future..... As a statesman he had deep understanding of the practical problems of nation-building. He contributed significantly to the consolidation of our political and parliamentary tradition.[1]

Sarvepalli Radhakrishnan was born on Sept.5,1888 in a small town Tiruttani, located 50 miles to the north west of Madras, in a Telugu speaking Brahmin family. His father Sarvepalli Veeraswami and mother Seetamma belonged to the sect of Telugu Brahmins known as *Prangnadu Niyogis* of Sarvepalli village in Nellore of Andhra Pradesh. Veeraswami's father Sitaramayya and mother Kondamma had left the family home in Sarvepalli in the early nineteenth century and had settled down in Tiruttani. Veeraswami worked in the tahsildar's office with a meagre salary. He had three sons and a daughter, Radhakrishnan being the second son. Inspite of the family's humble economic status, the atmosphere of his house was deeply religious. "My approach to the problems of philosophy," Radhakrishnan recalled later, "from the angle of religion as distinct from that of science was determined by my early training. I was not able to confine philosophy to logic and epistemology."[2] A reluctant Veeraswami had conceded to the pressure of his relatives and family friends to put Radhakrishnan in a Missionary School to learn English instead of Sanskrit, as he originally desired. Hence Radhakrishnan joined Lutheran Mission High School at Tirupati to complete his Secondary School Education after finishing his primary education in Allamaram School.

At the age of fifteen when he was doing his F.A. (Fellow of Arts) course from Voorhes College at Vellore, he married Sivakamamma aged ten; his cousin, the daughter of T. Chenchuramiah, who was the station master of Tirupati railway station. Radhakrishnan joined Madras Christian College. One of his senior cousins gave Radhakrishnan a gift of his old books – Stout's *Psychology*, Welton's *Logic* and Mackenzie's *Ethics*. When Radhakrishnan finished reading them he decided to choose philosophy as the main subject of his studies. "The subject of philosophy which I happened to take up by sheer accidents," wrote Radhakrishnan, "has been of considerable help to me in giving me a goal to work for."[3] He had a phenomenal memory, insatiable intellectual curiosity and a prodigious urge for details. He was serious and had a meditative frame of mind, which was responsible for his love of loneliness. He had an unflinching faith in the "Divine Sovereignty in God, who is the Creator of the world, the Ruler of nations, the Inspirer of all that is true and beautiful."[4] As a student he was hard working. He always tried to and aimed at doing his best.[5] He was liked by all his teachers.

If Tiruttani and Tirupatti, (the two places of Hindu pilgrimage, where the tender period of Radhakrishnan's life was spent) and the spiritual fervour of his family were responsible to generate a deep understanding of Hinduism in him, it was his education in Missionary schools and colleges that familiarised him not only with *The New Testament* and Christianity but also "with the criticisms leveled by Christian missionaries on Hindu beliefs and practices."[6] He was hurt and was impelled to react rashly but was prevented from doing so, guided by the Hindu tradition. In his own words:

My pride as a Hindu roused by the enterprise and eloquence of Swami Vivekananda was deeply hurt by the treatment accorded to Hinduism in missionary institutions.

My religious sense did not allow me to speak a rash or a profane word of anything which the soul of man holds or has held sacred.... Religious tolerance marked the Hindu culture from its very beginnings. The challenge of Christian critics impelled me to make a study of Hinduism and find out what is living and what is dead in it. The spirit of the times, in which India, so to say was turning in its sleep, strengthened this reserve.[7]

In addition to this, the insignificant status of his contemporary Indian philosophy and lack of its recognition in the philosophy courses of studies of the Madras University for B.A and M.A. Degrees, impelled him to choose a topic pertaining to Indian thought, entitled *Ethics of the Vedanta*, for his thesis in partial fulfillment of the conditions for the M.A. Degree examination. The Principal of Madras Christian College, William Skinner himself was the Head of the Department of Philosophy which consisted of William Meston and Alfred G. Hogg and others. In 1908, when he was only twenty years old, Radhakrishnan's thesis *Ethics of the Vedanta* was published. Prof. A.G. Hogg acclaimed, "The thesis which he prepared in the second year of his study for this degree shows a remarkable understanding of the main aspects of the philosophical problems, a capacity for handling easily a complex argument besides more than the average mastery of good English."[8] All his teachers exercised some influence in moulding his thought and in helping him to realise his potential. But to Radhakrishnan Alfred Hogg was the most distinguished teacher, a very distinguished theologian, and of the greatest Christian thinkers India ever had, particularly in theological matters.[9] According to Radhakrishnan, Prof Hogg "was undoubtedly one of the greatest Christian teachers of his generation," who "left a permanent mark on the minds of those who came under his influence."[10]

As a student of philosophy, he read Plato, Plotinus, Kant, Hegel, Bradley, and M.Bergson. His European teachers introduced him to Western literary classics. He passed M.A. in 1909 and was blessed with a son in the same year. He entered the Madras Provincial Education Service and joined the post of *Malayalam Master* in the Madras Presidency College but taught in the Department of Mental and Moral Sciences. The impact he left on his students while teaching was highly remarkable. He passed the Licentiate in Teaching (L.T.) examination from the Teachers' College, Saidpet, in 1911, in order to qualify for a permanent post of Asistant Professor.

Having secured a permanent post, Radhakrishnan intensified his study of the classical texts of Hinduism and Indian philosophy and started writing articles and research papers with an aim to interpret these to western readers. He wanted to convey to them the nuances of Hindu thought and Indian philosophy in the idiom and terminology of Western philosophy which they understood.[11]

Most likely it was in this period of life that Radhakrishnan seriously studied the *Bhagavadgita* for academic purposes, though he might have read it earlier, purely as a religious practice common in the Hindu families. If Gandhi studied translated and commented upon the verses of the

Bhagavadgita (1926) to enable the common Indian to perceive their meaning in the true spirit, and Sri Aurobindo (in 1916-20), by the call of his inner voice (though he cited the *Gita* to arouse patriotism in the *Arya* during the *Vande Mataram* days); Radhakrishnan studied and wrote his article on the *Bhagavadgita* (1911) purely for academic purposes, with an intention to meet the challenges of the criticism of Western scholars of Hindu philosophy by interpreting and bringing out the meaning of Indian scriptures in its true spirit, perceptible to the western readers. While serving the Madras Presidency College, Radhakrishnan, "studied the classics of Hinduism, the *Upanishads*, the *Bhagavadgita* and the commentaries on the *Brahmasutra* by the chief *acaryas*, Samkara, Ramanuja, Madhva, Nimbarka and others, the dialogues of Buddha as well as the scholastic works of Hinduism, Buddhism and Jainism".[12]

As a writer he proved to be prolific. By the time he was twenty seven, he had already contributed a number of essays reflecting the range and diversity of his interests, a such as *Karma and Free Will, Nature and Convention in Greek Ethics, The Ethics of the Bhagavad Gita and Kant, Bergson's Idea of God, Morality and Religion in Education, A View from India on the War I.*[13] These Essays were published in journals of international repute like *The Monist, The Quest, Mind, Journal of Philosophy* and the *International Journal of Ethics*. Besides reestablishing the ethical character of the Hindu religion, the purpose of all these writings was to prove that:

Philosophy in India is not an abstract study remote from the life of man. It is intimately woven into the texture of human existence. The civilisation in India is an effort to embody philosophical wisdom in social life.... Spiritual values are realised on earth through the empiric means of family love, of love and friendship, of loyalty and reverence. To the truly religious all life is a sacrament, modern attempts to improve the general condition of the community, to transform society so that hope and happiness might be brought within the reach of the needy and the down trodden, are not inconsistent with the Hindu religion but are demanded by it.[14]

Needless to say his articles secured him a warm reception. His article *The Ethics of Bhagavadgita and Kant* which was published in the *International Journal of Ethics* in July 1911, was appreciated by Bal Gangadhar Tilak and it encouraged Radhakrishnan a "good deal." Radhakrishnan was well acquainted with the writings and thought of great writers and thinkers of the west like Artistotle, Epicures, Voltaire, Byron, Johnson, Muller, Deussen, Wordsworth, Lange, Hegel and Baile and many others before he embarked upon the task of translating and commenting on the *Gita*.[15] He derived a great support for his views on Hindu ethics and the doctrine of *maya* from the writings of Rabindranath Tagore.

In 1916 he was promoted to the post of a Professor and transferred to the Government Arts College, Rajahmundry where he stayed upto 1918. Those two years were the "happiest and most fulfilling years" of his life.[16] At Rajahmundry he worked on the manuscript of his book *The Philosophy of Rabindra Nath Tagore* which was published in 1918. In this book Radhakrishnan was unwittingly rehearsing his own future fights in the domain of international literature.[17] This reflects the deep influence that Tagore had exerted on the mind of Radhakrishnan.

In 1918, Radhakrishnan joined Maharaja's College of Mysore University, and was promoted to the Imperial Grade by the Madras Government. Radhakumud Mukerjee, K.T.Shah and A.R.Wadia joined the College as the Professors of their respective subjects and became close friends, not knowing at that time that they were destined to be the Members of Parliament in free India.[18] Other eminent scholars who were the colleagues of

Radhakrishnan were C.R.Reddy, N.S.Subba Rao, M.Hiriyanna, Mahamuhopadhyaya Lakshimpuram Srinivasa Acharya, and many others-all together creating an excellent environment – congenial for flourishing scholarship.[19] At Mysore Radhakrishnan wrote, articles on Bergson, Leibniz, James Ward, William James, Rudolf Eucken, Hastings Rashdall, Bertrand Russell and Lord Balfour and pointed out that "their implicit support of the pluralism or pluralistic theism is traceable to the interference of religion with the pursuit of philosophy."[20] These studies came out as his second major work in the form of a book titled *The Reign of Religion in Contemporary philosophy* in 1920. In his own words :

Noted critics praised it beyond its merit. Apart from many favourable reviews by men of established reputation in philosophy like J.H. Muirhead, J.S. Mackenzie, and J.E.C. Mc Taggart, among others, Prof. Hinman of America in his presidential address to the American Philosophical Association selected for treatment *Two Represervative Idealists, Bosanquet and Radhakrishnan*. To be coupled with Bosanquet is an honour which more eminent men would covet. The book was used by students in metaphysics not only in Indian Universities but in which British and American ones, and I became somewhat known as a writer on philosophy.[21]

Radhakrishnan resigned from the Maharaja's College Mysore in February 1921 to join the prestigious King George V Chair of Mental and Moral Science in the University of Calcutta. While at Calcutta in 1923, his monumental work Indian Philosophy Vol. I was published in the *Library of Philosophy* etided by J.H. Muirhead. The second volume of the same book was published in 1927. The book made him internationally known. In this book he made it clear by expounding in modern philosophical idiom all the schools of Indian thought with sympathy and reverence, that it had an indisput able claim to be called

Philosophy even in the Western sense of the term.[22] While Radhakrishnan was felicitated in 1936 in Madras he spoke:

My endeavour in my book was not so much to chronicle as to interpret, critics will find a lot of mistakes, so many follies, in all those volumes but my main attempt was to render the vibration of life, to reveal the movements of mind, to unfold the forces of India's mind in the profound and secret space of mens' nature. I wanted to make out that Indian thought was not to be treated as something strange, quaint and antiquated. I wanted to establish that India's answers to the questions which are enjoying the attention of the world today have also their effective contribution to make to the world's spiritual awakening...... My main idea was to bring about a fresh breath of life in Indian philosophy by reconstructing the atmosphere of philosophizing and by tracing the path on which the ideas moved in Indian philosophy.[23]

The credit of establishing the Indian philosophical congress in 1925 also goes to him. Radhakrishnan was elected as the Upton Lecturer at Manchester College, Oxford for 1926. In the same year he delivered a series of lectures on Indian Philosophy and Hinduism at the British Institute of Philosophical Studies, Aristotelian Society of Cambridge University. The University of Chicago elected him as the Haskel Lecturer in Comparative Religion. He delivered lectures at the Universities of Yale, Harvard, Princeton and Columbia and at the Union Theological Seminary of New York and the Pacific School of Religion, California. His objective was to show to the world that Hinduism is not a rigid set of doctrines or imperatives fixed once for all, but a way of life. To him Hinduism seeks unity of religions not in common creed, but in common quest.

Radhakrishnan's popularity abroad made him a charismatic personality. He was elected President of All Bengal College and University Teachers' Association. In his presidential address he criticised the Government's education policy and emphasised the needs for educational reforms. In 1929 he went to U.K. again on invitation and the stable way in which he expressed his solidarity with the freedom movement in India right in London, the home of the alien imperial rulers of India was remarkable and reflected his courage and patriotism.[24]

Radhakrishnan was knighted in 1931 and assumed the office of the Vice Chanellor of Andhra University on May 1, the same year when he was only fourty three and served as such for more than one term. In 1931 he was nominated a member of the International Committee and Intellectual Cooperation of the League of Nations. In 1936 Radhakrishnan was offered the Oxford Chair for Eastern Religions and Ethics and the Spalding Professorship which he accepted. His book *Eastern Religions and Western Thought* was published in 1939. He returned to India in July 1939 from Oxford and was unanimously elected the Vice-chancellor of Banaras Hindu University succeeding Madan Mohan Malviya on 24th of Sept, 1939. In 1941 he relinquished the George V Professorship at Calcutta and became the wholetime Vice-Chancellor of Banaras Hindu University. He was thrice elected to the post and continuously endeavoured to improve the status of the University in every sphere of its activity. In 1944 he visited China and delivered a series of lectures on Indian and Chinese philosophy and religion.

In July 1946 he became a member of the constituent Assembly In addition to giving him access to active politics, Radhakrishnan's membership of the Constituent Assembly gave him an opportunity to come into closer and almost daily contact with the leading political personalities of India, and to involve himself not only in the task of framing the constitution but also in the legislative proceses and debates.[25]

In December 1948, the Government of India appointed a University Education Commission consisting of some leading educationists under the chairmanship of

Radhakrishnan, to suggest and devise ways of making higher education in India relevant to its changing needs,[26] which under the able guidance of its Chairman submitted its report as quickly as by August 1949. Radhakrishnan in the meantime was appointed India's Ambassador to the U.S.S.R. in July 12, 1949. Immediately after submitting the report of the University Education Commission, Radhakrishnan resigned from the Constituent Assembly and went to Moscow. Within a very short time he made a positive impression on Stalin. Consequently there was a definite improvement in the diplomatic relations between the two nations. After the failure of Bijaylakshmi Pandit, the first Ambassador from India to U.S.S.R., to establish any rapport between the two nations, Radhakrishnan's achievements were well recognised by Pt. Jawaharlal Nehru, the first Prime Minister of free India. On his request, Radhakrishnan agreed to be nominated as the Vice-Prisident of India by the Congress Party, Radhakrishnan left Moscow for India. In May 1952 he was elected the Vice-President. He successfully expounded in an illuminating manner India's policies of secularism and non-allignment, through his epoch-making speeches and writings in India and abroad. He presided over and managed the proceedings of the Rajya Sabha very efficiently. His success was unprecedented and unsurpassed.

In 1956 his wife passed away, leaving behind Radhakrishnan with one son and five daughters. In May 1957 he was re-elected as the Vice-President of India. He was an aspirant to succeed Rajendra Prasad to the Presidency but due to some differences of opinion in the Congress, inspite of Pt. Nehru's sincere desire, Radhakrishnan had to concede the chair to Rajendra prasad again and reluctantly accept the Vice-Presidency for the second term. Nevertheless, he continued to manage the affairs of the Rajya Sabha and his tours abroad with equal commitent and efficiency. His broad vision and nonpartisan out-look impressed one and all who were associated with Radhakrishnan.

In 1962, after successfully completing the second term as the Vice-President, Radhakrishnan was elected as the President of India and assumed office on 13th May, 1962. On this occasion Bertrand Russell declared :

It is an honour to Philosophy that Dr. Radhakrishnan should be the President of India and I, as a philosopher, take special pleasure in this. Plato aspired for philosophers to become kings and it is a tribute to India that she should make a philosopher her President.[27]

He worked with Pt. Nehru, Lal Bahahdur Sashtri and Indira Gandhi, who were the Prime Ministers of India when he was the President. Innumerable highest honours of many countries were conferred on him. He laid down the office of the President of India to Zakir Hussain on 13th May, 1967. He spent a non-political retired life in Madras. In 1975 he became the first non-Christian to be awarded the Templeton Foundation Prize for Religion. On 7th April, 1975 he passed away.

His Philosophical Outlook:

Sarvepalli Radhakrishnan was probably the best and the greatest amongst the Indians of his times as a writer on philosophy.[28] Radhakrishnan did not receive early education abroad like Sri Aurobindo and Gandhiji. Nevertheless he studied Western philosophy for his B.A. and M.A. Degrees. As already pointed out, harsh criticism against Hindu thought and Hindu religion, during his student life in missionary schools and colleges had hurt his sentiments. His young yet matured mind had decided to take up this as a challenge. His ultimate aim, while deciding to study Hindu systems of metaphysics was to disprove the allegations of Westerners and the Christians : that Hinduism provided no firm basis for practical conduct : hence an abstract study remote from the life of man.

Some critics do not consider Radhakrishnan a philosopher in its real sense of the term, because he did not propound any 'ism' original and independent of the prevalent systems of metaphysics. According to Leonard Woolf, (Quack, Quack !, Hogarth Press London, 1935. pp.184-192) Radhakrishnan's philosophy was an extreme form of intellectual quackery, though he was a writer of considerable intellectual power. Woolf further charged that Radhakrishnan used his potentiality as a writer, "to decorate this (the kind of mysticism indigenous and endemic in the Asiatic mind during the last two thousand years) sterile oriental mysticism with the flowers and purity of Western rationalism."[29]

The other school of critics view that by nature and training, Radhakrishnan was moulded to successfully synthesise the philosophy of India and the West. Basically to interpret Indian thought in the light of Western metaphysics was a necessity for Radhakrishnan, to fulfill the goal of his life, that is to convey the message of the Indian scriptures in a way, understandable to the Western readers, in its true perspective, intelligible, fathomable so as to eradicate the fallible notion many of them groomed towards Hinduism and Hindu philosophy. In the process, he enlightened not only the West, but also the Indian intellectuals who could delve easily deep into the ocean of ancient Hindu metaphysics, 'When he speaks of Indian Philosophy', writes C.E.M. Joad, "it is as if a freshening wind blew through those musty chambers whose walls are scaled with sacred texts, whose air is thick with the dust of dogma. The shutters are opened and sun, air and light stream into the room in whose corners has mouldered the spirit of a dead past."[30]

It is not the sense of revenge or retaliation that drove Radhakrishnan to take up the task of reformulating ancient Hindu philosophy. It is his deep rooted fundamental convictions in the Indian traditions and the feeling of an academic necessity to present them in the idioms and models of Western thought in order to make them universally more apparent, that prompted him to deviate from unreflectively following the 'dictates of populist Hinduism'. "A critical study of Hindu idea was thus forced upon me, said Radhakrishnan, "..... The need for philosophy arises when faith in tradition is shaken."[31] This gave him a goal to work for and sustained him both intellectually and spiritually. Emphasising the role of providence in his life Radhakrishnan wrote ;

To all appearances this is mere accident. But when I look at the series of accidents that have shaped my life, I am persuaded that there is more in this life than meets the eye. Life is not a more chain of physical causes and effects. Chance seems to form the surface, but deep down other forces are at work. If the universe is a living one, if it is spiritually alive, nothing in it is merely accidental. The moving in finger writes and having writ moves on.[32]

Though Radhakrishnan did not propound any new theory or ism, his claim as a philosopher still stands, for he provided an academic and scientific presentation of Indian thought in a western format which remains till date unmatched. He was almost encylopaedic in his treatment of Indian philosophical heritage.

Thinking through Radhakrishnan's *An idealist View of Life*, C.E.M. Joad upholds that Radhakrishnan has successfully reformulated the ontological argument by showing that human religious aspirations are grounded in reality and that they are the result of interaction between man and his surrounding.[33] Radhakrishnan was assiduously permeated with the traditional theory of absolute spiritual idealism, drawing sustenance from the *Upanishads*, *Ramayana*, Tagore, Gandhi, Plato, Plotinus, Bergson, and Bradley. He was also deeply influenced by Samkara.[34] In the words of B.K.Lal :

He takes up the monistic character of the Vedantic reality and combines it with some of the important aspects of Absolute Idealism. Like *Vedanta* he believes that the reality is one, like absolute Idealism he shows that everything is a necessary aspect of the One. Consequently one finds it difficult to reduce his philosophy to any of the current metaphysical models. It can broadly be described as a philosophy of Monistic Idealism.[35]

To Radhakrishnan ancient scriptures like the *Dhammapada*, the *Upanishads*, the *Bhagavadgita* and the *Brahmasutra*, etc. must have "to be understood by each generation in relation to its own problems."[36] He finds two aspects of its applicability in every scripture – one temporary and the other eternal. He writes :

Every scripture has two sides, one temporary and perishable, belonging to the ideas of the people of the period and the country in which it is produced, and the other eternal and imperishable, and applicable to all ages and countries. The intellectual expression and the psychological ideas are the products of time while the permanent truths are capable of being lived and seen by a higher than intellectual vision at all times. The vitality of a classic consists in its power to produce from time to time men who confirm and correct from their own experience truths enunciated in it. The commentators speak to us form and express in a new form, a form relevant to their age and responsive to its needs, the ancient wisdom of the scripture. All great doctrine, as it is repeated in the course of centuries, is coloured by the reflections of the age in which it appears and bears the imprint of the individual who restates it.[37]

Though he admired great masters of all times and places and was influenced by many, his thought proceeded from his own experience, which is not quite the same as that which is acquired by mere study and reading. It is born of spiritual experience rather than deduced from logically ascertained premises.[38] He claimed that he had tried to communicate his insight into the meaning of life.

Quoting the ancient Hindu philosophers, Radhakrishnan upholds the view that the world has no existence in the absolute sense (of unchangeable, immovable, infinite and uncaused) of the term. *Maya* is just a term which is given to the world by the propounders of *Jaganmithya* philosophy to connote its relativity.[39]

He traces the distinction between the *Nirguna Brahma* (Impersonal Absolute) and the *Saguna Isvara* in the *Vedanta* and the *Upanishads* and adheres to the concept. But he discards the attempts to stratify them into higher and lower planes. He finds vindication of the authenticity of spiritual experience in the lives of Uddalaka, Buddha, Samkara, Socrates, Plato, Mohammad, St. Paul, Plotinus, Porphyry, Augustine, Dante, Eckhart, St. Bernard of Chairaux, St. John, Spinoza, Blake, Ruysbroeck and other seers and sages of humanity.[40] The fact that these leaders in different climatics and ages testified to the certitude and illuminating transforming potency of spiritual experience is too massive and almost appears as an evidence for an objective fact.[41]

While Sri Aurobindo describes ignorance as the root of evil, to Radhakrishnan, "Ignorance is the cause and knowledge the cure of the moral imperfection."[42] Like Sri Aurobindo, Radhakrishnan also was aware of the limitations of the physical mind or intelligence to fully perceive the nature of ultimate reality. One has to seek an explanation in terms of a non-physical principle. Intuition, to Radhakrishnan, "carries our intellect to a deeper synthesis....... It is the most complete experience we can possibly have."[43] To Radhakrishnan Absolute has to be spiritual in nature. He conceived the Absolute as "Pure consciousness and pure freedom and infinite possibility."[44] The creation is the actualisation of one of the inherent possibilities of the Absolute. Therefore, according to Radhakrishnan the world is an accident, because it is not necessary for the Creator. But the creation is not an illusion, it is an accidental reality, because it is willed by God accidentally. The cosmos is an ordered whole, with a tendency towards a greater interrelationship of its organisms and its environment. It is dynamic but not mechanistic. It is continuously changing with a purpose, perhaps to reach a state of total spiritualisation of the entire cosmic process. God is Absolute viewed from the point of view of the creation, that is an actualisation of one of the possibilities of the Absolute. Radhakrishnan also adheres to the Upanishadic view that the creation is *Lila*. But he refutes the Upanishadic view that *Lila* (divine play) is *Maya* or Illusion, by advocating the theory that *Lila* is real and *Maya* is relative.

To Radhakrishnan, man in the body is aware of its limitations and capable of surpassing this 'State' to reach the goal of perfect contentment and consummate happiness. This inability and awareness is indicative of his supernatural destiny and his consciousness of eternity.[45] "The destiny of the human soul is to realize its oneness with the Supreme."[46] However, to Radhakrishnan individual soul's realisation of goal does not serve the purpose of ultimate human destiny which is *Sarvamukti* or universal redemption, (a Mahayanic concept).

Treatment of the *Gita* :

Having generally surveyed Radhakrishnan's life and metaphysical outlook, the focus may be shifted now to his treatment of the *Bhagavadgita*. It is felt that keeping in view the principal issues like the concept of reality, cosmos, man, theory of knowledge, etc. as identified earlier it is pertinent to retain the format developed by Radhakrishnan himself in his translation of the *Bhagavadgita*.

In other words it is designed to treat the major questions within Radhakrishnan's own framework : adopted in his translation of the *Bhagavadgita* published in 1948. Retaining his subtitles the forth coming discussion will be continued under the following headings : The importance of the work, date and text of the *Gita*, the chief commentators of the *Gita*, the setting, the Ultimate Reality, Krsna – the Teacher, Status of the world and the concept of *Maya*, the Individual Self, *yoga-shastra*, *Jnana* (or saving wisdom), the Way of devotion or *Bhagavadgita*, the way of Action or *Karma-marga* and the Goal. The discussion on these aspects shall be followed by a general treatment of the *Gita* as evinced from his translation and commentaries thereof. However, in view of the proceeding chapters, where setting of the *Gita* and the crisis of Arjuna have been discussed at the outset before treating the metaphysics, it is porposed to analyse Radhakrishnan's treatment of the setting of the *Gita* after his comments on the various commentaries on the *Gita* and before analysing his treatment of the *Gita* concept of Reality.

Importance of the *Gita* :

The work of Radhakrishnan on the *Bhagavadgita* aims at a restatement of the truths of eternity in the accents of our time.[47] Gandhiji's mind was preoccupied by the concurrent intersecting forces of the freedom struggle and the socio-political problems of India while he studied and delivered discourses on the *Bhagavadgita*.[48] Gandhi attempted to draw support from *Gita* to sustain his views on non-violence, non-cooperation, *Satyagraha-* , and untouchability, etc. Sri Aurobidno took up the writing of the *Essays on the Gita* with the objective of evolving a guidance for the practitioners of his system of *Yoga*. Though, earlier when he was politically active, like other stalwarts of the freedom struggle, Sri Aurobindo also cited examples from the *Gita* to invoke the mass for participation in the freedom struggle. Radhakrishnan's first study of the *Gita* in his article *The Ethics of the Bhagavadgita and Kant* which was published in the *International Journal of Ethics* in July 1911 and was designed to establish the ethical character of Hindu religion and to prove that, "Philosophy in India is not an abstract study remote form the life of man."[49] *The Theism of the Bhagavadgita* in the first volume of Radhakrishnan's major work *Indian Philosophy* published by the Oxford University Press in 1929 forms a chapter and the work intended to bring Indian views within the focus of Western traditions of thought.[50] As a matter of fact, treatment of the *Bhagavadgita* by Radhakrishnan has been basically academic in nature. The philosopher in Radhakrishnan had experienced the devastation of two world wars. To him, human action and happiness ultimately depend on the study of the concepts of right and wrong.[51] Radhakrishnan believes that the *Gita* is a "valuable aid for the understanding of the supreme ends of life."[52] The world wars projected the destructive side of the scientific achievement, reviving the faith of man in religion and philosophy. Misinterpretations of the *Bhagavadgita* and other Indian scriptures by the western readers and the apprehensions following the wars impelled scholars, seers and leaders of India to seek the solutions in the ancient scriptures. Radhakrishnan was no exception to it. In his words :

The problem facing us today is the reconciliation of mankind. The *Gita* is specially suited for the purpose, as it attempts to reconcile varied and apparently antithetical forms of the religious consciousness and emphasizes the root conceptions of religion which are neither ancient nor modern but eternal and belong to the very flesh of humanity, past, present and future. History poses our problems, and if we restate old principles in new ways, it is not because we will to do so but because we must. Such restatement of the truths of eternity in the accents of our time is the only way in which a great scripture can be of living value to mankind. From this point of view, the general Introduction and the Notes may perhaps be found useful by the intelligent reader. There are many points in the detailed interpretations of the *Gita* where there are differences among scholars, I have not done more than call attention to them in the Notes as the book is intended for the general reader who wishes to enlarge his spiritual environment rather than the specialist.[53]

The works of Radhakrishnan though do not designate him as a scholarc, they are undoubtedly scholastic and scholarly. Unlike Sri Aurobindo and Gandhiji, Radhakrishnan translated the *Gita*, stanza by stanza. His translation of the contents are not literal. He for example had preferred to express the *akshara brahma yoga* as 'the course of cosmic Evolution' instead of "The *Yoga* of Imperishable *Brahma;*" and the *Vibhuti Yoga* as 'God is the Source of All; to know Him is to Know All' rather than the '*Yog* of Divine Manifestations,' so on and so forth. This approach of translation is vindicative of the motive behind Radhakrishnan's translation of the *Bhagavadgita* which was to make the scripture presentable in a format suitable for all the readers of the world, more so for the western readers. Radhakrishnan has adopted a selected Bibliography comprising of : I- *The Bhagavad Gita* by K.T. Telang (1882), II- *The Song Colestial* by Edwin Arnold (1885), III- *The Bhagavad Gita* by A.Mahadeva Sastri (1901), IV- *The Bhagavad Gita* by L.D.Barnett (1905), V *Bhagavad Gita* by Annie Besant and Bhagavan Das (1905), VI-*Essays on the Gita* by Sri Aurobindo (1928), VII – The *Bhagavad Gita* by W.Douglas P.Hill (1928), VIII – *The English Translation of Gitarahasya* by B.G.Tilak (1935), IX – *The Bhagavad Gita* by D.S.Sarma (1937), X- *The Bhagavad Gita* by Franklin Edgarton (1944), XI – *The Bhagavad Gita* by Swami Prabhavananda and Christopher Isherwood (1945) and-, XII – *The Gita According to Gandhi* by Mahadev Desai (1946).

As it is evident from the dates of their publications, Radhakrishnan has referred to all major translations of the scripture published prior to his own. In addition, his work is also impregnated with innumerable notes and references from the works of scholars and philosophers of the world belonging to almost all sects, religions and schools of thought. He has drawn on the *Vedas*, and *Upanishads*, the *Puranas*, works of Samkara, Ramanuja, Tukaram, Jnaneswar, Yamunacharya, Vrittikara, Anandagiri, Kalidasa, Spinoza, Proclus, John Woolman, Plontinus, Chaitanya, Rumi, Vallabha, Lao Tze, Angelius, Silesius, Tauler John, St. Thomas Aquinas, Manu, Luther, Vyasa, Sridhara, Plato, Wordsworth, St. Thomas, Amarsinha, St. Augustine, Abul Fazl, Madhusudana, Brother Lawence, Nilakantha, Mahatma Gandhi, Abhinavagupta, Tulsidas and Goethe, to substantiate his views while commenting on various verses of the *Bhagavadgita*. Evidently his purpose was to establish an all connecting universality and the vitality of the *Bhagavadgita*. The *Bhagavadgita* to quote Radhakrishnan himself, "gives utterance to the aspirations of the pilgrims of all sects who seek to tread the inner way to the city of God."[54]

The scholar in Radhakrishnan made him to approach the *Bhagavadgita* systematically as an ardent student of history, literature and philosophy. Analysing its nature, Radhakrishnan accepts the *Bhagavadgita* as 'the most popular religious poem of Sanskrit literature,' 'the most beautiful, perhaps the only true philosophical song existing in any known tongue.'[55] 'conveying lessons of philosophy, religion and ethics,' 'a *smrti* or a tradition,' not a '*srti*' or a revealed scripture'[56] 'more a religious classic than a philosophical treatise.'[57] The most influential work in Indian thought, its message of deliverance is simple, its method of deliverance through *Bhakti* or devotion to God is within the reach of all.[58] The *Bhagavadgita* 'sets forth in precision and penetrating words the essential principles of a spiritual religion which are not contingent or illfounded facts, unscientific dogmas or arbitrary fancies.'[59] The profound wisdom of the *Gita* insists on a world wider and deeper than wars and revolutions can teach. 'It is a powerful shaping factor in the renewal of spiritual life and has secured an assured place among the world's great scriptures.'[60].

Radhakrishnan was troubled to see the spiritual disharmony as a major cause of the problems pertaining to the reconciliation of mankind. He was also aware that agreement in mind and spirit was essential for keeping together the world, 'which has become materially one by the universal acceptance of the externals of civilization.'[61] That is probably why he was keen to establish the universal applicability and acceptability of the system of metaphysics propounded in the *Bhagavadgita*. He emphasises that the *Gita* does not teach the metaphysics of an individual or a school of thinkers. In his own words:

It is set forth as a tradition which has emerged from the religious life of mankind. It is articulated by a profound seer who sees truth in its many sidedness and believes in its saving power. It represents not any sect of Hinduism but Hinduism as a whole, not merely Hinduism but religion as such, in its universality, without limit of time or space, embracing within its synthesis the whole gamut of the human spirit, from the crude fetishism of the savage to the creative affirmations of the saint. The suggestions set forth in the *Gita* about the meaning and value of existence, the sense of eternal values and the way in which the ultimate mysteries are illuminated by the light of reason and moral intuition provide the basis for agreement in mind and spirit so very essential for keeping together the world which has become materially one by universal acceptance of the externals of civilization.[62]

To establish his point, Radhakrishnan makes a reference to Aldous Huxley's (a non Indian/non Hindu) comment on the *Bhagavadgita*- "The Gita is one of the clearest and most comprehensive summaries of the perennial philosophy ever to have been made. Hence its enduring value, not only for Indians, but for all mankind...... The *Bhagavadgita* is perhaps the most systematic spiritual statement of the perennial philosophy."[63] Radhakrishnan's eager tendency to refer to and draw comparision with non-Hindu scriptures and writings in addition to the Indian scriptures, in order to establish a point while interpreting the *Bhagavadgita* or the other scriptures whatsoever as we shall see with the progress of this chapter is an ample evidence of his sincerity in providing the spiritual harmony to the world as an aid for the reconciliation of mankind or to establish the efficacy of the teachings of the *Bhagavadgita* to lead the mankind towards spiritual unanimity. It is rightly observed by the contemporary critics that, "the function, the unique function which Radhakrishnan fulfills today is that of a liaison officer. He seeks to build a bridge between the traditional wisdom of the east and the new knowledge and energy of the West."[64] "This statement does contain some elements of truth," affirms Professor B.K.Lal, "and that is apparent from the fact that Radhakrishnan makes persistent efforts to bring about an East-West synthesis."[65]

Radhakrishnan gives the *Bhagavadgita* the status of both ethics and metaphiysics on the basis of the colophon of the scripture at the end of each chapter. The colophon of chapter I of the *Bhagavadgita* which reads as follows : *ity srimadbhagavadgitasupanisadsu brahmavidyayam yogasotre sri krsnarjuna samvade arjunavisada yoga nama prathamodhyayah,* means in the *Upanisad* of the *Bhagavadgita,* the science of the Absolute, the scripture of *Yoga* and the dialogue between Sri Krishna and Arjuna, this is the first chapter entitled The Depression of Arjuna. As per the colophon, the *Gtia* is *Brahmavidya* , the science of reality and also a *Yogasastra* the art of union with reality. It is also called an *Upanishad*. The *Gita* derives its main inpiration from the *Upanishads* and accepts assumptions laid down by the Upanishadic tradition. It crystallises and concentrates the thoughts and feelings which were developing among the thinking people of its time. The fatricidal struggle is made the occasion for development of a spiritual message based on the ancient wisdom, *prajna purani* of the *Upanishads*.[66] Radhakrishnan finds in the author of the *Gita* a man of deep culuture, catholic rather than critical. He is sympathetic to all forms of worship and thought which were competing within the prevailing Hindu system, brings them together and integrates them into a "comprehensive synthesis, free and large, subtle and profound. The author of the *Bhagavadgita* is not a leader of any missionary movement. He is not a representative of any sect or school of thought. Radhakrishnan describes him to be "well fitted for the task of interpreting the spirit of Hinduism which is unwilling to break up culture into compartments and treat other forms of thought and practices in a spirit of negation."[67] To Radhakrishnan, the teachings of the *Bhagavadgita* are nothing but a refined reconciliation of various currents of thought like, "the vedic culture of sacrifice, the *Upanishad* teaching of the transcendent Brahman, the *Bhagavata* theism and tender piety, the *samkhya* dualism and the *Yoga* meditation;" drawing all these living elements of Hindu life and thought into an organic unity. It "adopts the method, not of denial but of penetration and shows how these different lines of thought converge towards the same end."[68] In due course of the analysis of his treatment of the *Gita*, the approach of Radhakrishnan to bring about a reconciliation of contradictions in the *Gita* shall be highlighted.

The scope of the message of the *Bhagavadgita* is universal. And Radhakrishnan has brought into limelight the influence it had exerted on China and Japan through Buddhism. In this considered opinion the principal works of Mahayana Buddhism *viz Mahayana Sraddhotpatti* (The Awekening of Faith in the Mahayana) and *Saddharmapundarika* (The Lotus of the True Law) are deeply indebted to the teachings of the *Gita*.[69]

To quote Radhakrishnan, "The Mahayana found that it could capture the peoples' minds only if it gave up the icy coldness of some forms of early Buddhism and framed a religion which could appeal to the human heart. It imitated the successful experiments of Hinduism embodied in the theism of the *Yoga*, of the later *Upanishads* and of the *Bhagavadgita*.[70]

Though the question whether Buddhism entered China in its older form of the *Hinayana* or the Younger form of the *Mahayana*, is still unsolved, the predominance of the *Mahayana* form of Buddhism and its growing popularity in China till today is beyond any elment of doubt.[71]

Radhakrishnan also observes how 'the official exponent of the German faith,' J.W. Hauer has given the *Bhagavadgita* a central place in the German faith. In the words of J.W.Hauer himself, the *Bhagavadgita* is "a work of imperishable significance." He further declares that :

(the book) gives us not only profound insights that are valid for all times and for all religious life, but it contains as well the classical presentation of one of the most significant phases of Indo-Germanic religious history. It shows us the way as regards the essential nature and basal characteristics of Indo-Germanic religion. Here Spirit is at work that belongs to our spirit.[72]

The intention of Radhakrishnan to emphasise on these influences of the *Bhagavadgita* on systems of thought outside India is not to establish the superiority of the text over the others but to establish its universality of application and to prove the existence of its parallels elsewhere. A serious scholar of Indian philosophy who is fully acquainted with Western philosophy, Radhakrishnan is naturally and agreeably surprised to see how philosophic minds everywhere have travesed more or less the same path and how the same philosophical concepts which developed in later times in Europe were so closely anticipated in India.[73]

In the *Introductory Essay* to his translation of the *Bhagavadgita*, Radhakrishnan has systematically analysed the date of the composition of the *Bhagavadgita*. Taking his earlier stand while coping up with this problem for his eassy on 'The Theism of the *Bhagavadgita*' in *Indian Philosophy*, Vol. I. Radhakrishnan upholds the view that the date of *Bhagavadgita* can be assigned to fifth century B.C., "though the text may have received many alteractions in subsequent times."[74] In order to justify his conviction, Radhakrishnan points forward the following arguments :[75]

I. The *Mahabharata* has referred to the *Bhagavadgita* and these references indicate that the *Gita* has been treated as a genuine part of the epic from the date of its composition.[76]

II. The archaic construction and internal reference of the *Bhagavadgita*, and the stylistic resemblances between the *Gita* and the *Mahabharata* show that they belong to one whole and to the pre-christian era.[77]

III. Both in the *Gita* and the *Mahabharata* the main views about various systems and practices of philosophy and religion tally with each other. In both, *Karma* is preferred to *akarma*.[78] "The attitude to the vedic sacrifices,[79] the statements of the order of creation,[80] the account of the *Samkhya* theories of *Guna*,[81] *patanjali's yoga*[82] and the description of *Visvarupa*[83] are more or less the same. Nor can we say that the principles of reconciliation are peculiar to the *Gita*."[84]

IV. Telang assigns the *Gita* to a period earlier than the 3rd Century B.C.

V. Sir R.G. Bhandarkar thinks that *Gita* is atleast as old as 4th Century B.C.

In addition to these, Radhakrishnan refutes, the theory of Garbe, who assigns the original *Gita* to 200 B.C. and believes that the present form was given to the text by the later composers in 200 A.D. In the opinion of Radhakrishnan, the *Bhagavadgita* belongs the 5th Century B.C. However, he says that, "If the references in the *Dharma Sutras* are regarded as interpolated texts, then the *Gita* may be assigned to the third or second Century B.C., He adopts the text followed by Samkara, the oldest extant commentary of the poem."[85] Since the objective of this work is to highlight the treatment of the philosophy of the *Gita* by the stalwarts like Sri Aurobindo, Gandhi and Radhakrishnan in its historical perspective against the wider canvass of India's socio-political senario, it is necessary to preface, Radhakrishnan's treatment of the chief commentaries on the *Gita* with his analysis of *Gita's* relation with other Indian systems of thought prevalent in the age of its composition. In the opinion of Radhakrishnan, "The Gita does not throw overboard the authority of the *Vedas*."[86] The *Gita* also upholds the ordinances and injunctiosn of the *Vedas* to be quite valid for men of a particular cultural status and considers them to be inevitable for one to attain perfection. In this connection Radhakrishnan refers to the twelfth stanza of chapter XVII of the *Bhagavadgita* which accords sanction to the vedic sacrificial acts which are required to be performed without any expectation or reward.[87] However, while translating the 11th stanza which reads thus :

Aphalakanksibhir yajno
Vidhidrsto ta ijyate
Yastavyam eve'ti manah
Samadhaya sa sattvikah.XVII.11.

That sacrifice which is offered according to the scriptural law, by those who expect no reward and believe firmly that it is their duty to offer the sacrifice, is good. Radhakrishnan opts to comment that :

The *yajna* of the *Gita* is not the same as the ceremonial sacrifice of the *Veda*. It is sacrificial action in general by which man dedicates his wealth and deeds to the service of the One Life in all. People with such a sacrificial spirit will accept even death gladly, though unjustly meted out to them, so that the world may grow through their sacrifice...... they do the right but are indifferent to the consequences. A Socrates or a Gandhi is concerned only whether he is doing right or wrong acting the part of a good man or of a bad, and not whether he has a chance of living or dying.[88]

The *Bhagavadgita* also says :

Abhisamdhaya tu phalam
Dambhartham api cai¯vayat
Ijyate bharathasrestha
Tam yajnam viddhi rajasm.XVII.12

This is translated by Radhakrishnan as : "But that which is offered in expectation of reward or for the sake of display, know O'best of the *Bharatas* (Arjuna), that sacrifice to be 'Passionate'."

In this connection the following canto of the *Gita* has also specific relevance :

Vidhinam astrannam
Mantrahinam adakhsinam,
Sraddhavirahitam yajanam
Tamasam paricaksate.XVII.13.

"The sacrifice which is not in conformity with the law, in which no food is distributed, no hymns are chanted and fees are paid, which is empty of faith, they declare to be dull."

Referring to these verses of the *Gita*, Radhakrishnan comments that "the distribution of food and the payment of fees are symbolic of help to others without which all work is self regarding."[89] Interestingly this interpretation positively recommends the chanting of the vedic hymns, approves *Yajna* in the *Gita* sense, not of the Vedic sense and Radhakrishnan had taken recourse to both mystic and symbolic interpretations and directly discards the literal sense of the distribution of food and payment of fees (*daksina*). To Radhakrishnan after a particular stage, when the secret of salvation is known, and the self is discovered, the observation of vedic rites and the performance of vedic *karma* become obsolete for one's life.[90]

The theism of the *Bhagavadgita* to Radhakrishnan is nothing but an idealisation of *Varuna* worship propounded by the *Rgveda*.[91] The system of caste is neither Aryan nor Dravidian to Radhakrishnan, but was introduced to enable the different racial types to coexist in amity. It was a way to conserve the culture of the vedic Aryan race from being absorbed by the superstitions of the large numbers of native cultures. It was evolved with a noble view to prevent the social organisation from decay and death. But ultimately the rigidity of the caste system prevented the social organisation from growing. Analysing these aspects, Radhakrishnan aptly comments :

India solved peaceably the inter-racial problem which other people did by a decree of death. When European races conquered others, they took care to efface their human dignity and annihilate their self respect. Caste enabled the Vedic Indians to preserve the integrity and independence of the conquering as well as the conquered races and promote mutual confidence and harmony.[92]

Radhakrishnan believes that the author of the *Bhagavadgita* took its philosophic background from the *Upanishad*. He refers to many verses to be common to both the *Gita* and the *Upanishad*.[93]

He finds the Verses 29 and 20 of Chapter.II, Verse 2 of the Chapter.VIII, Verse 42 of the Chapter.III of the *Bhagavadgita* to be common to the Verses 7,19 and 15 of Chapter.II and Verse 10 of Chapter.III of the *Kathaupanisad* respectively. Similarly, to him the Verses 11 and 13 of the Chapter.VI of the *Bhagavadgita* and Verses 10 and 8 of the second Chapter of the *Svetasatvara Upanisad* are similar to each other respectively.

He also refers to the oft quoted verse of the *Gita dhyanam* :

Sarvaponisadogabho
Dogdha gopalanandana,
Partha vachcha sudhirbhokta
Dugdham gitamritam mahat[94]

While the *Bhagavadgita* rests on the *Upanishadic* philosophy, some *Upanisads* (e.g *Kathaupanisad*) contain in them the elements of the *Samkhya* and *Yoga* systems quoted from the *Bhagavadgita.*[95] He finds a parallel of the discussion on *Ksetra and Ksetrjna* in Chapter.XIII of the *Bhagavadgita, Ksara and Aksara* in Chapter.VIII of the *Bhagavadgita* in the *Upanishads. Bhakti* is a direct development of the *Upasana* of the *Upanishads.* According to him, the *Upanishad* also advocates the *niskama karma* (work without attachment) so vehemently propounded by the *Bhagavadgita.* The *Chandogya Upanishad* and the *Brhadaranyak Upanisad* also brought the theory of non-attachment which results from an elevated state of mind. The influence of the *Bhagavata* religion inspired the author of the *Bhagavadgita* 'to give a glow and a penetrating power to the absolute of the *Upanisads*. He made it into a personal *Isvara,* called by the different names of *Siva, Vishnu,* etc. All the same the author is aware that he is only revivifying a dead past and not propounding a new theory."[96] This is evident from the following cantos of the *Gita* :

Imam vivasvate yogam
Proktavan aham avyayam
Vivasvan manav praha
Manur iksvakave'bravit.IV.1.
Evam paramparapraptam
Imam rajarsayo viduh
Sa kalene'ha mahata
Yogah proktah puratanah

Bhakto'si me sakha ce'ti

Rahasyam hy etad uttamam.IV.3.

"I proclaimed this imperishable *yoga* to Vivasvan. Vivasvan told it to Manu and Manu spoke it to Iksvaku."

"Thus handed down from one to another the royal sages knew it till that *yoga* was lost to the world through long lapse of time, O oppressor of the foe (Arjuna)."

"This same ancient *yoga* has been today declared to thee by Me; for thou art My devotee and my friend; and this is the supreme secret."

Explaining the term *rajarsayah* as royal sages, Radhakrishnan refers to Ram, Krishna and Buddha, all sons of Kings, who taught the highest wisdom and hence can be called as *rajarshis* (royal sages). He also refers to *Kalena Mahahta*, (by the great efflux of time and affirms that, "this teaching has become obscure by the lapse of ages. To renovate the faith for the welfare of humanity, great teachers arise. Krishna now gives it to his pupil to reawaken faith in him and illumine his ignorance."[97]

While translating this aspect of the continuity of spirit, Radhakrishnan does not leave the chance of establishing a chord common to the Hindu, Buddhist and Christian thoughts. The teacher in Krishna of the *Bhagavadgita* declares that he is not propounding a new doctrine. He is simply restoring the *yogahpuratanah* (ancient *yoga*), the old tradition, the eternal truth; handed down from the teacher to the disciple. Radhakrishnan emphasises :

The teaching is a renewal, a rediscovery, a restoration of knowledge long forgotten. All great teachers like Gautama, the Buddha and Mahavira, Samkara and Ramanuja are content to affirm that they are only restating the teachings of their former masters. *Milindapanha* explains that it is an ancient way that had been lost that the Buddha opens up again...... the great teachers do not lay claim to originality but affirm that they are expounding the ancient truth which is the final norm by which all teachings are judged, the eternal source of all religions and philosophies, the *philosophia perennis,* the *sanatanadharma,* what Angustine calls the 'wisdom that was not made; but is at this present, as it hath ever been and so shall ever be. *Bhaktosi me sakha ceti*: Thou art My devotee and My friend. Revelation is never closed.......So long as the human heart has qualities of devotion and friendship, God will disclose His secrets to them......... 'Everyone that is of the Truth heareth my voice' said Jesus to Pilate;[98]

Radhakrishnan appeals the religions of the world to retain the quintessential religious sense to make feasible a world community. He invites the humanity to join in unity of spirit, a "unity which embraces the richness in which religious realities which have found expression in other faiths are not destroyed but cherished as valued expression of the One truth."[99] His eagerness to guide the world towards the fulfillment of his dream motivates him to touch upon the unity of spirit prevalent in ancient thoughts of the world.

Some of the views of the *Gita* are like those of Budhism even though there is no mention of Buddhism in the *Gita.* Both denounce the absolute authority of the *Vedas,* the rigours of caste system and the foundation of ritualistic religion. However, Radhakrishnan believes that the teachings of Buddha are not true to the principles of golden middle path announced by him. He writes :

To prefer celibacy to marriage, fasting to feasting, is not to pracice the golden mean. The *Gita* denounces the religious madness of the hermits and the spiritual suicide of saints who prefer darkness to daylight and sorrow to joy. It is possible to attain salvation without resorting to the cult of narrowness and death. The word *nirvana* occurs in the *Gita*.IV.15, but this does not show any borrowing from Buddhism, since it is not peculiar to it. In the descriptions of the ideal man the *Gita* and Buddhism agree. (Chapter.II,

Verses 55-72, Chapter.IV Verses 16-23, V-18-28, XII.13-16. cf. *Dhammapada*, 360-423; *Suttanipata, Munisutta*, I, 7 and 14). As a philosophy and religion the *Gita* is more complete than Buddhism, which emphasises over much the negative side. The *Gita* adopts the ethical principles of Buddhism while by implication it condemns the negative metaphysics of Buddhism as the root of all unbelief and error. It is more in continuity with the past and therefore had a better fortune than Buddhism in India.[100]

Radhakrishnan, as we shall see while discussing his treatment of the metaphysics and ethics of the *Bhagavadgita*, constantly harps on his concern regarding the widening of the gulf between our intellectual progress and moral stagnation, as the potential threat of self-destruction of the human race. He writes :

The main cause of our malaise is our uprootedness. We are detached from our spiritual foundations, which give us poise and balance. Many of us have lost our historical roots and become exiles from our past. Things nearest to us in time are not nearest to us in spirit. The froth or the surface of history does not count so much as the deep underlying current.[101]

He feels that had Buddhism carried forward the deep underlying features and eternal values of Indian culture and Hinduism, it would not have lost its ground. The reverse is true for the *Gita*. He writes, "It (the *Gita*) is more in continuity with the past and therefore had a better fortune than Buddhism in India."[102]

While analysing the relation of the *Bhagavadgita* with *Samkhya-yoga* and the *Vedanta*, Radhakrishnan does not agree with the argument of Garbe that the philosophical observations of the *Bhagavadgita* are based entirely on the teachings of the *Samkhya-yoga*, and that the vedantic constituents of the *Bhagavadgita* are later interpolations. Canto 39 of Chapter, II, Canto 3 of Chapter, III, Canto 4 and 5 of Chapter, V, Canto 24 of Chapter, XIII and Canto 13 of Chapter, XVIII of the *Bhagavadgita* refer to *Samkhya-yoga*. Radhakrishnan comments :

Samkhya in the *Gita* does not mean the system of philosophy known by that name; nor does *Yoga* mean *Patanjalayoga*. The scholastic version of the *Samkhya* is a frank dualism of *Purusa* (self) and *Prakriti* (not self) which is transcended in the *Gita*, which affirms the reality of a Supreme Self who is the Lord of all. *Samkhya* gives an intellectual account of the intuition of the unchanging One.[103]

Referring to Madhva's commentary on the Canto 40 of Chapter, II of the *Gita*, where he quoted a verse from *Vyasa Smriti (Suddhatmatattvavijnanam samkhyam ity abhidhiyate)*, Radhakrishnan opines that the terms *Samkhya-yoga* of the *Gita* do not represent the classical schools but "only the reflective and meditative methods of gaining salvation."[104] At the time of the *Gita*, the *Samkhya* philosophy and the Vedantic systems were not yet clearly distinct from each other, which justifies Garbe's interpretation. *Samkhya* and *Yoga* in the *Gita* are not discordant systems. They aim at the same goal but are different in their methods to achieve it.

Nevertheless, the evident influence of the scholastic *Samkhya* which was in the making at the time of the *Gita* is categorically recognised by Radhakrishnan.[105] Radhakrishnan believes that though the psychology and the order of creation of the *Samkhya* are accepted by the *Gita*, the meaphysical implications of the *Samkhya* deliberately avoids the question of the existence of God, the *Gita* is most anxious to establish it."[106]

Na tvevva' ham jatu na'sam
Na tvam ne'me janadhipah
Na cai'va bhavisyamah
Sarve vayam atah param.II.12.

"Never was there a time," translates Radhakrishnan, "When I was not, nor thou, nor these lords of men, nor will there ever be a time hereafter when we all shall cease to be." Commenting on this verse, Radhakrishnan further says, "While the *Samkhya* system postulates a plurality of souls, the *Gita* reconciles this with the unity, the one *Ksetrajna* in whom we live, move and have our being."[107]

Apart from this the *Samkhya* system and the *Gita* also differ from each other in their outlook while analying the concepts of *Purusha* and *Prakriti*. *Samkhya* looks upon *Prakrti* or nature, in the words of Radhakrishnan :

Phenomena implying a permanent subject to whom they appear and for whom they exist. Though *Prakriti* or nature is unconscious, its activities are purpositive, meant as they are for the freedom of soul. The teleological character of its activities is not in accord with its alleged unconsciousness. In the *Gita* the difficulty is overcome. There is a spiritual fact behind the play of *Prakriti* or nature. *Purusa* or soul is not the independent reality which it is in the *Samkhya* system. Its nature is not mere awareness, but bliss also. The *Gita* does not recognize any ultimate distinctness of individual souls. (VII.4,& XIII. 20-22, of the *Bhagavatgita*). It also believes in the existence of an *uttamapurusa* or Supreme Soul. Yet the character of the individual soul and its relation to nature as given in the *Bhagavatgita* show the influence of the *samkhya* theory..... The physiological account of the internal organs and the senses is found here as in the *samkhya*, XVIII. 40 of the *Bhagavatgita*).[108]

Having analysed the nature, scope, date of composition and relation with other Indian systems of thought of the *Bhagavatgita*, Radhakrishnan briefly touches upon the views of the chief commentators of the scripture. The supportive authority from the *Prasthanatraya* (triple canon) consisting of the *Bhagavatgita*, the *Brahmasutra* and the *Upanisads* has been constantly drawn by the teachers of the *Vedanta*, to justify the special doctrine of their respective traditions (*sampradaya*) and to refule those of others. Unlike the *Upanisads* which contain many different suggestions about the nature of the Absolute and its relation to the world and the *Brahmasutra* which is so terse and obscure that it has been used to yield a variety of interpretations the *Bhagavatgita* gives a more consistent view and the task of the commentators, who wish to interpret the text to their own ends, becomes more difficult. Nevertheless, Radhakrishnan commets that, all writers are able "to find in the *Gita* their own systems of religious thought and metaphysics, since the author of the *Gita* suggests that the one eternal truth which we are seeking, from which all other truth derives, cannot be shut up in a single formula. Again, we receive from the study and reflection of the scripture as much living truth and spiritual influence as we are capable of receiving."[109]

Samkara's commentary on the *Bhagavatgita* is the most ancient of the available ones. Though mention has been made about the commentators like Vrittikara who belonged to a period prior to Samkara, their commentaries are not available to us, Samkara (A.D. 788-820) believes that Reality or *Brahman* is one without a second, (*Ekobrahma dwitiyonasti*) and the world of manifestation and multiplicity is not real, though it seems real to those who live in *avidya* (ignorance). Work binds us to this unreal cosmic process. The wisdom of *Aham Brahmosmi*, (the universal reality and the individual self are identical) can only bring redemption from this bondage, leading to bliss. To Radhakrishnan, "the aim of the Gita, according to Samkara, is the complete suppression of the world of becoming in which all action occurs, though his own life is an illustration of activity carried on after the attainment of wisdom."[110] Samkara's views are upheld by Anandagiri, Sridhara and Madhusudana.

Ramanuja (eleventh century A.D.) discards the doctrine of the unreality of the world and the path of renunciation of action propounded by Samkara. Radhakrishnan believes that Ramanuja adopted the interpretation of Yamunacharya, the author of *Gitarthasamgraha;* and that he developed a type of 'personal mysticism' in his commentary on the *Gita*. Radhakrishnan writes :

Ramanuja admits that the paths of knowledge, devotion, and action are all mentioned in the *Gita,* but he holds that its main emphasis is on devotion....... The Supreme is *Visnu* for Ramanuja. He is the only true god who will not share his divine honours with others. Liberation is service of and fellowship with God in *Vaikuntha* or heaven.[111]

Madhava (1199 to 1276 A.D.) propounded the *dvaita* (dualistic) philosophy from the *Gita* in his two works on the scripture-*Gitabhasya* and *Gitatatparya*. By giving up the distinction between mine and thine, and adopting the path of devotion, liberation can be achieved. However, Madhva contended that the *Gita* did advocate individual soul to be identical to the Supreme. In the opinion of Radhakrishnan, "it is self contradictory, he (Madhava) contends, to look upon soul as identical with the Supreme in one sense and different from Him in another. The two must be regarded as eternally different from each other and any unity between them, partial or entire, is untenable."[112]

Radhakrishnan analyses the interpretation of Nimbarka (1162 A.D.) from his commentaries on the *Brahmasutra* and conjecturises it with the commentaries of *Kesavakasmirin* (Nimbarka's disciple) on the *Bhagavatgita* known as *Tattvaprakasika*. In this way Radhkrishnan concludes : "Nimbarka holds that the soul (*jiva*), the world (*jagat*) and God are different from each other; yet the existence and activity of the soul and the world depend on the will of God. Devotion to the Supreme is the principal theme of Nimbarka's writing."[113]

While Nimbarka adopted the theory of *dvaitadvaita* (dual-non-dual) doctrine, Vallabha (1479 A.D.), Radhakrishnan believes, developed on the *sudhadvaitavada,* the principles of pure non-dualism.

In addition to the above mentioned commentaries on the *Gita* by ancient seers, Radhakrishnan recognises Tilak and Sri Aurobindo as the chief commentators of the Gita "in our own times" and adds, "Gandhi has his own views."[114]

The Setting:

Radhakrishnan deals with the metaphysical aspects of the *Bhagavatgita* in his introductory essay to his English version of the scripture. He has not given a special heading to his treatment of the setting of the *Bhagavatgita* which has been the most popular, yet controversial subject among its commentators, past and the present. He has analysed the war setting in his treatment of the concept of *jnanamarga* and concept of the individual self of the scripture particularly in the introduction to his English rendering of the *Bhagavatgita*. In addition he has raised the issue of the war setting of the *Bhagavatgita* at the time of commenting on its first chapter, 'The Hesitation and Despondency of Arjuna.'

Being a *brahmavidya* (metaphysics) as well as a *yogasastra* (ethics) the *Bhagavatgita* does not talk about only the transcendental aspects of life and spirit, but also the empirical order of reality has been emphatically expounded in the scripture. In the opening chapter, Radhakrishnan points out, the *Gita* raises the question of the problem of human action. The genesis of the answers in the *Gita* given to this question has been traced by Radhakrishnan to the *prajnapurani* (ancient wisdom) of the *Upanisads*. And the factricidal war is made the occasion, (it does not matter whether it was historical) for the development and presentation of a spiritual message, by organising the various elements of thought lying scattered and disorganised in the various systems of metaphysics of India through the ages.

Like Sri Aurobindo, Radhkrishnan is also least perturbed by the choice of the war setting of the *Gita* by its author. To him, by enacting the war scene as the preface to the delivery of the message of the *Gita* where Krsna, the Divine Teacher advises Arjuna to fight, the author of the *Bhagavatgita* does not support the validity of warfare. The author only indicates the spirit in which all work including warfare should be performed. Arjuna's problem in the *Gita* is not to establish whether war is right or wrong. He has the experiene of warfare as a *Kshatriya*. He declares against this particular war where he has to destroy his own relatives (*Svajanam*), who have turned out to be his enemies. According to the *Gita* Arjuna's despondency and reluctance to fight is due to his ignorance and passion. The root cause of his aversion to war is not to upkeep the principle of non-violence. It is not a *sattvik* spiritual transformation of mind. It is *tamasik* (due to the nature of dullness). The *Gita* declares:

Niyatasya tu samnyyasah
Karmano no' papadyate
Mohat tasya parityagas
Tamasah parikirititah. XVIII.7.
Dukham ity eva yat karma
Kayaklesa bhayat tyajet
Sa krtva rajasam tyagam
Naiva tyagaphalam labhet. XVIII. 8.

"Verily the renunciation of any duty ought to be done is not right. The abandonment of it through ignorance is declared to be of the nature of 'dullness'.

He who gives up duty because it is painful or from fear of physical suffering, performs only the relinquishment of the 'passionate' kind and does not gain the reward of relinquishment."

Radhakrishnan feels, the occurrence of the *Mahabharata* war was a necessity, in harmony with the cosmic purpose.[115] And Arjuna's aversion to fight is due to his own weakness, confusion and ignorance. He is conscious of his imperfections. His soul is alive and has all the possibilities of improvement. He expresses his own state of mind in the *Gita* thus :

Karpayadosopahatasvabhavah
Prcchami tvam dharmasammudhacetah
Yacchreyah syam niscitam brutitane me
Sisyaste' ham sadhi mamtvam prapamam II.7

"My very being is stricken with the weakness of (sentimental) pity. With my mind bewildered about my duty, I ask thee. Tell me, for certain, which is better. I am Thy pupil; teach me, who am seeking refuge in Thee."

Arjuna in the *Gita* is seen by Radhakrishnan to have overcome by false passion, ignorance and confusion. This is an impediment that goes against the process of his evolution, for the attainment of the goal *lokasamgraha* (world solidarity) or *sarvamukti* (total emancipation). He declines to participate in a fight for truth and justice. This is against cosmic purpose. To Radhakrishnan, what Krshna, the teacher explains, advises and implores Arjuna to do, is the ideal of *ahimsa* or non-violence. He writes :

Krishna advises Arjuna to fight without passion or ill will, without anger or attachment and if we develop such a frame of mind violence becomes impossible. We must fight against what is wrong but if we allow ourselves to hate, that ensures our spiritual defeat. It is not possible to kill people in a state of absolute serenity or absorption in God. War is taken as an illustration. We may be obliged to do painful work but it should be done in a way that does not develop the sense of a separate ego........The *Gita* requires us to lay stress on human brotherhood.... In the conflict betweent he self affirming law of good and the forms that impede it, force is sometimes necessary to give the law of good a chance of becoming a psychological fact and an historic process.......If we act in the spirit of the *Gita* with detachment and dedication, and have love even for our enemy, we will help to rid the world of wars.[116]

Radhakrishnan derives the following conclusions from the setting and the issues of the *Gita* raised in its first two chapters :

Only man has the quality of deciding what is right or *dharma*.

The world is a battleground for a moral struggle and evolution of man. The battles are fought daily and hourly in the hearts of men.

The duties of civic and social life can not be separated from the ambit of religion. *Dharma* is what promotes world prosperity and spiritual freedom. Instead of rejecting the duties and relationships of life as an illusion the *Gita* accepts them as opportunities for the realisation of spiritual freedom.

Life is a perpetual battle, against the spirit of evil. In the words of Radhakrishnana :

Creative process is one of perpetual tension between two incompatibles, each standing against the other. By their mutual conflict, the development is advanced and the cosmic purpose furthered. In this world are elements of imperfection, evil and irrationality, and through action, *Dharma*, we have to change the world and convert the elements, which are now opaque to reason, transparent to thought. War is a retributory judgemnet as well as an act of discipline.[117]

The *Pandavas* and the *Kauravas* represent the divine and the demoniac, the conflict between the two great movements, the upward and the downward respectively. But they are not irreconcilable as they spring from the same source. They are cousins and have a common ancestry.

The crisis of Arjuna is his realisation that a war inevitably entails abandonment of the whole scheme of life, the great ideals of race and family, of law and order, of patriotism and reverence for the teachers.

It is not so much slaughter but slaughter of his own people that causes distress and anxiety to Arjuna.

Arjuna's despondency is due to his aspiration for realisation which was catalysed by the presence of the Teacher, the consciousness of the Divine, Krsna, the charioteer. Radhakrishnan affirms, "This intolerable sadness is generally the experience of all those who aspire for the vision of Reality."[118]

Arjuna's social conventions and customary morality are the crux of his problem, a malady to be eradicated by individual perception of truth and realisation of the spirit, the lack of which is instrumental for his inability to take the right decision.[119]

The *Gita,* which has a practical programme in addition to its theoretical analysis of the questions of metaphysics believes in the improvement in the individual nature as the way to social betterment.

The spiritual tension of Arjuna as a result of his bondage with social obligations, makes him feel isolated and insecure. These feelings must be overcome and thence shall he be able to function successfully as a co-sharer in the work of creation and for the establishment of the kingdom of God on earth.

Ultimate Reality :

Unlike an average academician Radhakrishnan is not pre-occupied with logic, arguments and dialectics in his analysis of metaphysical questions, though he is no less brilliant at it. For him logic is not the last word. In fact this approach is in keeping with the Indian perspective in philosophical analysis. Recognising this aspect he says :

The *Gita* does not give any argument in support of its metaphysical position. The reality of the Supreme is not a question to be solved by a dialectic which the vast majority of the human race will be unable to understand. Dialectic in itself and without reference to personal experience can not give us conviction. Only spiritual experience can provide us with proofs of the existence of spirit.[120]

To Radhakrishnan the *Gita* endeavours to synthesise and reconcile varied and antithetical form of the religious consciousness and emphasises the root concepts of religion which are neither ancient nor modern but eternal. For him philosophy is the vision of truth and not a matter of logical arguments. He recognises intuition to be higher than intellect as Samkara recognised the importance of *Anubhava* (experience) or *Buddha* (intelligence) that of *prajna* (wisdom). For him intuitive realisation is identical to freedom and leads to salvation.[121] He views the *Gita* as an attempt to derive religion from the Upanishadic philosophy. He finds a spirit of unity rather than a stream of contradictions in the *Bhagavadgita*.[122] Radhakrishnan did not intend his writing on the *Gita* for the intellectuals, though incidentally they find it useful. He intended it for the general reader who wish to enlarge his spiritual environmental. Emphasing the importance of the spiritual content of the *Gita*, he recognises the limitations of a translator, he feels, "The translator's anxiety render the thought, but he can not convey fully the spirit. He cannot evoke in the reader the mood in which the thought was born and induce in him the ecstacy of the seer and the vision he beholds."[123]

Ultimate reality for Radhakrishnan is naturally not a matter of mere description but is of a supreme spiritual experience. Speaking of the same he says :

Spiritual experience centers round a sovereign unity which overcomes the duality between the known and the knowing...... Strictly speaking we cannot give any description of *Brahmam* : The austerity of silence is the only way in which we can bring out the inadequacy of one halting descriptions and imperfect standards.[124]

Radhakrishnan prefaces the *Gita's* analysis of the concept of reality with that of the *Upanishads*. He profusely quotes from various *Upanishads* to describe the link between the duality of the knowing and the knowable characters. He finds a correlation between the Upanishadic description of the Absolute Real through the principle of negation (*Na-iti, Na-iti*) with the *Bhagavadgita's* description of the Supreme as the 'unmanifest,' 'Unthinkable' and 'Unchanging,' 'neither existent' nor 'non-existent' and 'It does not move' yet 'It moves', 'It is farway' yet 'It is near.'[125] These concepts are derived from the following stanzas of the *Bhagavadgita*.

Avyaktoyam acintyo'yam
Avikaryo'yam ucyate
Tasmad evam viditvai'nam
Na' musocitum arhasi. II. 25.

"He is said to be unmanifest, unthinkable and unchanging. Therefore, knowing him as such, thou shouldst not grieve."

Jneyam yat tat pravaksyami
Yaj jnatvva martamasmute
Anadimat parambrahma
Na sat to na'sad ucyate. XIII. 12.

"I will describe that which is to be known and by knowing which life eternal is gained. It is the supreme *Brahman* who is beginningless and who is said to be neither existent nor non-existent."

Bahir antas ca bhutanam
Acaram caram eva ca
Suksmatvat tad avijneyam
Durastham ca'ntike ca tat. XIII. 15.

"He is without and within all beings. He is unmoving as also moving. He is too subtle to be known. He is far away and yet is he near.

Avibhaktam ca bhutesu
Vibhaktam iva ca sthitam

Bhutabhartr ca taj jneyam
Grasisnu prabhavisnu ca. XIII. 16.

"He is undivided (undivisible) and yet He seems to be divided among beings. He is to be known as supporting creatures, destroying them and creating them afresh".

Jyatisam api taj jyotis
Tamasah param ucyate
Jnanam jneyam jnanagamyam
Hrdi sarvasya dhisthitam. XIII, 17.

"He is the light of lights, said to be beyond darkness, knowledge, the object of knowledge and the goal of knowledge – He is seated in the hearts of all."

While analysing the above aspects of the *Brahman*. Radhakrishnan intrinsically compares the concept of reality of the *Gita* with the concept of the *Purusa* of the *Samkhya* philosophy and that of the *Brahman* of the *Upanishads*. He finds the concept of reality of the *Gita* more akin to the *Purusa* of the *Samkhya*, Radhakrishnan also refers to Dionysius' contention i.e. "undivided in things divided" and believes that many of these passages of the *Gita* are quoted from *Svetasvatara Upanishad, Isa Upanishad, Mundaka Upanishad* and *Brihadaranyaka Upanishad*. He is of the opinion that all contradictory predicates are attributed to the Supreme to indicate the inapplicability of empirical determinations.[126]

Radhakrishnan recognises the theistic aspect of the *Brahman* and states that :

The impersonality of the Absolute is not its whole significance. The *Upanishads* support Divine activity and participation in nature give us a God who exceeds the mere infinite and mere finite...... In the words of the *Taittiriya Upanishad*, the Supreme is that "from which these beings are born, that by which they live and that into which, when departing they enter." According to the *Veda*, "He is the God who is in fire, in water, who pervades the entire universe; He who is in plants, in trees, to Him we make our obeisance again and again".....The theistic emphasis becomes prominent in the *Svetasvatara Upanishad*." He who is one and without any colour (visible form), by the many fold wielding of his power, ordaining many colours (forms) with a concealed purpose and into whom in the beginning and the end, the universe dissolves, he is the God"...... The Eternal Reality not only supports existence but is also the active power in the world. God is both transcended, dwelling in light inaccessible and yet in Augustine's phase more initimate to the soul than the soul itself......... Impersonality and personality are not arbitrary constructions or fictions of the mind. They are two ways of looking at the Eternal. The Supreme in its absolute self-existence is *Brahman*, the Absolute and as the lord and creator containing and controlling all is *Isvara*, the God....... The Supreme is at once the transcendental, the cosmic and the individual reality. In its transcendental aspect, it is the pure self unaffected by any action or experience, detached, unconcerned. In its dynamic cosmic aspect, it not only supports but governs the whole cosmic action and this very self which is one in all and above all is present in the individual.[127]

Radhakrishnan finds a parallel for the Self in its transcendental, cosmic and individual aspects with the Christian Trinity of Father, Son and Holy Ghost. He refers to Jacob Boehme who states that "creation was the act of the Father, the incarnation that of the Son, while the end of the world will be brought about through the operation of the Holy Ghost.[128] Radhakrishnan finds a perceptible emphasis in the *Bhagavadgita* on the Supreme as the God who resides in the heart of every being. The *Gita* says :

Isvarah sarvabhutani
Hrddese' rjuna tisthati

Bhrramayan sarvabhutani

Yantrarudhani mayaya. XVIII. 61.

"The Lord abides in the hearts of all beings, O Arjuna causing them to turn round by his powers as if they were mounted on a machine ."

To Radhakrishnan , He is the Enjoyer and Lord of all sacrifices. He stirs our hearts to devotion and grants our prayers. He enters into the personal relations with us in worship and prayer. In the *Bhagavadgita* he finds sustenance of his concept in the following verses.

Aham hi sarvayajnanam

Bhokta ca probhur eva ca

Na tu man abhijananti

Tattrenatas cyavanti te. IX. 24.

This is translated by Radhakrishan thus : "for I am the enjoyer and Lord of all sactrifices. But these men do not know me in my true nature and so they fall."

The *Gita* also says ;

yo-yo yam yam tanum bhaktah

Sraddhaya raitum icchati

iasyya-tasya' calam srddham

tam eva vidadhamyaham. VII. 21.

"Whatever form any devotee with faith wishes to worship, I make that faith of his steady." Radhakrishan upholds the view that the *Bhagavadgita* depicts the world as the scene of an active struggle between good and evil in which God is deeply interested, though *Isvara* is not responsible for evil except in an indirect way for he is not a dictator. He is completely good, he is concerned about the suffering of the world. God is omnipotent because there are no external limits to His power. The *Gita* according to Radhakrishan also emphasises the concept of the Supreme as the personal God, who creates the perceptible world by His nature or *prakriti*. In the 19th canto of chapter -XIII of the *Bhagavadgita*, Krishna says to Arjuna,

prakritim purusam caiva
viddhy anadi ubhare api
vivkarams' ca gunams' caiva
viddhi prakrtisambhavain. XIII. 19.

Which means "know thou that *Prakrti* (nature) and *Purusa* (soul) are both beginningless; and know also that the forms and modes are born of *Prakriti* (Nature)." While translating the verse thus, Radhakrishan explains that the Supreme is eternal and hence His *prakritis* are also eternal. Through the possession of two *prakritis*, nature and soul, *Isvara* creates, preserves and destroys the Universe. *Prakriti* is the cause of the body and the sense and the *Purusa* is the experiencer of the pleasures and pain. *Gita* does not distinguish between the known of the field and the Supreme Reality.[129] Radhakrishan recognises the two natures of the Supreme as *para* and *apara* (or the higher and the lower respectively) *prakritis*, which are respectively represented by the living souls and the material medium. In this connection he refers to the following verses of the *Gita* :

Bhumir apao'nalo vayuh
Kham mano buddhir eva ca
Ahamkara iti'yam me
Bhinna prakritir astadha. VII. 4.

Apare'yam itas treanyam
Prakritim viddhi me param
Jivabhutam mahabaho
Yaye'dam dharyati jagat. VII. 5.

"Earth, water, fire, air ether, mind and understanding and self-sense-this is the eightfold division of My nature. This is My lower nature. Know My other and higher nature which is the soul, by which this would is upheld, O Mighty-armed (Arjuna)."

Identifying the Supreme with the personal *Isvara,* here Radhakrishan draws support from Samkara and the *Bhagavata* and compares this aspect with the Old Testament which believes in creation out of nothing; Plato and Aristotle who assume a primitive matter to which God gives form. In any case this verse emphasises the higher *(para)* and lower (*apara*) aspects of God which is embodied in the individual as the *Ksetrajna* (knower of the field) and the *Ksetra* (the field) respectively. These are the two natures of *Isvara* who is superior to them both. The universal being of God includes the totality of the conscious in his higher nature (*apara*). "The *jiva,*" (the embodied self) according to Radhakrishan, "is only a partial manifestation of the Supreme." Reflecting the synthetic tone of the *Bhagavadgita* Radhakrishan notes :

God with his creative ideas is *Brahma*. God who pours out his love and works with patience which is matched only by his love is *Vishnu,* who is perpetually at work saving the world. When the conceptual becomes the cosmic, when heaven is established on earth, we have the fulfillment represented by *Siva*. God is at the same time wisdom, love and perfection. The three functions cannot be torn apart. *Brahma, Vishnu* and *Siva* are fundamentally one though conceived in a threefold manner. The *Gita* is interested in the process of redeeming the world. So the aspect of *Vishnu* is emphasised. Krishna represents the *Visnu* aspect of the Supreme.[130]

The supra-cosmic, eternal, spaceless, timeless *Brahman* who supports this cosmic manifestation is space and time. He is the Universal spirit, *Paramatman,* who ensouls the cosmic forms and movements. He is the *Paramesvara* who presides over individual souls and movements of nature and controls the cosmic becoming. He is also the *Purusottama,* the supreme person, whose dual nature is manifested in the evolution of the cosmos. He fills our being, illumines our understanding and sets in motion its hidden springs.[131]

Referring to the *Gita* in particular, Radhakrishan believes that the boundless universe in an endless space and time rests in Him and not He in it. The Lord in the *Gita* says :

Maya tatam idam sarvam
Jagad avyaktamurtina
Masthani sarva bhutani
Na ca' ham tesreavasthitah. IX. 4.

"By me all this universe is pervaded through my unmanifested form. All beings abide in me but I do not abide in them." Radhakrishan does not identify the God of the *Gita* with the cosmic process for he extends beyond it. The Lord says in the *Gita* :

yad yad uibhutimat sattvam
srimad urijitam eva va
tad tad eva' vagaccha tvam
mama tejomsasambhavam. X.41.
athava bahunai tena
kim jnatena tavarjuna
vistabhya'ham idam kritsnam
ekamsona thita jagat. X.42.

"Whatever being there is, endowed with glory and grace and vigour, know that to have sprung from a fragment of my splendour. But what need is there, O Arjuna for such detailed knowledge by you ? I support this entire universe pervading it with a single fraction of myself." A single fraction does not a mean broken part of the Divine. This cosmos is only a partial revelation of the Infinite, is illuminated by one ray of His effulgence. The transcended light of the Supreme dwells beyond all this cosmos, beyond time and space.

To Radhakrishan the *Gita* concept holds, that in the cosmos the Supreme is manifest more in some aspects than in others. Referring to the verses from 21 to 37 of Chapter-X of the *Bhagavadgita* he affirms that though the Supreme is in all things, He is more prominent in some than in others. To him God is more revealed in life than in matter, in consciousness than in life. He is more revealed in individuals who are preminent to others within their same order. In the words of Radhakrishan, "while all things are supported by God, things of beauty and splendour reveal Him more than others. Every deed of heroism, every life of sacrifice, every work of genius, is revelation of the Divine."[132] Having spelt out Radhakrishan's treatment of the concept of Ultimate Reality in his own words through references to the relevant stanzas of the *Gita* identified by him, an humble attempt in generalising his concept and approach may be made.

Ultimate reality is not a matter of debate. Its knowledge can only come through a spiritual experience.

The spiritual experience of Reality centres around a unity of all contradictions.

Intuition is the only instrument of such an abounding experience.

The process of naming the Supreme is always incomplete. Thus one is forced to describe it through negations or contradictory predicates.

The Ultimate Reality is both the being and becoming. It is not double but a single with dual aspects.

He is also the Lord of the Universe. He is at once the transcendental the cosmic and the individual reality.

He is not directly responsible for the evil. He is also the personal God. With his two *prakritis-para* and *apara*, He creates the world, sustains it and He also is the destroyer.

The three functions of *Brahma, Vishnu* and *Siva* are fundamentally one.

Though He has an active nature through which he exercise his control over the ever changing world He has also an unchanging aspect and He remains the impersonal Absolute.

Radhakrishan as a whole confirms the spiritual understanding of the Ultimate Reality as the great seers of India had held through the ages, not withstanding their apparent differences on metaphysical stand. The only exception to this line of thinking was probably that of Gandhiji.

Krsna, the Teacher :

Radhakrishan, like other interpreters of the *Bhagavadgita,* also does not find any relevance to prove the historicity of Krsna, the teacher, the charioteer and friend of Arjuna of the *Mahabharata*. To him that which matters "is the eternal incarnation of the Divine, the everlasting bringing forth of the perfect and divine life in the universe and the soul of man."[133] None-the-less, he cites the following to establish the historicity of Krsna.

Chandogya Upanishad refers to Krsna the son of Devaki, a disciple of Ghora Angirasa, who is described as the priest of the Sun in the *Kausitaki Brahmana*. There is a great similarity between the teachings of Ghora Angirasa in the *Upanishad* with that of Krsna in the *Gita*. *Harivansa* also speaks of Krsna who was opposed to the sacerdotalism of the Vedic religion. Krsna, who is also known as Vasudeva belonged to the ancient *Vrsni* or *Satvata* branch of the family of *Yadu*, whose home was in the neighbourhood of Mathura. The Buddhist work *Niddesa* of 4th Century B.C. included in the Pali Canon refers to worshippers of Vasudeva and Baladeva (Krishna's elder brother as described in the *Mahabharata*). There is a mention of Vasudeva in the works of Megasthenes (320 B.C) in the Besnagar Inscription of Heliodorus (a Greek *Bhagavata* of Taxila) and in the Nanaghat Inscription. Patanjali in his *Mahabhasaya* commenting on *Panini* also calls Vasudeva Bhagavat. So to

Radhakrishan Krsna was not a imaginary but a historical figure. He does not find any difficulty in identifying a historical Krsna with the Supreme God. He says :

As an individual Krsna is one of millions of forms through which the Universal Spirit manifests Itself...... The *avatara* is the demonstration of man's spiritual resources and latent divinity. It is not so much the contradiction of Divine majesty into the limits of the human frame as the exaltation of human nature to the level of Godhead by its union with the Divine."[134]

To Radhakrishan, Krsna is an incarnation (*avatara*) or descent of the Divine, the human embodiment of *Vishnu.* Krsna is the Divine limiting Himself to human form but possessing the fullness of knowledge. He takes birth to break the deadlock of the chaotic conditions prevalent in His creation, and to bring in order, not only in the form of human body but also in the various other forms like a fish a tortoise or a boar. In any case, at the time of calamity, chaos and enslavement, when all seems lost, light from heaven breaks, enriching life more than words can describe. The episode of the birth of Krsna described in the *Bhagavata* is representative of this aspect. The *Bhagavata* describes, "at midnight, in the thickest darkness the Dweller in every heart revealed Himself in the Divine Devaki for the Lord is self hidden in the hearts of all beings." (X. 20; XVIII. 61) Radhakrishnan also finds a parallel of this episode with the birth of Christ.[135] To him "the glorious radiance arises from the blackest of the black nights. The meaning of the birth of Krsna is the fact redemption in the dark night. In the hour of calamity and enslavement the Saviour of the world is born."[136]

In the *Gita,* Krsna is the teacher who guides his pupil Arjuna, who is the struggling soul fighting with the forces of darkness, falsehood, limitations and morality which bar one's way to the higher world. Krsna is also the charioteer. Radhakrishnan emphasises this aspect and writes :

The rider in the chariot of the body is Arjuna but the charioteer is Krsna and He has to guide the journey. Every individual is a pupil, an aspirant for perfection, a seeker of God and if he seeks earnestly with faith, God the goal becomes God the guide. It is of little moment, so far as the validity of the teaching is concerned, whether the author is a figure of history or the very god descended into man, for the realities of spirit are the same now as they were thousands of years ago and differences of race and nationality do not affect them. The essential thing is truth or significance, and the historical fact is nothing more than the image of it.[137]

In other words Radhakrishnan finds no relevance in establishing the historicity of Krsna, so far as the revelation of truth is concerned. However, he has cited references of historical sources which mention Krsna, Vasudeva as the son of Devaki and a descendent of *Yadu* family. According to Radhakrishnan, Krsna was an incarnation (*avatara*). This theory brings to mankind a new spiritual message. It is an eloquent expression of the law of the spiritual world. Unlike Gandhi, to Radhakrishnan *avatara* is a descent of God into man, but not an ascent of man into God. Though God assumes a limited form for the work of redemption, which though a constant activity, becomes accentuated on some occasions; He is in possession of the fullness of knowledge. Hence the descend is not a fall of the God head to manhood. Krsna, the charioteer of Arjuna, his friend, philosopher and guide, exhorts him to enter into the warfare of the world. In the ordinary sense, to Radhakrishnan, God is never born. When He manifests, it only means that it takes place with reference to a finite being.

For Radhakrishnan Krsna signified the descent of the Divine, the Divine intervention to remove the deadlock in the creation, the charioteer who shows the way, the freedom of the Absolute Reality to take the form – human or otherwise; revelation of the Spirit in us, the Divine hidden in the gloom, the transcendent and immanent aspect of the Divine and the latent divinity and its spiritual resources.

The Status of the World and the Concept of *Maya* :

Radhakrishnan gives a spiritual account of the creation by conceiving God or *Isvara* as the Intermediary between the Absolute Being and the cosmic process. God is identified with the Divine Intelligence – the creative power of the Absolute. Absolute is without attributes and hence to Radhakrishnan, the world which is an appearance cannot be logically related to Him. The creation exists by It though It causes nothing. The world is dependent on *Brahman*, but *Brahman* does not depend on the world. The logical inconceivability of the relation between the ultimate Reality and its creation is explained by the word *maya*. God, the Creator, the Sustainer, and the Destroyer has the immutability of *Brahman* as well as the mutation of becoming. To substantiate this Radhakrishnan refers to the 19th verse of chapter-IX of the *Bhagavadgita* which says :

Tapamy aham aham varsam
Nigrhnamy utsrjami ca
Amrtam cai va mrtyus' ca
Sad asac ca'ham arjuna.

"I give heat; I withhold and send forth the rain. I am immortality and also death, I am being as well as non-being, O Arjuna."

Radhakrishnan comments further and writes : "*Sat* is the absolute reality and *asat* is the cosmic existence and the Supreme is both. He is being when manifested and non-being when the world is unmanifested."[138] *Maya* is the power by which God produces the mutable nature. It is also called *sakti*, the energy of *Isvara* or *atmabibhuti*, the power of self becoming. *Isvara* and *Maya* are mutually dependent and beginningless. *Isvara* creates the universe by means of two elements of His being – *Prakriti* and *Purusa* which are the higher *maya* and lower *maya* of God. *Purusa* seems to be the seed which the Lord casts into the womb of *prakriti* for creation. The manifested world hides the real from the vision of the mortals and hence becomes delusive. The world is not an illusion but a source of delusion for the mortals for whom the *maya* becomes *avidya maya*. To Radhakrishnan, though the *Gita* mentions that to the ignorant God seems to be enveloped in the immense cloak of *maya*, the author of the *Gita* was not aware of the concepts of *vidya maya* and the *avidyamaya*. But for God who knows all and controls, - *maya* becomes *vidyamaya*. Radhakrishnan finds these principles of the creation in the following verses of the *Gita*.

Ajo'pisann avyayatma
Bhutauam isvaro' pisan
Prakritim savam adhisthaya
Sambhavamy atmamayaya". IV. 6.

"Though (I am) urborn, and Myself (is) imperishable, though (I am) the lord of all creatures, yet establishing Myself in My own nature, I come into (empiric) being through My power (*Maya*)."

Daivi hy esa gunamayi
Mama maya duratyaya
Mam eva ye prapadyante
Mayam etam tarantite. VII. 14.

"This divine *maya* of Mine, consisting of the modes is hard to overcome. But those who take refuge in Me alone cross beyond it ."

Na' ham prakasah sarvasya
Yoga maya samavrtah
Mudho' yam no' bhijanati
Loko mam ajam avyayam VII. 25.

"Veiled by My creative power (*yogamaya*) I am not revealed to all. This bewildered world knows Me not, the unborn, the unchaning ."

To Radhakrishnan, embodiments of human beings are born again driven by the *prakriti* through ignorance. This process is not voluntary. But the Lord controls the *prakriti* and assumes form through His own will as an *avatara*, through His own power or free will which is termed as *Yogamaya* in the *Bhagavadgita*. The Supreme is not only in the cosmos, but also He transcends beyond it. In the world of experience *Gita* to Radhakrishnan, finds a struggle of opposites, though the Real is above all opposites.

Radhakrishnan believes that the world is described in the *Gita* as a real emanation from Supreme *Purusottama*, though from the ultimate point of view it is not real because of its ever ranging strife with itself. To him *Gita* does not believe in the theory that "the world is untrue, without any fixed basis, devoid of any other ruler, brought about by union caused by lust ."[139] Pointing at the similarity of the concept of cosmos in the *Bhagavadgita, Katha Upanishad* and the *Rg Veda* Radhakrishnan cites the first verse of Chapter-XV of the *Gita* which says :

Urdhvamula adhahsakham
Asvatham prahur avyayam
Chandamsi yasya parnani
Yastam yeda sa vedavit. XV.1.

"The speak of the imperishable *asvatham* (peepal tree) ashaving its roots above and branches below. Its leaves are the *Vedas* and he who knows this is the knower of the *Vedas*."

The cosmic process is compared here to a tree. As this cosmic tree originates in God, it is said to have its roots "above", as it extends into the world, its branches are said to go "downwards." "The world is a living organism united with the Supreme."[140]

In short Radhakrishnan understands the cosmic process of creation as an effect of God who is the cause. Since the cause is more real, the world seems to be less real. This relative unreality of the world is accentuated by the self contradictory nature of the process of becoming. *Isvara* is the Creator, but it is not necessary for Him to create. The cosmic process is an accident of the Absolute or His free will. The creative power of God is *Maya*. The world is an ordered whole. Matter, life and mind are the expressions of the reality. The world is dynamic, "never satisfied with the levels it has reached, it always aspires to other levels."[141] Radhakrishnan conclusively writes :

It is in the nature of the Absolute to grow into the world........ The question as to why the Absolute limited itself...... is irrelevant. For there is no such thing as the Infinite which first was an Infinite and then transformed itself in the finite...... We do not have the Infinite and the finite, God and the world, but only the Infinite as and in the finite, God as and in the world.[142]

The Individual Self :

Radhakrishnan in his analysis of the metaphysical concepts of the *Bhagavadgita*, clearly applies his own metaphysical understanding which he has imbided from a wide reading of the philosophy of the West as well as the East. He identifies a concept as evinced by the *Gita*, refers to the prevalent commentaries like those of Samkara, Ramanuja and othes. He meticulously establishes the root of such concepts in the *Upanishads* and their echo in the philosophy of the West. An idealist, Radhakrishnan believes in the spiritual nature of the reality and in the process of the spiritual evolution of the cosmic process.

For Radhakrishnan the cosmic process has assumed five stages of matter, life, mind, intelligence and bliss. It is the man who carries forward the principles of matter, life and mind. Man has mastered the world of matter to a great extent by using his mind and intelligence. Radhakrishnan holds that the progressive self enlargement of man is a continuous process and man shall go beyond intelligence into a still higher Divine life manifesting the principle of bliss. The Divine dwells in man and moves on through birth to birth, untouched by death in greater harmony and is ascending to its spiritual destiny.

Referring to Arjuna, Radhakrishnan finds that Arjuna's problem is having found himself a specific place in the social world, having given a meaning to his life and gaining a sense of security and belongingness. He is sticking to the social bondage and in the process is not able to express himself completely. In otherwords, bound by the social morality he is at conflict with the inner freedom of his spirit. Radhakrishnan writes that ,"Arjuna does not conceive of himself except through the social medium. Arjuna could have overcome his feeling of helplessness and anxiety by submitting completely to the social authority."[143] Radhakrishnan goes ahead to draw a parallel to the modern concept of totalitarianism where the individual is supposed to attain true freedom by sacrificing his individuality, both inner and outer in the altar of the State or Society. In fact for Radhakrishnan Arjuna disentangles himself from the social context and the moral context. He overcomes loneliness and anxiety by developing the inner spiritual nature. Arjuna for him, grows into the freedom and develops a new kind of relatedness to the world where the integrity of the self is not compromised. Describing the effect of such change Radhakrishnan says, "We then become ourselves as active, creative Individuals, living, not by the discipline of external authority but by the inward rule of free devotion to truth."[144] Expanding the concept of Individuality he further comments, "no individual is quite like his fellow; no life repeals another and yet a single pattern runs through them all."[145] Any form that the individual assumes is bound to be suppressed and transcended until it reaches its end in being. Referring to man Radhakrishnan believes that man through the development of his mental principles and intelligence understands the cosmos.

The problem of man is integration of his personality through attainment of spiritual mastery over the body and the soul. Man must discover that there is no ultimate difference between the body and the soul. In the integrated personality there is victory of the spirit over nature, of freedom over necessity. Determinism has no applicability for the Divine. For Radhakrishnan even though man has many limitations of hereditary environment, moral judgement, etc. freedom supersedes all these. The whole teaching of the *Gita* for him "requires man to choose the good and realize it by conscious effect."[146] Radhakrishnan emphasises to a great extent the principle of freedom and the need for man to consciously choose the Divine, to make his nature a medium for the spirit. He writes, "Through struggle and suffering, man can pass from his freedom to choose good or evil to the higher freedom that abides in the steadfastly choosen good. Liberation is a return to inward being, to subjectively; bondage is enslaving to the object world, to necessity, to dependence."[147]

Without compromising the absoluteness of the *Brahman* Radhakrishnan believes that it chooses to woo the consent of man but never compels. He writes : "while the movements of matter, the growth of plants and the acts of animals are controlled more completely, man has understanding which enables him to co-operate consciously with the work of the world."[148]

He recognises that the ego is a distorted expression of the Supreme Self. Referring to the *trigunas* (tripple nature) of man as expounded in the *Bhagavadgita*. Radhakrishnan advocates that, it is not sufficient to be guided by *sattva* (the noblest nature) alone subordinating *rajas* (the nature of passion) or *tamas* (the lowest of all *gunas*, or the nature of dullness). It is necessary even to go beyond all the three including *sattva*, to become *trigunatita*, to be free from the bonds of the world; "of course not by abandoning it any way." One must become one with the Supreme and submit to His will completely. That is the significance of Arjuna for Radhakrishnan. As a whole Arjuna to him is a representative of man. His problems are the problems of humanity. The answers provided in the *Gita* for Arjuna's problems are also the answers to the problems of all mankind.

Unless the individual personality of all men are integrated with the Divine the problem of births and rebirths shall continue for them. The following verses of the *Gita* are referred to by Radhakrishnan :

Puravabhyasena tenai'va
Hriyate hyavaso'pisah
Jijnasurr api yogasya
Sabdabrahma 'tivartate. VI.44.
Prayatnad yatamanas tu
Yogi samsuddha kilbisah
Aneka janmasansiddhas
Tato jati param gatim. VI.45.

"By his former practice, he is carried on irresistibly. Even the seeker after the knowledge of yoga goes beyond the vedic rule."

But the Yogi who strives with assiduity, cleansed of all sins, perfecting himself through many lives, then attains to the highest goal."

Harping on his understanding of the teachings of the *Gita* as to the goal of the world being the perfection of all and liberation of all, Radhakrishnan writes :

God's purpose will not be accomplished until all human beings are redeemed by forgiveness, repentance and healing discipline and restored into communion with the Supreme. Every soul will be won back to God who created him in His own image. God's love will finally restore into harmony with itself even the most rebellions elements. The *Gita* gives us a hopeful belief in the redemption of all.[149]

Even after individual liberation, man retains his individuality and continues to take births until the universal liberation is achieved. What next after *sarvamukti* (universal liberation) ? It is irrelevant for Radhakrishnan. He however, believes that in the infinite possibilities of the Supreme Spirit may express itself in some form – "some other plot may commence."[150]

Yoga-sastra :

Like many other seers and saints of th world Radhakrishnan also feels that a mere awareness of man that he is a part of the Divine is not enough. He needs an integral consciousness to force the passage from narrow ego to the transcendent personality. In the words of Radhakrishnan:

Perfection at the human level is a task to be accomplished by conscious endeavoured. The image of God operating in us produce a sense of insufficiency. Man has a haunting sense of the vanity, the transience and the precariousness of all human happiness. Those who live on the surface of life may not feel the distress, the laceration of spirit, and may not feel any urge to seek their true good. They are human animals (*purusapasu*), and like animals they are born, they grow, they mate and leave offspring and pass away. But those who realize their dignity as men are acutely aware of the discord and seek a principle of harmony and peace.[151]

The technique, by which man reminds himself that he is essentially a part of God and is required to attain Divine perfection, is also proided by the *Bhagavadgita* like other systems of Indian philosophic thought. The *Gita* gives a comprehensive discipline (*Yogasastra*), "large feasible and many sided." The different methods of *yoga* (binding one's psychic powers, balancing and enhancing them) propounded by the *Gita* are special applications of the inner discipline to achieve the liberation of the soul and to acquire a new understanding of unity and meaning of mankind. They are the *Jnana yoga* or the way of knowledge, *Bhakti yoga* or the way of devotion and *Karmayoga* or the way of action. However, the end is the same which ever method may he adopt. The *Gita* synthesises various methods of the *yoga* by recognising "that different men are led to the spiritual vision by different approaches, some by perplexities of the moral life, some by the doubts of the intellect, and some by the emotional demands of perfection."[152]

Jnana or Saving-wisdom :

Samsara, or the cosmos to Radhakrishnan is nothing but 'historical becoming', 'the temporal procession of changes from one state to the other', 'ebb and flow' and is prevailed by action or *Karma*. At the level of *jiva* action is caused by desire or *kamai* arising out of *avidya* or ignorance. Whether good or bad desire remains a question of bondage. *Vidya* or wisdom is the means of liberation from this chain of bondage caused by *avidya-kama-karma* (ignorant desire and action).

Since ignorance is not intellectual error, wisdom is not correct beliefs acquired out of theoretical learning. Ignorance is spiritual blindness and one must "cleanse the soul of its defilement and enlighten the spiritual vision." The *Gita* says:

Sraddhavanl labhante jnanam
Tatparah samyatendriyah
Jnanam labdhva param santim
Acirena' dhigacchati. IV. 39.

"He who has faith, who is absorbed in it (i.e. wisdom) and who has subdued his senses gains wisdom and having gained wisdom he attains quickly the supreme peace."

Radhakrishnan in this light affirms that *sraddha* or faith is necessary for gaining wisdom for which the soul aspires. *Jnana* or wisdom is free from all doubts while intellectual knowledge which depends on sense data and logical inference, and where doubt and scripticism, have their place can not give wisdom. Only way to acquire knowledge is through faith and self control. Through faith and self control the senses are brought under control and the mind is steadied and enabled to reflect the wisdom from above. Wisdom is a direct experience which comes as soon as obstacles to its realisation are removed. It is inherent and it needs to be revealed by utter silence of mind and the will. An emptying of the ego produces illumination, wisdom, the light which enables the soul to realize the true Self. At this point Radhakrishnan quotes from Boethius and equates this state of illuminated wisdom with the completely simultaneous and perfect possession of unlimited life at a singe moment. When wisdom descends, ignorance dies and the liberated soul overcomes the world and lives in the Supreme.[153]

This *Jnana* or saving wisdom or saving truth, according to Radhakrishnan is the goal of perfection. The paths leading to this goal according to *Gita* are by a knowledge of Reality (*Jnana*) adoration and love (*bhakti*) of the Supreme or by the subjection of the will to the Divine purpose (*karma*).

The Way of Knowledge : *Jnana-marga* :

Though all the three *margas* (paths) for Supreme realisation, at the end mingle with each other, they are initially classified on the basis of theoretical, emotional and practical aspects of life. No man is exclusively reflective or emotional or practical. God Himself is *sat, cit* and *ananda* (reality, truth and bliss). Depending on the nature of the seeker, Light, or External Righteousness or External Love and Beauty of Holines. Thus the aim of man as a part of the Divine is also to achieve an integral life of Spirit. Cognition, will and feeling, though distinguishable logically, are different aspects of the one movement of the soul.

Jnana, according to Radhakrishnan is both the goal and the path. To him *Gita* recognises two kinds of knowledge : the intellectual understanding of the details of existence or *vijnana* and the intuitive apprehension of the ultimate principle, the common foundation of all existence. Both are the knowledge of God, different sides of one pursuit. *Vijnana* or scientific knowledge is dominated by *rajas*, where as spiritual knowledge is permeated by the quality of *sattva*. If scientific knowledge which is partial is mistaken for the whole truth, it ends in an inferior knowledge which is predominated by the lowest *guna* of *tamas*.

The *Gita* says :

Sarvabhutesu yenai' kam
Bhavam avyayam iksate'
Avibhaktam vibhaktesu
Taj jnanam viddhi sattvikam. XVIII. 20.
Prthaktvvena tu yaj jnanam
Nana bhavan prthagvidhan
Vetti sarvesu bhutesu
Taj jnanam Niddhi rajosam. XVIII.21.
Yat tu krtsnavad ekasmin
Harye saktam aheetukam
Atattvarthavvad alpam ca
Tad tamasam udahrtam. XVIII.22.

"The knowledge by which the one Imperishable Being is seen in all existences, undivided in the divided, know that knowledge is of goodness."

The knowledge which sees multiplicity of beings in the different creatures, by reason of their separateness, know that the knowledge is of the nature of passion."

But that which clings to one single effect as if it were the whole, without concern for the cause, without grasping the real, and narrow is declared to be of the nature of "dullness."

Referring to above, Radhakrishnan also believes that spiritual knowledge is not discontinuous from scientific knowledge. Scientific knowledge is also useful as a dispeller of the ignorance of mind by showing it the incompleteness of its own world and as a motivator of the mind for something beyond the empirical.

Radhakrishnan lays emphasis on the *Gita* concept of acquiring wisdom :

Tad viddhi pranipatena
Pariprasnena sevaya
Upadeksyanti te jnanam
Jnaninas tattvadarsinah.IV.34.

"Learn that by humble reverence, by inquiry and by service. The men of wisdom who have seen the truth will instruct thee in knowledge."

Furthering this Aspect Radhakrishnan Comments:

Until we realize the God within, we must act according to the advice of those who have had the experience of God. If we accept what is said in the *sastras* of taught by the teacher in unthinking trust, that will not do. Reason must be satisfied...... we must combine devotion to the teacher. With the most unrestricted right of free examination and enquiry. Blind obedience to an external authority is repudiated. Today there are several teachers who require of their dictates. They seem to believe that the death of intellect is the condition of the life of spirit. Many credulous and simple minded people are drawn to them not so much by their spiritual powers as by the publicity of their agents and the human weakness for novelty, curiosity and excitement. This is against Hindu tradition........ Truth achieved is different from truth imparted. Ultimately what is revealed in the scriptures (*pranipatasravana*), what is thought out by the mind (*pariprasnamanana*) and what is realized by the spirit through service and meditation (*seva-nididhyasana*) must agree. We must consort with the great minds of the past, reason about them and intuitively apprehend what is of enduring value in them. This verse makes out that in spiritual life, faith comes first, then knowledge, and then experience. Those who have experienced the truth are expected to guide us. The seers owe a duty to their less fortunate brethren and guide them to the attainment of illumination which they have reached.[154]

Radhakrishnan also draws sustence for his convictions quoted above from the writings of Plato and Plotinus. To him the *Gita* prescribes the following for the attainment of spiritual knowledge which are also akin to *Samkhya* philosophy and *Patanjala yoga*.

The individual should learn to live within and fix his mind on the highest reality with a deep passion for knowledge.

He has to, by a mighty exercise of will, suppress the 'clamour of ideas' and 'the rabble of desires.'

The aspirant has to avoid bodily excesses of indulgence or abstinence and go to a place free of external distractions, choose a comfortable seat, regulate his breath, focus his mind on one point and become harmonized (*yukta*). By unceasing care and fostering, by developing purity of intention, which subsequently kills the passions directed towards mundane objects producing tranquility of mind, which in turn gives rise to the inward silence in which the soul begins to establish contact with the eternal from which it is sundered, and experience the presence of the Indwelling God-in stillness he shall experience the insight and become what he is.

Once he attains this unity he understands his fellow beings through sympathy and love, not because it is a matter duty. Radhakrishnan cites the example of Gautama Buddha, who was enlightened by the spiritual wisdom and says, "We have the example of Gautama the Buddha, the greatest *Jnani* or seer whose love for humanity led to his ministry of mankind for forty years."[155]

Emphasising the synthetic aspect of all the three paths for realisation Radhakrishnan refers to the seventeenth verse of chapter seventh of the *Bhagavadgita* and affirms that the knower of the truth also becomes a best devotee (*Bhakta*) of God, because to know the truth is to lift up our hearts to the Supreme and adore Him. The said verse of the *Gita* says :

Tesam jnani nityayukta
Ekabhaktir visisyate
Priyo hi jnanino' tyartham
Aham sa ca mama priyah. VII.17.

"Of these the wise one, who is ever in constant union with the Divine, whose devotion is signle minded, is the best. For I am supremely dear to him and he is dear to me."

At the level when man is a seeker of wisdom the paths are differentiated because he still remains in the world of duality. But once he attains wisdom he also becomes a devotee or *bhakta* and is identified with the *purusottama*, losing the sense of all dualities of *margas* or paths he has adopted. Before analysing the way of Devotion for self-realisation as put forth by the *Gita* Radhakrishnan cautions the seekers of the incidental development of supernatural powers which are distractive and futile so far as the realisation of the divine is concerned. So according to him, a seeker has to concentrate on Krsna, who is the lord of *Yoga* (*yogeswara*), to help for attaining truth and gaining contact with Reality.

The Way of Devotion : *Bhakti marga* :

As pointed out earlier, an academic approach is found in Radhakrishnan's analysis of every aspect of the *Bhagavadgita*. While dealing with the way of knowledge or *Bhagavadgita* propounded by the *Gita* Radhakrishnan traces the linguistic origin of the word *Bhakti*, cites various definitions of *bhakti marga*, brings out the salient features of the *bhakti yoga* as laid down by the *Gita* and compares them with other works of philosophy of the East and the West and finally draws his own conclusions.

Radhakrishnan finds the root of the word *bhakti* in *'bhaj'* which means to serve. The meaning of *bhakti* is service to Lord, loving attachment to God. Ancient Indian *rshis* (seers) like Sandilya defined *bhakti* as supreme longing for God for its own sake, Narada defined it as intense love for God. It is *Isvarapranidhana* of *Yogasutra*. To Bhoja it is, "the love in which, without seeking results, such as sense enjoyments, etc. all works are dedicated to the teacher of teachers."

The way of devotion according to Radhakrishnan has been in vogue since the hoary past. In his opinion, "The praises and prayers of the *Rg Veda*, the *Upasanas* of the *Upanishads* and the ardent piety of the *Bhagavata* religion influenced the author of the *Gita*."[156] *Avyoktopasana* or worship of the unmanifested is difficult for ordinary human beings, hence the *Gita* recommends worship of the personal God as an easier way open to all. To Radhakrishnan the sacrifice of love is easier than the tuning of the will to the Divine purpose or ascetic discipline or the strenuous effort of thinking. In the following verses of the *Gita*, Krsna explains how a *bhakta* (a devotee) is capable of attaining the highest spiritual goal by adopting *bhaktimarga* or the way of devotion.

Mam hi partha vyapasritya

Ye' pi syuh papayonayah

Striyovaisyas tatha sudrs

Te' pi yanti param gatim. IX.32.

"For those who take refuge in Me, O *Partha* (Arjuna) though they are lowly born, women, *vaisyas*, as well as *sudras*, they also attain to the highest goal ."

Na'ham vedair na tapasa
Na danena na ce 'jyaya
Sakya evamvidho drastum
Drstavan asi mam yatha. XI.53.
Bhaktya tv ananyaya sakya
Aham evamvidho' rjuna
Jnatum drastum ca tattvena
Pravestum ca param tapa. XI.54.
Matkarmakrn matparamo
Madbhak tah samgavarjitah
Nirvairah sarvabhutesu
Yah sa mam eti pandava. XI.55.

"In the form in which thou hast seen Me now, I can not be seen either by the Vedas or by austerities or by gifts or by sacrifices."

But by answering devotion to Me, O Arjuna, I can be thus known, truly seen and entered into, O oppressor of the foe (Arjuna).

He who does work for Me, he who looks upon Me as his goal, he who worships Me, free from enmity to all creatures, he goes to Me, O Pandava (Arjuna). Radhakrishnan analyses these verses and writes:

This is the essence of *bhakti*....... This verse is the substance of the whole teaching of the *Gita (gitasastrasya sarvabhuto 'rthah)*. We must carry out our duties directing the spirit to God and with detachment from all interest in the things of the world, and free from enmity towards any living being. Whatever be our vocation and character, whether we are creative thinkers or contemplative poets or humble men and women with no special gifts, if we posses the one great gift of the love of God, we become God's tools, the channels of His love and purpose. When this vast world of living spirits becomes attained to God and exists only to do His will, the purpose of man is achieved.[157]

The chapter XII of the *Bhagavadgita* which the author calls *bhakti yoga,* Radhakrishnan in his translation calls it, "Worship of the Personal Lord is better than meditation of the Absolute." In this chapter to Arjuna's querry as to know who have the greater spiritual experience, out of these who worship God with earnest devotion and those who meditate on the imperishable and the unmanifest the Lord answers :

Mayyavesya mano ye mam
Nityayukta upasate
Sraddhaya parayo' petas
Te me yuktatama matah. XII.2.

"Those who fixing their minds on Me worship Me, ever earnest and possessed of supreme faith them do I consider most perfect in *Yoga.*"

Kleso' dhikataras tesam
Avyaktasaktacetasam
Avyaktahi gatir dukham
Dehavadbhir avapyate. XII.5.

"The difficulty of those whose thoughts are set on the unmanifested is greater, for the goal of the unmanifested is hard to reach by the embodied beings."

Translating the verses as above Radhakrishnan further draws the reader's attention to other scriptures and systems of philosophy who have also similar views. In the words of Radhakrishnan :

Search for the Transcendent Godhead is more difficult than worship of the Living Supreme God, the soul of all things and persons. In the *Avadhutagita,* Dattatreya asks : "How can I bow to Him who is formless, undifferentiated, blissful and indestructible, who has through Himself and by Himself and in Himself filled up everything ?" The Immutable does not offer an easy hold to the mind and the path is more arduous. We reach the same goal more easily and naturally by the path of devotion to the personal God by turning godward all our energies, knowledge, will and feeling." Radhakrishnan further quotes from Dattatreya who says, "With minds rapt in meditation, if the mystics see the unqualified actionless light, let them see. As for myself, my only yearning is that there many appear before my gladdened eyes that bluish some one who keeps romping on the shores of the Yamuna." Radhakrishnan also finds similar thoughts in the writings of St. John of Damascus who wrote : "By the visible aspect our thoughts must be drawn up in a spiritual flight and rise to the invisible majesty of God."[158]

To Radhakrishnan the Supreme is not a God sleeping in serene abstraction while the creatures cry out for help but a saving God of love. He bestows salvation on those who take refuge in him with unwavering faith. In the *Gita*, the Lord says :

Ksipram bhavati dharmatma
Sasvacctantim nigacchati
Kaunteya pratijanihi
Na me bhaktah pranasyati. IX.31.

"Swiftly does he become a soul of righteousness and obtain lasting peace. O Son of Kunti (Arjuna), know thou for certain that My devotee perishes never."

Commenting on this Radhakrishnan says, "Once we place ourselves in the hands of the Divine, we cannot fall into utter darkness."[159] Referring to the *navadhabhakti* (nine stages of devotion) of the *Bhagavata*, Radhakrishnan points out that by contemplation of God's power, wisdom and goodness, by constant remembrance of Him with a devout heart, by covering about Gods qualities with others, by singing His praises with fellowmen and by doing all acts as His service, the human soul is drawn nearer to the Divine. Though, the path of devotion involves a duality between the worshipper and the worshipped it does not mislead the seeker who has the proper understanding. This duality for the sake of worship is more beautiful and hundred times greater than liberation. To Radhakrishnan adoration is the essence of religion and the distinction between creature and the creator is the ontological basis of the religion of *bhakti*. "The Eternal one is viewed" writes Radhakrishnan, "In the *Bhagavadgita* not much as the God of philosophical speculation as the God of grace such as the heart and the soul need and seek, who inspires personal trust and love, reverence and loyal self surrender."[160]

To Radhakrishnan the *Gita* concept of *bhakti* is not *amour intellectualis* which is more reflective and contemplative. It is sustained by knowledge but not knowledge. It does not involve any *yoga* technique or longing for speculative knowledge of the Supreme. God loves the humility, meekness and the utter prostration of the self of the devotee.

The *bhakti marga* or the way of devotion emphasises on the feminine qualities like humility, obedience, readiness to serve, compassion, sense of surrender and renouncement of self and passivity, etc. Feminity is in all beings. In relation to God, *bhaktas* (followers of the way of devotion) are more like women. To them the Supreme Lord is the only man and all others have the aspirations of a woman to be loved by Him. *Bhakti* is active love for Divine who enters into the world for redeeming it when a *bhakta* surrenders himself to the Divine will and is possessed by Him living Him to deal with him as He elects, with a humble and direct attitude of trust, he is said to have reached the level of *prapatti*. The impediments on the way of such total surrender, to Radhakrishnan, are the devotee's own virtues, pride, knowledge, subtle demands, unconscious assumptions and prejudices. One must empty himself of all desires and wait in trust on the Supreme Being. The difference between *bhakti* and *prapatti* is symbolised by the 'ape way' and the 'catway'. A little effort of the young ape is called for who clings to its mother fast and is saved. But for the kitten, the mother cat takes it in her mouth while the young one does nothing to secure its safety. Radhakrishnan writes, "*In bhakti*" "the grace of God is earned to an extent; in *prapatti* it is freely bestowed. There is no reference in the latter to one's own worthiness or the service performed."[161] The difference of *prapatti* and *bhakti* relates to the issue in christian thought, which is as propounded by St. Augustine and Plegagius. Plegagius believed in free will, questioned the doctrine of original sin and asserted that men acted of their moral effort. The *Gita* according to Radhakrishnan, is inclined to the Pelagian doctrine. Total surrender to the Supreme requires man's effort. It can not be possible without man's intention to do so. The doctrine of grace is not to be understood as one of special election, as propounded by Augustine and Calvine who adopt the view of universal guilt and God's mercy on few elected ones, because the *Gita* affirms the principle that the Supreme is the same to all beings. The Lord in the *Gita* says :

Samo' ham sarvabhutesu
Na me dvesyo' sti na priyah
Ye bhajanti tu mam bhaktya
Mayi te tesu ca' py aham.IX.28.

"I am the same in (alike to) all beings. None is hateful nor dear to Me. But those who worship Me with devotion they are in Me and I also in them." On this Radhakrishnan comments : "God has no friends or foes. He is impartial. He does not damn any nor elect any by His capricious will. The only way to win His Love is by faith and devotion and each must tread the path by himself."[162]

If faith or *bhakti* is there even to lower gods, it leads to some amount of devotion and love which is better than none, though, in the lower stages, one prays for wealth, and protection regarding the Divine as the provider of material needs. Later with greater perfection of mind and meditation, the devotee is identified with the Divine and all his attachment and anxiety for material gain vanishes. When the emotional attachment to God becomes highly ecstatic the devout lower forgets himself in God.

Bhakti leads to *Jnana* or wisdom. The devotee identifies himself with the Lord, finds Him every where. Participation in God's work for the world becomes his duty. God becomes the ruling passion of his mind. All his work is done for the glory of God. Radhakrishnan concludes :

"*Bhakti* in the *Bhagavadgita* is an utter self-giving to the Transcendent. It is to believe in God, to love Him, to be devoted to Him, to enter into Him. It is its own reward. Such a devotee has in him the content of the highest knowledge as well as the energy of the perfect man."[163]

The Way of Action : *Karma-marga* :

In the introductory essay of his translation of the *Bhagavadgita* Radhakrishnan refers to the problem of Arjuna in the war setting of *Mahabharata* while analysing the way of action for the *Gita*. Radhakrishnan holds that one must give due weightage to the introduction (*upakrama*) and the conclusion (*upasamhara*) of a treatise in order to determine its purpose. In the introductory chapter, the *Gita* begins with a problem – where Arjune puts forth a plausible plea for abstention from action (his duty to fight). To Radhakrishnan, at the time of composition of the *Gita*, retreat from the world of action "was an ideal which dominated certain sects." The purpose of the *Gita* is to convert him. *Gita* discusses on the question whether action or renunciation of action is better and comes to a conclusion that action is better. Arjuna himself is totally convinced and satisfied. He decides to fight. Thus right through the author of the *Gita* stresses the need for action. Action is neither a 'snare' for him nor is he prepared to accept the solution of dismissing the world as an illusion. Radhakrishnan says :

The *Gita* is therefore, a mandate for action. It explains what man ought to do not merely as a social being but as an individual with a spiritual destiny. It deals fairly with the spirit of renunciation as well as with the ceremonial piety of the people which are worked into its code of ethics.[164]

Radhakrishnan here refutes the argument of Samkara and his interpretation of the *Gita* where he identified Arjuna with a *madhyamaḍhikari* for whom renunciation fo action was dangerous, so he was asked to take to action. For Radhakrishnan the *Gita* in the light of the *Bhagavata* adopts the view, gives the theory of liberation through *Jnana* and action. This is an ancient methods of Hindu thought. Accordingly the *Gita* asks us to live in the world and save it.

To Radhakrishnan, the extreme subtlety of the problem of action has been recognised by the *Gita* in the following verse :

Karmano by'api boddhavyam
Boddhavyam ca vikarmanah
Akarmanas' ca boddhavyam
Gahana karmano gatih.IV.17.

"One has to understand what action is, and likewise one has to understand what is wrong action and one has to understand inaction. Hard to understand is the way of work."

Total abstention from action is neither possible nor is it desirable. The binding quality of action lies not in its mere performance but in the motive and desire that prompts it. Renunciation to Radhakrishnan means absence of desire. The *Gita* advocates detachment from desire but not cessation from work. By persuading Arjuna to fight, the *Gita* does not support the validity of war. In the words of Radhakrishnan :

War happens to be the occasion which the teacher uses to indicate the spirit in which all work including warfare will have to be performed...... Arjuna does not raise the question of right or wrong of war. He declares against war and its horrors because he has to destroy his own friends and relations (*svajanam*)..... His reluctance to fight is not the outcome of spiritual development or the predominance of *sattvaguna* but is the product of ignorance and passion. The ideal which the *Gita* sets before us is *ahimsa* or no-violence..... Krsna advises Arjuna to fight without passion or ill-will, without anger or attachment and if we develop such a frame of mind violence becomes impossible. We must fight against what is wrong but if we allow ourselves to hate, that ensures our spiritual defeat. It is not possible to kill people in a state of absolute serenity or absorption in God. War is taken as an illustration. We may be obliged to do painful work but it should be done in a way that does not develop the sense of a separate ego. Krsna tells Arjuna that one can attain perfection even while doing one's duties. Action done devotedly and whole heartedly, without attachment to the results makes for perfection. Our action must be the result of our nature. While Arjuna is a householder belonging to the warrior caste, he speaks like a *samnyasin* not because he has risen to the stage of utter dispassion and love for humanity but because he is overcome by false compassion. Everyone must grow upward from the point where he stands. The emphasis of the *Gita* on *lokasamgraha*, world solidarity, requires us to change the whole pattern of our life..... The *Gita* requires us to lay stress on human brotherhood...... The *Gita* belongs to a period of upheaval through which humanity periodically passes in which intellectual, moral, social and political forms are at strife and when these are not properly adjusted, violent convulsions take place. In the conflict between the self affirming law of good and the forms that impede it, force is some times necessary to give the law of good a chance of becoming a psychological fact and an historic process. We have to act in the world as it is, while doing our best to improve it..... if we act in the spirit of the *Gita* with detachment and dedication, and have love even for our enemy, we will help to rid the world of wars.[165]

To Radhakrishnan, if the *Gita* spirit of detachment from result is cultivated, one becomes a perpetual *samnyasin*. However, he also believes that the wisdom is the sovereign remedy of ignorance or *avidya* which is the root of all evil. Wisdom is pure and perfect but it is not the fruit of any action. Wisdom which is an eternal achievement devoid of change, can not be the result of a temporary act. But action prepares for wisdom. Action performed in the spirit of sacrifice or *yajna* does not become a source of bondage.[166]

Radhakrishnan finds in the *Gita* a religion by which the rule of *karma* (action), the natural order of deed and consequence, can be transcended. By developing detachment and faith in God one becomes the master of his actions. God acts through him for the sake of world maintenance and progress. The question of right or wrong ceases for him.[167] He becomes the doer of all works as an instrument of God. Krsna advises Arjuna to become an instrument of God in the *Bhagavadgita* :

Tasmat tvam uttistha yaso labhasva

Jitva satrum bhuksva rajyam samrddham

Mayai vai' te mihatah pulvam eva

Nimitta-matram bhava savvyasacin.XI.33.

"Therefore arise thou and gain glory. Conquering thy foes, enjoy a prosperous kingdom. By Me alone are they slain already. Be thou merely the occasion, O *savyasacin* (Arjuna)."

The author of the *Gita*, according to Radhakrishnan seems to uphold the doctrine of Divine predestination and indicates the futility of the individuals will and effort. He states :

The writer here is affirming the meaning of eternity in which all moments of the whole of time, past, present and future are present to the Divine spirit. The radical novelty of each moment of evolution in time is not inconsistent with Divine Eternity.[168]

Unlike Buddhist ideal which advocates a life of contemplation, the *Gita* is the ideal for those who relish action and adventure. To Radhakrishnan one has to know the truth of one's own highest and inner most existence himself and live accordingly. He should not follow any outer standards. His action will be free, spontaneous and easy if his *svabhava* (inner being) tallies with his *svadharma* (outward life of action).

Karma marga (way of action) or *bhaktimarga* (the way of devotion) both culminate in wisdom leading to spiritual freedom. But negating the view of Samkara, Radhakrishnan believes that spiritual freedom is not inconsistent with activity. The liberated souls act for the sake of the welfare of the world. Work for them becomes a *laksana* (symptom) not a *sadhana* (austerity). While analysing the concept of *karmayoga* of the *Gita*, Radhakrishnan finds its echo in many other Indian scriptures and western treatises. He draws sustence from the the *Bhagavata*, the *Upanishads* like *Isa Upanisad, Jaiminiya Upanisad*, the *Veda* the *Vishnu Purana, Yajnavalkye smrti, Nyaya sutra*, and *Brahmasiddhi* of Madana Misra. He compares the theory of action of *Gita* with Samkara's philosophy and also Buddhism. He finds similarity of thought between the *Gita* theory of action with the thoughts of western writers of Christian philosophy like Tauler, St. John, St. Thomas and Aquinas. He also refers to Wordsworth, Aristotle, Plato and the works of Narada, Manu, Astavakra, Vyasa many other saints of India to substantiate his interpretations. Man must act, keeping in mind the nature of his innermost self, dedicating all his actions and the results there of to the Supreme, as his instrument towards achieving the ultimate goal of the

Divine, the Universal welfare and solidarity. This is the *summum bonnum* of Radhakrishnan's interpretation of the way of action of the *Bhagavadgita*.

The Goal :

Diverge may be the various paths prescribed in the *Gita* but they are complimentary to each other and their goal is one. The *Gita* also mentions the age old idea of the goal of transcedence as the ascent to the world of the *creator* (*brahmaloka*) or the attainment of the status of the Impersonal Supreme (*brahmabhava*) or isolation from the world (*kaivalya*). But according to Radhakrishnan, the main emphasis of the *Gita* is not only a state of release where duality disapperars and where the soul attains a condition beyond all qualities and modes, impassives, free and at peace, where the spirit and the body are unreconciled. For the *Gita* to Radhakrishnan :

The state of spiritual freedom consists in the transformation of our whole nature into the immortal law and power of the Divine. Equivalence with God (*sadharmya*) and not identity (*sayujya*) is emphasised. The freed soul is inspired by Divine knowledge and moved by the Divine will. He acquires the mode of being (*bhava*) of God. His purified nature is assimilated into the Divine substance. Any one who attains this transcendent condition is a *Yogin*, a *siddha purusa*, a realised soul, a *jitatma*, a *yuktacetas*, a disciplined and harmonised being for whom the Eternal is ever present. He is released from divided loyalties and actions. His body mind and spirit, the conscious, the preconscious, and the unconscious, to use Freud's words, work flawlessly together and attain a rhythm expressed in the ecstasy of joy, the illumination of knowledge and the intensity of energy........ All his activities are for the holding together of the world, *cikirsur lokasmagraham*.[169] He cites the following verses of the *Gita* to describe the activities of a liberated soul.

Saktah karmary avidvamso
Yatha kurvanti bharata
Kuryad vidvams tatha' saktas
Cikirsur lokasmgraham.III.25.

"As the unlearned act from attachment to their work, so should the learned also act. O *Bharata* (Arjuna), but without any attachment, with the desire to maintain the world order."

These liberated souls are to lead the mankind by taking up themselves the burden of the redemption of the whole world lost in ignorance and bewilderment. Though Radhakrishnan finds it very different to say as to what happens if and when the cosmic process reaches fulfillment, to him when all individuals acquire wisdom of spirit and the kingdom of God is established on earth, then this cosmic process may take into that which is beyond all manifestations. The Supreme which is infinite possibility may take another possibility for expression. He further writes :

The freed soul is beyond all good and evil....... It would be a dangerous doctrine if these freed man, who has no patience with the weak and the unfit, the defective and the delinquent. Though they are freed from social obligations the free spirits of the *Gita* freely approved of them. The liberated do not suffer any vexation in themselves or cause vexation to others........ While the *Gita* insists much on social duties it recognises a supra social state. It believes in the infinite destiny of the individual apart from human society. The *samnyasin* is above all rules, caste and society...... he may be aloof from the society, yet he has compassion for all. Mahadeva, the ideal ascetic, seated in the Himalayan snows, readily drinks poison for the saving of humanity.[170]

Treatment of Key Verses of The *Gita* :

Having followed the format as developed by Radhakrishnan in analysing his treatment, one may yet turn to an assessment of his interpretation of key verses of the *Bhagavadgita*. In this attempt there is bound to be some overlapping and repetition. To minimise the same only essentials are drawn and the choice of the key verses are limited to a few only.

In the thirtysixth canto of chapter. I of the *Bhagavadgita* Arjuna says :

Nihatya dhartarastran nah

Ka pritih syaj janardana

Papam eva' srayed asman

Hatvai' tam atatayinah.I.13

"What pleasure can be ours, O Krsna, after we have slain the sons of Dhrtarasta ? Only sin will accrue to us if we kill these malignants."

Radhakrishnan feels that this verse summarises the setting and the problem of Arjuna – the setting of the *Gita*, the discourse of the *Gita* and the problem of *Visada* (despondency). Arjuna's crisis is whether to be guided by the social conventions and customary morality or by his individual perception of truth. From this crisis Arjuna is ultimately led to the knowledge that he sould act with out his will having its roots in desire.

Radhakrishnan also finds the twelfth verse of the second chapter of the *Gita* to be significant both to Ramanuja as well as to Samkara. The verse reads :

Na tueva' ham jatu na' sam

Na tvam ne' me janadhipah

Na cai' va na bhavisyamah

Sarve vayam atah param. II.12.

"Never was there a time when I was not, nor thou, nor these lords of men, nor will there ever be a time hereafter when we all shall cease to be."

For Radhakrishnan this verse enumerates how the *Gita* reconciles the plurality of the souls with the unity of the One who is *kstrjna* (the knower of the field) "in whom we live, move and have our being. *Brahman* is the basis of all things and is not itself a thing."[171]

Speaking of the *Jnana Yoga* Lord Krishna advances that He shall unveil the supreme secret to Arjuna for his devotion and friendship.[172] And the secret of Radhakrishnan is the glorious assurance of Krsna which says :

Yada yada hi dharmasya
Glanir bhavati bharata
Abhyuthanam adharmasya
Tada' tmanam srjamy' ham. IV.7.

"Whenever there is a decline of righteousness and rise of unrighteousness, O Bharata (Arjuna), then I send forth (create incarnate) myself."

For Radhakrishnan the Supreme manifests in human embodiment to over-throw the forces of ignorance and selfishness. The verse also signifies the concept of *Avatara* or the descent of the Divine to facilitate the ascent of man. It also defines *dharma*. To Radhakrishnan, "*Dharma* literally means mode of being. It is the essential nature of being that determines its mode of behaviour."[173] The God of the *Gita* for him is the upholder of righteousness and not above or beyond good and evil and remote and unconcerned with man's struggle with unrighteousness.

The verse nine of chapter -IV of the *Gita* says :

Janma karma ca me divyam
Evam yo vetti tattvatah
Tyaktva deham punarjanma
Nai ti mam eti so 'rjuna. IV.9.

"He who knows thus in its true nature My divine birth and works, is not born again, when he leaves his body but comes to Me, O Arjuna."

The birth of the birthless for Radhakrishnan means the revelation of mystery in the soul of man. For him it signifies that there is no opposition between spiritual life and life in the world.

The eleventh verse of the same chapter says :

Ye yatha mam prapadyante
    Tamstathai' va bhajamy ahham
Mama vartma' nuvartante
    Manusyah partha sarvasah.IV.11.

"As men approach Me so do I accept them : Men on all sides follow My path, O *Partha* (Arjuna)." Radhakrishnan postulates that this verse brings out the catholicity of the *Gita* religion. "God meets every aspirant with favour and grants to each his heart's desire."[174]

Radhakrishnan lays emphasis on the seventh and eighth verses of the sixth chapter of the *Gita*, which describe the nature and qualities of a *Sthitaprajna* (a man with steadfast intellect) or a *Jitatman* (conquerer of one's lower self).

The verses say, "When one has conquered one's self (lower) and has attained to the calm of self mastery, his Supreme Self abides ever concentrate, he is at peace in cold and heat, in pleasure and pain, in honour and dishonour. The ascetic (*yogi*) whose soul is satisfied with wisdom and knowledge, who is unchanging and master of his senses, to whom a clod, a stone and a piece of gold are the same, is said to be controlled in *Yoga*."

One who has established himself in unity with the Universal Self is satisfied with the knowledge and experience of the Reality behind the appearances. He is unperturbed by things and happenings of the world and is therefore, said to be equal minded to the events of this changing world."[175]

While the first verse of the Chapter-IX of the *Bhagavadgita* is the key to the chapter, its twenty seventh verse provides the gist of the practical message of the *Gita* as a whole.

The verses are :

Idam tu te guhyatamam

Pravaksyamy anasuyave

Jnanam vijnanasahitam

Yaj jnatva moksyase' subhat.IX.1.

"To thee, who dost not cavil, I shall declare this profound secret of wisdom combined with knowledge, by knowing which thou shall be released from evil."

Yat karosi yad asnasi

Yaj juhosi dadasiyat

Yat tapasyasi kaunteya

Tat kurusva madarpanam.IX.27.

"Whatever thou doest, whatever thou eatest, whatever thou offerest, whatever thou givest away, whatever austerities thou dost practice – do that, O Son of Kunti (Arjuna) as an offering to Me."

Enumerating the above verse Radhakrishnan writes : "Self-giving results in the conscretion of all acts to God."[176]

The other two verses of this chapter which are important and which emphasise the need of an undistracted devotion to Lord are :

Api cet suduracaro

Bhajate mam ananyabhak

Sadhur eva sa mantavyah

Samyag vyavasito hi sah.IX.30.

"Even if a man of the most vile conduct worships Me with undistracted devotion, he must be reckoned as righteous" for he has rightly resolved.

Manmana bhava madbhakto

Madyaji mam namaskuru

Mam evai' syasi yuktvai' vam

Atmanam matparayanah.XVIII.65.

"On Me fix thy mind; to Me be devoted; worship Me; revere Me; thus having disciplined thyself, with Me as thy goal, to Me shall thou come."

Repentence has an infallible power of eradicating sin. Radhakrishnan finds parallels of the 30th verse of Chapter -IX, with the sayings of Samkara, *Baudhayana, Dharmasutra* and Tukaram. He reflects :

Karma never binds completely. The sinner in the lowest depths of degradation has the light in him which he can not put out, though he may try to stifle it and turn away from it utterly. God holds us, fallen though we be by the roots of our being and is ready to send His rays of light into our dark and rebellious hearts. The very consciousness of our imperfection and sin betrays the presence of the Divine on our hearts..... Error, imperfection and selfwill are difficult to overcome, but when the soul gives up its ego and opens itself to the Divine, the Divine takes up the burden and lifts the soul into the spiritual plane.[177]

Commenting on the last two verses of Chapter-IX of the *Gita*, Radhakrishnan postulates that for the existentialist the life of man is a tragic reality and man is left to his own resources. But the teacher of the *Gita* shows a way out of the transitoriness of things, curse of age and death. "He asks us to take refuge in the Divine." Devotion to the Unborn, Beginningless, Eternal who speaks through Krisna is the way to rise out of our ego-centred consciousness to the divine plane. "Joy and peace are the result of self-oblivion, of utter abandonment, of absolute acceptance."[178]

In the Chapter-XI of the *Bhagavadgita*, Radhakrishnan finds verses 32, 33 and 55 having unique significance. The verse 32 explains the essence of the concept of time spirit. The Lord says : "Time am I, world destroying grown mature, engaged here in sub-during the world. Even without thee (thy action), all the warriors standing arrayed in the opposing armies shall cease be."

This verse outlines how time is the prime mover of the Universe. Explaining the verse Radhakrishnan writes, "Time is the streaming flux which moves unceasingly."

In the following verse of the *Gita* how God works out his thoughts through human instruments is explained : "Therefore, arise thou and gain glory," says Krsna the *Gita,* "Conquering thy foes, enjoy a prosperous kingdom. By Me alone are they slain already. Be thou merely the occasion, O *Savyasacin* (Arjuna)."

Radhakrishnan comments on the verse and says ,"The God of destiny decides and ordains all things and Arjuna is to be the instrument, the flute under the fingers of the Ommnipotent One who fulfils His own purpose and is working out a mighty evolution."[179]

In the last verse of the Chapter-XI of the *Gita* the Lord says:

Matkarmakrn matparama

Madbhaktah sangavarjitah

Nirvairah sarvabhutesu

Yah sa mamm eti pandava.XI.55.

"He who does work for Me, he who looks upon Me as his goal, he who worships Me, free from attachment, who is free from enmity to all creatures, he goes to Me, O *Pandava* (Arjuna)."

Radhakrishnan attaches great importance to this verse. To him this verse contains the essence of *bhakti* (devotion). He writes :

This verse is the substance of the whole teaching of the *Gita*..... what ever be our vocation and character,......... if we possess the one great gift of the love of God, we become

God's tools, the channels of His love and purpose. When this vast world of living spirits becomes attuned to God and exists only to do His Will, the purpose of man is achieved.[180]

To Radhakrishnan the fifth verse of Chapter-XIV of the *Gita*, which expounds the three modes (*gunas*) of goodness (*sattva*), passion (*rajas*) and dullness (*tamas*) also explains the objective of the creation. The verse reads :

Sattvam rajas tama iti
Gunah prakrtisambhavah
Nibadhnanti mahabaho
Dehe dehinam avyayam.XIV.5.

"The three modes (*gunas*) goodness (*sattva*), passion (*rajas*) and dullness (*tamas*) born of nature (*prakrti*) bind down in the body, O Mighty-armed (Arjuna), the imperishable dweller in the body." Radhakrishnan feels that the *gunas* or the modes are the cause of the appearance of the immortal soul in the cycle of births and deaths. The cosmic trinity of *Brahma, Vishnu* and *Siva* are represented by the three *gunas, rajas, sattva* and *tamas* respectively. *Sattva* contributes to the preservation and stability of the cosmos, *tamas* represents the tendency of things to decay and die and *rajas* contributes to the creative movement of the Universe. Radhakrishnan writes :

The application of the *gunas* to the three aspects of the personal Lord shows that the latter belongs to the objective or the manifested world. God is struggling in humanity to redeem it and the god like souls co-operate with Him in this work of redemption. To rise above bondage, we must rise above the modes of nature, become *trigunatita,* then we put on the free and incorruptible nature of spirit. *Sattva* is sublimated into the light of consciousness, *jyoti, rajas* into austerity, *tapas* and *tamas* into tranquility or rest, *santi.*[181]

Radhakrishnan points out the universal application of the four fold order propounded by the *Gita*, in the following verse :

Brahmanaksatriyavaisam
Sudranam ca paramtapa
Karmani pravibhaktani
Svabhavaprabhavairgunaih.XVIII.41.

"Of Brahmins, of *Ksatriyas*, and *Vaisyas* as also of *Sudras*, O conqueror of the foe (Arjuna), the activities are distinguished, in accordance with the qualities born of their nature."

To Radhakrishnan, the fourfold order is not peculiar to Hindu society alone, but is of universal application. However, the *Gita* can not be used in support of the existing rigid social order which is in a very confused state today. The inborn nature of very individual (*svabhava*) is to be made effective in his duty (*svadharma*), which will finally enable.

God to express Himself in the free volitions of human beings. All that is essential for the world will be done without a conflict……. The problem that human life sets to its truth; otherwise we would sin against our nature. The emphasis on *svabhava* indicates that human beings are to be treated as individuals and not as types.[182]

He further emphasises that the four broad types of nature represented by four kinds of social living and the four classes are not to be determined by heredity or race but by psychological characteristics which fit the individual for a specific function in the society. Every category of individual is necessary for the society. All contributions of man fromt heir respective quarters are of equal value.

The verse 34 of Chapter-IX of the *Gita* which epitomises the essence of the *Bhagavadgita* according to Radhakrishnan, is repeated in Chapter XVIII, as a prelude to the verse which is regarded as the *carama sloka* or the final verse of the whole book by Ramanuja. As a matter of fact, the *Gita* itself has made it clear that the concept propounded in the verses of Chapter-XVIII from 64 to 66 are the supreme words, the most secret of all. Krishna in the *Gita* says to Arjuna : "Listen again to my supreme word, the most secret of all. Well beloved art thou of Me. Therefore, I shall tell thee what is good for thee XVIII.64."

"Fix thy mind on Me; be devoted to Me, sacrific to Me; prostrate thyself before Me; so shall thou come to Me. I promise thee truly for thou art dear to Me, XVIII.65."

"Abandoning all duties, come to Me alone for shelter. Be not grieved, for I shall release thee from all eveils,XVIII.66."

Radhakrishnan like Sri Aurobindo also confirms the view of the *Gita* that in these lies the final appeal of the Lord, a Divine assurance to man in the process of evolution. Radhakrishnan expounding the verses further holds that Divine help is necessary to transcend all the laws of the world (*dharma* according to nature, station and time, etc.) by which man is bound to nature and the help or the extended hand of God comes only when man surrenders and waits upon the help in all intensity.

Conclusion :

To conclude the discussion on Radhakrishnan's treatment of the *Gita*, a brief summary of the preceeding pages is appended along with the reflections of the scholar.

Radhakrishnan was born and brought up in a traditional south Indian Brahmin family developing a due understanding of Hindu ethos and inculcating revernce for the essential Hindu faith and practices.

This was happily interwined with a training in the Western philosophy, religion, logic and epistemology under the best of the teachers. These gave him a breadth spread over India and the West to analyse, interpret and comment in a newer fashion on the Indian philosophy in general and the

Bhagavadgita in particular. Added on the this was Radhakrishnan's profession. He was by birth, by nature and by choice a brilliant teacher, which enabled him to present his understanding in a most compehensive and intelligible manner. He was an *Acharya,* a chip from the old block in modern times suitably altered in tune with time. He had a flare for writing in a style marked with clarity and lucidity.

Radhakrishnan's principal work is *Indian Philosophy* in two volumes. His other important works include *Region of Religion in Contemporary Philosophy, The Hindu View of Life, An Idealist View of Life, Religion in Transition, The Principal Upanishads, Recovery of Faith and The Brahmasutra,* to cite a few. Radhakrishnan aspired to present Indian Philosophy and thought in an Indian perspective answering the innumerable criticisms from the unsympathetic western reviewers and Christian missionaries. His translation and commentary on the *Bhagavadgita* is written for the common mass. Yet Radhakrishnan the scholar, the trained philosopher, persists in it in full vigour.

The *Bhagavadgita* for Radhakrishnan is a religious classic, less of a metaphysical treatise, a book of practical guidance, transcending all spatial and temporal limitations. It is a comprehensive synthesis of the subtle and profound systems of Indian philosophy. Radhakrishnan was well conversant with numerous interpretations, commentaries and translations of the *Gita,* including those of Gandhi and Sri Aurobindo.

Radhakrishnan's philosophical outlook is not necessarily original. It is more in keeping with the traditional Indian philosophical explanations. The God for him is an Absolute Void from the point of view of the creation and simultaneously God is capable of actualisation of His infinite possibilities. Creation is *Lila,* a game of cosmic bliss, *Maya* for him is relative and not an absolute illusion. The origin of evil is ignorance. Man for Radhakrishnan as a whole must move forward is knowledge and become more god-like. Mind and intellect are not the final tools of knowledge and understanding for Radhakrishnan. Ultimate Reality can only be understood in terms of spiritual experience. Pure consciousness pure freedom, infinite possibility and essential spiritual nature are the key concepts of Radhakrishnan's metaphysics. He is not satiated with individual attainment of the high ideal and goal but he aspired for *Sarvamukti* or universal redemption.

Radhakrishnan constantly refers to earlier works of traditional Indian commentators like Samkara, Ramanuja, Nimbarka and others. He also glenses echoes of the deeper truth from western metaphysical classics. He even corrects unsympathetic and shallow understandings either form the East or from the West.

Bhagavadgita for Radhakrishnan essentially deals with the problem of human action. The background for him is of agitation and despondency. He is not concerned with the historicity of the *Mahabharata*. It neither reduces nor enhances the importance of the text. Arjuna's refusal to fight was not out of his adherence to the principle of non-violence but due to ignorance and a *tamasik* renunciation.

War for Radhakrishnan is a necessity in harmony with the cosmic purpose. World is a battle ground through which man evolves. The duties of civic and social life may be at varience with divine will and the ultimate evolution of creation. The *Mahabharata* is not a fight between pure evil and pure divine. For Radhakrishnan does not distinguish between the two in the ultimate sense. Arjuna's problem is the problem of every soul who is in a threshold of a higher life.

In his analysis of the concept of Reality in the *Bhagavadgita* Radhakrishnan finds it akin to the concept of *Samkhya* philosophy and the principle of *Brahman* of the *Upanishads*. As to the contradictory predicates attributed to the

Supreme, he explains that they are necessitated by the inapplicability of empirical determinations to the Supreme. Radhakrishnan's understanding of the concept of Reality is not limited by the concepts of finite and infinite or the freedom of the Divine to act or His freedom to remain unmanifest. Radhakrishnan does not think that there is any contradiction in the concept of God as propounded in the *Vedas, Upanishads* and the *Bhagavadgita*. He recognises the Supreme both as *para* (higher) and *apara* (lower). The God of of the *Gita* to Radhakrishnan is not only the God of the cosmic process but He even transcends the cosmos. He accepts the concept of *Bibhuti* or pre-eminent powers of God in human beings and the concept of *avatara,* the descent of God-head in human form. God for him is not double or triple, but a dual and a triune. For Radhakrishnan Krishna signifies the descent of the Divine, the Divine intervention to remove the deadlock in the creation. Krishna is the Divine who is here to extend a helping hand to Arjuna who is waiting upon Him. He also signifies revelation of spirit in man hidden in gloom and manifestation fot he transcendent and the emmanent. Human beings for Radhakrishnan are born again and again. The Lord through his *Yogamaya* not only creates the cosmos but also controls the *Prakrti* and plays the *Lila* of opposites, remaining above all these. The world is less real as the effect is less real than the cause. But it is not non-existant.

The cosmic process evolves through five stages of matter, life, mind, intelligence and bliss. Man carries forward the principles of matter, life, mind and intelligence. Man to Radhakrishnan must transcend the mind and intelligence and manifest in full the inherent principle of bliss. Though Radhakrishnan does not expound this in great length, this concept of him is similar to that of Sri Aurobindo's theory of evolution. For Radhakrishnan man must consciously participate in his evolution. He calls man a co-sharer of God in the work of creation. As knowledge is a necessary component of man's transcend, his consent is a necessity. Both Radhakrishnan and sri Aurobindo derive this theory of evolution from the scriptures of India, though both of them may have been facilitated by the western theories of evolution. In dealing with the concept of man Radhakrishnan points out that the problem of man is of being caught in the principles of social life and the inner freedom to express one-self. The problem of man for him as depicted in the *Bhagavadgita* is the problem of integration of his personality through the attainment of a spiritual mastery through his body and soul. Yet another important aspect of man is to realize the Divine by conscious effort. Radhakrishnan refers to the *trigunas* and the need to transcend the limitations of these.

The practical aspects of attainment of the goals of life is always an important component of Hinduism. These practical techniques are known as the *Yoga. For* Radhakrishnan the *Gita* is an excellent *Yogasastra* which enables one to achieve a deep understanding of the meaning of mankind and cosmos. He finds the exposition of *Jnana, Bhakti* and *Karma Yogas* in the *Gita*. He also emphasiSes the unity of these ways as expounded in the *Bhagavadgita* itself. He wants man to break the chain of ignorance, desire and action for knowledge and action with devotion and surrender. Faith is a necessary corollalry of knowledge, for without faith knowledge can not free man completely from dbout. Wisdom may descend directly and result in realisation even in some who have not gone through the rigorous austerities for gaining knowledge. The highest knowledge or wisdom descends ripping open the clouds of ignorance and doubt. *Bhaktimarga* (way of devotion) for Radhakrishnan has been in vogue since hoary past. The prayers of the *Vedas* and the *Vedantas* attest to this. Love is always an easier and natural way of man for attaining the Supreme knowledge. The essence of *bhakti* for him is to work for the God, wait upon the God, worship Him free from attachment, free from enmity to any and marked by an intense desire to go to Him. From various stanzas of the *Bhagavadgita* Radhakrishnan emphasises the *Bhaktimarga* and he accepts it as a part of the supreme message. Radhakrishnan finds the essence of *vaishnavism* reflected in the *Bhagavadgita*. As noted earlier he also emphasises like many other thinkers that *Bhakti* leads to *Jnana*, and in turn to realisation or *Moksha*. Radhakrishnan also finds action to be an important message of the *Gita*. Action in a spirit of renunciation is the essence. Man must not act as a mere social being but must work for his spiritual destiny. Faith in God makes one master of his actions. A true *Karmayogi* allows God to act through him consciously with complete detachment. All the three *margas* (ways) lead to the same goal of spiritual freedom. One acts for the Divine and lives for the Divine. *Gita* recognises, for Radhakrishnan, the social aspect of realisation. In otherwords, the realised soul must discharge his social responsibility of lighting the lamp in others. The social responsibility of a realized soul must not be confused with the observance of social norms of his times.

Radhakrishnan, of the three thinkers under study, alone attempted a full-scale translation and stanza-wise commentary on the *Bhagavadgita*. Of the many verses that he considred to be more important than others, the most striking one for him is that where Krishna advises Arjuna to fix his mind on Him, be devoted to Him, sacrifice to Him and abandon all sense of duties and surrender completely to Him for the final release.

Radhakrishnan constantly refers to the works of Western thinkers including those of Spinoza, Plato, Proclus, John Woolman, Plotinus, St. Thomas Aquinas, St. Augustine, Tauler and many others. He quotes from them to find parallels of the meaning of the *Gita* in western thinking and realisation. He does not use western ideas to give a new twist to the meanings of the *Bhagavadgita* as Gandhi did partly. Radhakrishnan does not approach the *Gita* from the angle of his understanding of the West and Christianity. In other words, his readings of Western thought did not shape his understanding of the *Bhagavadgita*. Hence this aspect is not highlighted here further. Radhakrishnan partly drew the corollaries and parallels in order to cater to the intellectual curiosity of the western critics of Indian Philosophy.

In Radhakrishnan's translation and interpretation of the *Bhagavadgita* one finds an excellent exposition of generations of Indian wisdom presented in the beauty of English language. It is encyclopaedic. It carries forward the interpretation of the *Gita* and the spiritual experiences of various great seers including the Jaina and the Buddhist, various other schools of Indian philosophy and great individual commentators like Samkara, Ramanuja, Nimbarka, Madhva and others. Radhakrishnan's vision and understanding does not exclude an understanding of the contemporary indian thinking on the *Bhagavadgita*, including those of Gandhi and Sri Aurobindo. His work is immensely enriched with an equal mixture of the echoes of the eternal truth from other faiths like Islam and Christianity and the world of Western philosophers from Plato to the contemporary. Radhakrishnan's approach may be that of an intellectual and an academician, yet he was a seer par excellence with the highest realisation free from all doubts and with a firm conviction in the spiritual essence and destiny of mankind.

REFERENCES

1. K.S. Murty and Ashok Vohra, **Radhakrishnan : His Life and Ideas**; Delhi, 1989, p.193.
2. S. Radhakrishnan, "The Religion of the Spirit and the World's need : Fragments of a Confession, (Henceforth : Fragments of a Confession), P.A. Schilpp, ed. **The Philosophy of Radhakrishnan**; New York, 1952, pp.6-7.

3. S. Radhakrishnan, "The Aim of Education", **President Radhakrishnan's Speeches and Writings,** 1965, p.115.
4. Ibid., p.114.
5. Ibid.
6. S. Radhakrishnan, "My Search for Truth", **Radhakrishnan Reader : An Anthology,** (Henceforth. **An Anthology**) Ed. Dr. P. Nagaraja Rao and others; Bombay, 1990. p.4.
7. Ibid., pp.4-5.
8. Ibid., p.5.
9. S. Radhakrishnan, "Reply To Critics", **President Radhakrishnan's Speeches and Writings**, op.cit., p.806n. and p.65.
10. S. Radhakrishnan "Foreword", **The Theology of A.G. Hogg** by Eric Sarpe; Madras, 1971, p.IX.
11. K.S. Murty and A. Vohra, op.cit., p.14.
12. S. Radhakrishnan "Fragments of a Confession", op.cit., p.9.
13. K.S. Murty and V.Vohra, op.cit., p.14.
14. S. Radhakrishnan. **My Search For Truth**; Agra, 1956. p.3.
15. K.S. Murty and A. Vohra, op.cit., p.10.
16. Ibid., p.17.
17. Quoted in V.S. Narvane, "Radhakrishnan', Thought", **The Radhakrishnan Number**; ed. Vuppuluri Kalidas, Madras. 1962, p.55.
18. K.S. Murty and A. Vohra, op.cit., p.18.
19. Ibid.
20. S. Radhakrishnan, "My Search For Truth", **Anthology**; op.cit., p.6.
21. Ibid.

22. K.S. Murty and A. Vohra, op.cit., p.31.
23. Ibid., p.32.
24. Ibid., p.51.
25. Ibid., p.122.
26. Ibid., p.124.
27. Ibid., p.163.
28. S. Radhakrishnan, "My Search For Truth", **An Anthology**; op.cit., p.6.
29. Ibid.
30. S. Radhakrishnan, "Bridge Builder", **An Anthology**; op.cit., p.600.
31. S. Radhakrishnan, **The Philosophy of Radhakrishnan**; op.cit., p.9.
32. Ibid., p.6.
33. C.E.M. Joad, **Counter Attacks From the East**; Lodnon, 1933, p.73.
34. V.P. Varma, **Modern Indian Political Thought**; Agra, 1980, p.407.
35. B.K. Lal, **Contemporary Indian Philosophy**; Delhi, 1989.
36. S. Radhakrishnan, ***Dhammapada***; Oxford, 1954, Preface.
37. S. Radhakrishnan, Tr. **The *Bhagavadgita***; Delhi, 1989, Preface.
38. S. Radhakrishnan, **Fragments of a Confession**; op.cit., p.10.
39. Robert, N. Minar, **Radhakrishnan, A Religious Biography**; New york, 1987, p.18.
40. S. Radhakrishnan, **An Idealist View of Life**; London, 1947, pp.91-98.
41. V.P. Varma, op.cit., p.408.

42. S. Radhakrishnan, **The Ethics of the *Vedanta* and its Metaphysical presuppositions**; 1908, op.cit., p.66.
43. S. Radhakrishnan, **Regin of Religions in Contemporary Philosophy**; London, 1920, p.439.
44. S. Radhakrishnan, **An Idealist View of Life**; op.cit., p.343.
45. P.A. Schilpp, Ed. **The Philosophy of Sarvepalli Radhakrishnan**; New York, 1952, p.142.
46. S. Radhakrishnan, **Eastern Religion and Western Thought**; Oxford, 1939, p.96.
47. S. Radhakrishnan, (Tr.) ***The Bhagavadgita***; op.cit., Preface.
48. At Satyagraha Ashram from 24th Feb, 1926 to 27th Nov, 1926.
49. S. Radhakrishnan, **My Search For Truth**; op.cit. p.12.
50. S. Radhakrishnan, **Indian Philosophy** Vol.I; Delhi, 1991, p.10.
51. S. Radhakrishnan, **Occasional Speeches & Writings**, Vol.I; Govt. of India Publications, 1956, p.62.
52. S. Radhakrishnan, (Tr.) ***The Bhagavatgita***; op.cit., Preface.
53. Ibid.
54. Ibid., p.11.
55. S. Radhakrishnan, **Indian Philosophy**, Vol.I, op.cit., p.519.
56. Ibid.
57. S. Radhakrishnan, (Tr.) **The Bhagavadgita**; op.cit., p.11.
58. S. Radhakrishnan, **Indian Philosophy** Vol.I; op.cit., pp.519-520.
59. S. Radhakrishnan, (Tr.) ***The Bhagavadgita***; op.cit., p.11.

60. Ibid., p.12.
61. Ibid.
62. Ibid.
63. Ibid., p.12.fn.
64. C.E.M. Joad, **Counter Attacks From The East**; op.cit., p.38.
65. B.K.Lal, **Contemporary Indian Philosophy**; op.cit., p.258.
66. S. Radhakrishnan, (Tr.) ***The Bhagavadgita***; op.cit., p.13.
67. S. Radhakrishnan, **Indian Philosophy** Vol.I; op.cit., pp.521-22.
68. S. Radhakrishnan, (Tr.) ***The Bhagavadgita***; op.cit., pp.13-14.
69. Ibid., p.12.fn.
70. S. Radhakrishnan, **Indian Philosophy** Vol.I; op.cit., p.591.
71. Ibid., fn.
72. Ibid.
73. S.N. Dasgupta, "Philosophy", **A Cultural History of India**; d. A.L. Basham, Delhi, 1984. p.123.
74. S. Radhakrishnan, **Indian Philosophy** Vol.I; op.cit., pp.522-524.
75. Ibid.
76. ***The Mahabharata***, *Adiparva*, 2.69; 1.179, p.247.
77. Bal Gangadhar Tilak, (Tr.) **Gita Rahasya** (Eng.), 1935, Appendix, **Sacred Books of the East**, Vol.VIII; Introduction.
78. ***The Bhagavadgita***; Chapter.III and ***The Mahabharata***; *Vanaparva*, Chapter.XXXII.
79. ***The Mahabharata***; *Shantiparva*, and ***Manusamhita***; Chapter.III.

80. ***The Bhagavadgita,*** Chapter.VII and VIII; and ***The Mahabharata;*** *Shantiparva,* 231.

81. ***The Bhagavatagita,*** Chapter.XIV and XV; and ***The Mahabharata,*** *Asvamedhaparva;* 36-39, *Shantiparva,* 285 and 300-311.

82. ***The Bhagavadgita,*** Chapter.VI and *Shantiparva,* 239 and 300.

83. ***The Mahabharat,*** *Udyogaparva,* 170, *Asvamedhaparva* 55, *Shantiparva,* 339 and *vanaparva,* 99.

84. S. Radhakrishnan, **Indian Philosophy** Vol.I; op.cit., pp.523-524.

85. S. Radhakrishnan, (Tr) ***The Bhagavadgita***; op.cit., p.15.

86. S. Radhakrishnan, **Indian Philosophy**; op.cit., p.525.

87. Ibid.

88. S. Radhakrishnan, (Tr.) ***The Bhagavadgita***; op.cit., pp.345-346.

89. Ibid., p.346.

90. S. Radhakrishnan, **Indian Philosophy** Vol.I; op.cit., p.525.

91. Ibid., p.116.

92. Ibid., pp.112-113.

93. Ibid., p.525.fn.

94. ***The Bhagavadgita,*** *Gitadhyanam,* Canto-4.

95. S. Radhakrishnan, **Indian Philosophy** Vol.I; op.cit., p.142.

96. Ibid., pp.525 fn. And 526.

97. S. Radhakrishnan, (Tr.). ***The Bhagavadgita***; op.cit., p.151.

98. Ibid., p.152.

99. S. Radhakrishnan, **Religion In A Changing Wrold**; London,1967, as quoted by K.R.Srinivas Iyengar, **Indian Writing in English**, New Delhi, 1985, p.580.
100. S. Radhakrishnan, **Indian Philosophy** Vol.I; op.cit., pp.526-527.
101. K.R. Srinivas Iyengar, **Indian Writing in English**; op.cit., pp.580-581.
102. S. Radhakrishnan, **Indian Philosophy**; op.cit., p.27.
103. S. Radhakrishnan, (Tr.). *The Bhagavadgita*; op.cit., p.115.
104. S. Radhakrishnan, **Indian Philosophy** Vol.I; op.cit., p.527.
105. S. Radhakrishnan, (Tr.). *The Bhagavadgita*; op.cit., p.115.
106. S. Radhakrishnan, **Indian Philosophy** Vol.I; op.cit., p.528.
107. S. Radhakrishnan, (Tr.). *The Bhagavadgita*; op.cit., p.103.
108. S. Radhakrishnan, **Indian Philosophy** Vol.I; op.cit., p.528-29.
109. S. Radhakrishnan, *The Bhagavadgita*; op.cit., p.16.
110. Ibid., p.17.
111. Ibid., pp.18-19.
112. Ibid., p.19.
113. Ibid.
114. Ibid., p.20.
115. Ibid., p.354.
116. Ibid., pp.68-69.
117. Ibid., pp.80-81.
118. Ibid., p.90.
119. Ibid., p.95.

120. Ibid., p.20.
121. S. Radhakrishnan, **An Idealist View of Life**; op.cit., p.128.
122. Ronald Kapferer, "Contradiction and the Logic of Conversion In The Bhagavadgita", **New Essays In The Bhagavadgita**; Comp. Arvind Sharma, New Delhi, 1987, p.130.
123. S. Radhakrishnan, (Tr.) ***The Bhagavadgita***; op.cit., Preface.
124. Ibid., pp.20-21.
125. Ibid.. pp.109 & 305.
126. Ibid., pp.109 & 307.
127. Ibid., p.126.
128. Ibid., pp.24-25.
129. Ibid., pp.308-309.
130. Ibid., p.26.
131. Ibid., p.27.
132. Ibid., p.132.
133. Ibid., p.28.
134. Ibid., p.32.
135. Ibid., p.35.
136. Ibid.
137. Ibid., p.37.
138. Ibid., p.246.
139. Ibid., pp.336-337.
140. Ibid., p.326.
141. S. Radhakrishnan, **An Idealist View of Life**; op.cit., p.313.
142. S. Radhakrishnan, **The Reign of Religion In Contemporary Philosophy**; op.cit., pp.442-443.

143. S. Radhakrishnan, (Tr.) ***The Bhagavadgita***; op.cit., p.44.
144. Ibid., p.45
145. Ibid.
146. Ibid., p.48.
147. Ibid., p.47.
148. Ibid., pp.49 and 88.
149. Ibid., p.210.
150. S. Radhakrishnan, **An Idealist View of Live**; op.cit. p.310.
151. S. Radhakrishnan, (Tr.) ***The Bhagavadgita***; op.cit., p.51.
152. S. Radhakrishnan, **Indian Philosophy** Vol.I; op.cit., p.554.
153. S. Radhakrishnan, (Tr.) ***The Bhagavadgita***; op.cit., p.182.
154. Ibid., pp.169-170.
155. Ibid., p.58.
156. S. Radhakrishnan, **Indian Philosophy** Vol.I; op.cit., p.559.
157. S. Radhakrishnan, (Tr.) ***The Bhagavadgita***; op.cit., p.289.
158. Ibid., p.293.
159. Ibid., p.252.
160. Ibid., p.61.
161. Ibid., p.62.
162. Ibid., p.250.
163. Ibid., p.66.
164. Ibid.
165. Ibid., pp.68-69.

166. S. Radhakrishnan, **Indian Philosophy**; op.cit., p.570-572.
167. S. Radhakrishnan, (Tr.) ***The Bhagavadgita***; op.cit., p.72.
168. Ibid., p.281.
169. Ibid., p.76.
170. S. Radhakrishnan, **Indian Philosophy**; op.cit., p.580.
171. S. Radhakrishnan, (Tr.) ***The Bhagavadgita***; op.cit., p.103.
172. ***The Bhagavadgita,*** Chapter.IV.1, 2 & 3.
173. S. Radhakrishnan, (Tr.) ***The Bhagavadgita***; op.cit., p.155.
174. Ibid., p.158.
175. Ibid., pp.190-192.
176. Ibid., p.249.
177. Ibid., p.251.
178. Ibid., pp.254-255.
179. Ibid., p.280.
180. Ibid., p.289.
181. Ibid., p.317.
182. Ibid., p.365.

CHAPTER – VI

CONCLUSION

The *Bhagavadgita* as a singular work is the best illustrative embodiment of Indian religio-philosophic texts. The historian in dealing with such a text and its interpretation need not be a mere mechanical rag-picker, or a cataloguer of the dead authors and their writings but must undertake the work to educate the mind and enthrall the imagination. He should be a critic and an interpreter as well. Even though the present work may not completely stand upto the above tests, an humble attempt in this direction is being undertaken.

In their interpretations of the *Bhagavadgita* the three thinkers nauturally have correlated the text to an extent with their contemporary events and developments. Their interpretations were shaped largely by their individual personalities, and their general percepts of understanding of God, man and the world. Gandhi approaches the *Gita* mostly as an activist that is from the thick of his life of a politician, social reformer and an individual aspirant for God realisation. Radhakrishnan interprets *Bhagavadgita* in context of his deep and wide reading of earlier interpretations and classics on the western philosophy including the modern ones. He attempts to place the *Gita* by carrying forward the earlier interpretations, juxtaposing the same with similar philosophical and spiritual sayings and experiences from the western domain. Though he has eventually drawn parallels from the west, yet he does not give the *Bhagavadgita* a new interpretation in the western light. He only chooses those ideas and words which echo the Indian thinking and interpretation. Sri Aurobindo had a comprehensive understanding of the *Vedas, Upanisads* and the *Bhagavadgita*. He builds a theory of evolution and projects man's conscious participation in its evolution to a higher life – a life with the knowledge of divine nature of man as a living experience, a life conquering disease and death. He reads into the *Bhagavadgita* his vision and deep understanding of reality, cosmos and man. Even though he does not constantly refer to earlier Indian interpretation of the *Bhagavadgita* from the very ancient period to the present. Gandhi and Sri Aurobindo in particular could not divest their interpretation of the *Gita* from the political milieu in which they lived, wrote and participated. Though Sri Aurobindo's *Essays on the Gita* belongs to a later and mature period when he was no longer active politically and his earlier references to it came when he was deeply involved in Indian politics. The ideas of a 'chosen instrument of God', the 'hour of God', the 'periodic Divine Intervention for the establishment of *dharma*, upholding of righteousness', use of violence, necessity of sacrific or *Yajna* were invariably drawn from the *Bhagavadgita* by Sri Aurobindo. Of course Sri Aurobindo held out that the sword of the *Kshatriya* was not the only means, the pen of the *Brahmana* was no less potent. The gigantic mega conflict with the British was no less than a *'Dharma yuddha'* (the war for righteousness) similar to that of the *Mahabharata* on the wake of the *Gita*. Even in the later years, taking in a global view of the contemporary world, Sri Aurobindo held his time as a classic period of churning of the ocean. The whole world for him was on the threshold of a new age. In such a trying and potently creative age, the *Bhagavadgita* was a guide for a deeper understanding of the world, God and the man for Sri Aurobindo. For Gandhi, the political questions involved were partly similar and partly dissimilar to Sri Aurobindo's line of thinking. Like Sri Aurobindo, he considered India's freedom sruggle to be an epic struggle for the establishment of the righteous principles and upholding of truth and *dharma*. Of coruse, inspite of the fact that Duryodhana was not an evil incarnate and that good men like Bhisma, Drona and Karna fought on his side. And that Duryodhana was dear to goddess Lakshmi, yet he was destined to be defeated by the sheer weight of his sin. So also the English for him were not evil incarnates, but deserved to be driven out from India for their misdeeds and for the establishment of the self governing right of man.

For India, the western ideals which England represented were not necessarily in keeping with India's *swadharma*. Gandhi was naturally caught in the web of apparent contradictions of justifying his theory of non-violence against the war background of the *Bhagavadgita*. Gandhi was justified in holding that violence or non-violence was not the central question before Arjuna. But he was equally erroneous in holding out that the central question before Arjuna was the distinction between his kinsman and other. However, the central question remains is Arjuna's despondency, his feeling of depression, his refusal to perform his duty in an hour of crisis and his questioning of the whole ethical standard of his times. Gandhi had to read the question of violence and non-violence into the *Bhagavadgita* partly out of compulsion, in view of the totality of his thinking. Form the *Bhagavadgita* he drew his lessons of single mindedness in action, without attachments to the fruits or consequences there of. He learnt and made others learn the necessity of not losing sight of the central goal in life and to remain unperturbed by temporary successes and failures. We find him constantly referring to the spinning wheel and comparing the act of spinning to *Yajna*. He demanded a sense of complete sacrifice from every Indian in choosing *Swadeshi* clothes against the availability of cheaper cloth from Europe. He wanted the Indians as a whole to be proud of their own country, history and heritage. He endeavoured to instill the courage of a *Kshatriya* in the minds of his countrymen. He wanted to combat the despondency and lack of faith among the

Indians and he wanted to set aside their feeling and fear of failure. The *Bhagavadgita* was a handbook for him for achieving all these. Some even suggest that he believed in the spinning wheel as a replica of Lord Krishna's *Sudarsanachakra*. For Gandhi the spinning wheel alone was enough to drive out the English, as the *Sudarsanachakra* in the *Mahabharata* alone could annihilate the friends and the foes alike. A like parallel was drawn to the wheel, the symbol of the Janata party in the euphoria of the general parliament elections held in 1977 at the end of the emergency, a dark period of modern Indian history. For Gandhi, the *Bhagavadgita* was not a book for driving out political mileage. It was for him the most sacred religious book to which he constantly looked upon for comfort, solace and sustenance. Gandhi as an individual, and as a sincere aspirant of God-realisation drew the lessons of effacement of the ego, of complete devotion to God, and the lessons of a firm and living faith in the Divine power that controls the minutest details of life. He imbibed from the *Gita* a living faith that one must not get attached to the goals of action. He greatly developed the true characteristics of a *Sthitaprijna* as described in the *Bhagavadgita*. An understanding of Gandhi, the chief architect of India's freedom would remain incomplete without an analysis of his understanding of the *Bhagavadgita* one among the few books which shaped his life and personality, nay, India's destiny. Gandhi's overbearing attachment of importance to ethics, morality, in the form of *Yamaniyama, Brahmacharya* ,etc. was possibly erroneous. A true Hindu takes life more comprehensively and does not exclude the terrestrial goals of life. He does not aspire to annihilate the body or its demands and does not necessarily consider the body to be an impediment for the highest realisation. The concept of sin and virtue does not necessarily cloud his understanding and analysis of the inner most aspects of the ultimate reality. Morality is not the essential issue in any one of the classic metaphysical works of India or for their illustrious commentators. However, the average Indian, though has an intuitive understanding of this deeper truth constantly debates on the *papa* (sin) and *punya* (virtue) and is eager to uphold *dharma* which is partly social in its dimensions. Though issues like the ends and means, ethics and morality, violence and non-violence might have been overbearing with Mahatma Gandhi it would not be right to say that he altogether missed the Hindu ethos and Hindu understanding of life. Also for him God is far above such dualities, including that of virtue and vice. He confessed that in the absence of a deeper understanding and an esoteric spiritual revealing experience, he had to conduct himself with the two principles of truth and non-vilence. His essential emphasis that it is not possible to live with absolute non-violence yet to constantly realize that it is the good, it is the non-violence, it is the love; it is the sacrific that sustains and builds the beatitude of life was and is still valid. Gandhi must be taken as a whole. One must not over emphasise his logical inconsistencies or deficiencies otherwise, but it is more important for every student of Gandhi to see and experience the catholicity of his total fabric of life and action.

Sarvepalli Radhakrishnan in carrying forward the ancient heritage of Indian thought and culture become the modern ambassador of Indian metaphysics to the world. He is a classic example of the ability of the modern scholars of India to present the essence of her culture in lucid English language and western format. He widened the horizon of western readers of Indian philosophy and pointed out the metaphysical content of the Indian texts like the *Bhagavadgita* and the *Vedas*. He along with few others removed the misconception that the *Upanisads* alone contained metaphysics and other texts were mere babbling of black magic and occultism. He convincingly established the logical consistency marked in Indian scriptures in general and in the *Bhagavadgita* in particular. By drawing upon similar ideas from the West he was building in one of the finest ways the unity of spiritual experiences of the mankind. He was a par excellent synthesizer of the philosophy of the East and the West. He had a poetic vision of the unity of human thinking, transcending the barriers of time and space. He was at the same time the most modern academician and a *rshi* in the truest sense of the term. Not losing sight of individual *moksha* or liberation which may be the general attitude of the Hindus, Radhakrishnan advocated the emancipation of mankind as a whole. He, like Sri Aurobindo believed in the conscious participation of man in his own evolution as a 'Co-sharer of God.' He was firm in his faith that man having carried forward the principles of matter, life and mind shall yet scale the heights of bliss, intuition and will reach a fuller life with constant knowledge and living realisation of the ultimate reality. He aspired for a de-mystified word in which men and others shall live in perfect concord and harmony. An idealist and an utopian Radhakrishnan was capable of representing the very best of India's heritage.

Sri Aurobindo, Gandhi and Radhakrishnan had many divergent views as well as many meeting grounds. Yet all of them in a way did not miss the essence of the *Bhagavadgita*. All the three held the following verses of the *Gita* to stand for its central message :

Manmana bhava madbhakto
Madyaji mam namaskuru
Mam evai' syasi satyam te
Pratijane priyo' si me XVIII.65
Sarvadharman parityajya
Mam ekam saranam vraja
Aham tva sarvapapebhyo
*Moksayisyami ma sucah.*XVIII.66

The cost of repetition it may be said that the *Bhagavadgita* itself lends support to such a view. All the readers of the *Bhagavadgita* hold out the surrender to the Divine as the central aspect of its teaching. The varied interpretations in the details by the three thinkers is a pointer to the eternal freshness of the *Bhagavadgita*. There will be indeed no such time when the *Gita* would cease to lend itself for a newer interpretation of the deeper meanings of life and spiritual experiences.

In the present days the *Bhagavadgita* in addition to attracting interpreters from the domain of religion like Shivananda, Yogananda or Bhakti Vedanta Prahbupada, has newer adherents from the unconventional walks of life like managers. In a world where depression and despondency are rampant in the life of individuals in their mad and meaningless race of material comforts marked by spiritual and social aberration, the *Bhagavadgita* provides a link with the divine and serves many as a platform for a more meaningful life. The psychologists, the managers, the Human Resources Development personnel and information technologist all draw their lessons and injunctions from the *Bhagavadgita*. Even Swami Chinmoyananda, a saint, cites profusely illustrations from the *Bhagavadgita* in his discourses on management for the benefit of the managers of industries. Lessons of man management and material management are drawn today from the *Bhagavadgita*. Authors like O.P. Ghai, H.V. Divatia, M.P. Pandit and a host of others derive messages from the *Gita* as a guidance for modern life. Though the *Bhagavadgita* is no longer cited by the political activists in India, yet it has found new adherents from other walks of life. As a whole it continues to be the most widely read religious scripture of the Indians. Its use in the court by the Hindus for oath taking may not substantiate that the complexity of Hinduism is contained in a single text, yet it points out to its primacy in the lfie of the Hindus over other scriptures.

The present endeavour does not exhaust the possibilities of further studies on this topic. One may be critical of dealing on the three thinkers in a single treatise in view of their prolific and voluminous writings. One may be critical of the exclusion of numerous other treatments of the *Bhagavadgita* by equally illustrious sons of the soil. Not withstanding the validity of such criticism the attempt is limited and representative in character. To return to the objectives of the work, it establishes in a small way the link between thought and life. it is the mind which is behind all man's actions. No student of history can exclude the domain of thought from the purview of his study of events and processes that go to give shape to the material and cultural life of mankind. Gandhi, Arurobindo and Radhakrishnan exemplify the correlation between thought and action. Even through the present mind, eternal gifts of the domain of thought not only survive and live, but also influence and control; if not wholly, at least partially. The *Bhagavadgita* remains a classic of the Indian heritage and the interpretation of the three illustrious figures of the twentieth century is a pointer to its eternal value.

SELECT BIBLIOGRAPHY

Acharya, K.D. : **Guide to Sri Aurobindo's Philosophy**; Divya Jivan Prakashna, Pondicherry, 1973.

Agrwal, Sriman Narayan. : **The Gandhian Plan of the Economic Development**; Padma Publication, Bombay, 1944.

Alexander, H. : **Gandhi Through Western Eyes**; Asia Publishing House, 1996, Bombay.

Ambedkar, B.R. : **Gandhi & Gandhism**; Patrika Publications, Jullender, 1970.

Andrews, F.C. : **Mahatma Gandhi's Ideas**; Asia Publishing House, 1949.

Ashe, Geoffrey. : **Gandhi, A Study in Revolution**; Asia Publishing House, Bombay, 1968.

Bakhle, S.W. : **Hindusm, Nature & Development**; Sterling Publishers Pvt. Ltd. New Delhi, 1991.

Bandopadhyaya, J. : **Social & Political Thought of Gandhi**; Allied Publishers, Bombay, 1963.

Besant, Annie. : **How India Wrought for Freedom**; Theosophical Publishing House, London, 1915.

Birla, G.D. : **In the Shadow of Mahatma**; Orient Longmann, 1955.

Basham, A.L. (Ed.) : **Cultural History of India**; London, 1975.

Bazaz, Prem Nath : **The Role of Bhagavad Gid in Indian History**; Sterling Publishers, New Delhi, 1975.

Bhattacharya, Haridas. : **The Culture Heritage of India**, 6 Vol. IV, Calcutta, 1983.

Bose, A.C. : **The Call of The Vedas**; Bharatiya Vidya Bhavan, Bombay, 1970.

Bose, B.C. : **Gandhi Gita**; Thacker Spinick, Calcutta, 1948.

Bose, N.K. : **Gandhi : The Man & His Mission**; Bharatiya Vidya Bhavan, Bombay, 1966.

— : **Lectures on Gandhism**; Navajavan Publishing House. Ahmedabad, 1971.

Chakravarty, Nirodbaran. : **Correspondence With Sri Aurobindo**; Sri Aurobindo Ashram, Pondicherry, 1954.

Chatterjee, S.C., D.N. Dutta. : **An Introduction to Indian Philosophy**; University of Calcutta, Calcutta, 1968.

Chattopadhaya, D.P. : **Indian Philosophy: A Popular Introduction**; Peoples' Publishing House, New Delhi, 1986.

Chaturvedi, Laxmi Narayan. : **The Teachers of Bhagavad Gita**; Sterling Publishers, Pvt. Ltd., 1991. (New Delhi).

Choudhury, Haridas. : (Ed.) : **The Integral Philosophy of Sri Aurobindo**; George Allen & Unwin, Ltd. London, 1960.

Chidbhavananda Swamy. : (Ed.) : **Bhagavad Gita**; Sri Rama Krishna Tapovana Tiruchirapalli, 1982.

Cousins, Norman. : **Profiles of Gandhi**; Indian Book Company, Delhi, 1970.

Das, Adhar Chandra. : **Sri Aurobindo and the Future of Mankind**; Calcutta University, 1934.

Das, B.C. & G.P. Mishra, (Ed.) : **Gandhi in Today's India**; Ashish Publishing House, New Delhi, 1979.

Das, Manoj. : **Sri Aurobindo in The First Decade of the Century**; Sri Aurobindo Ashram, Pondicherry, 1972.

Dasgupta, S.N. : **A History of Indian Philosophy**; Motilal Banarsidass, Delhi, 1960.

Datta, D.M. : **The Philosophy of Mahatma Gandhi**; University of Calcutta, 1968.

Datta, Rajni Palme. : **India Today**; Victor Gollanie, London, 1940.

Desai, M. (Tr.) : **The Gospel of Selfless Action or The Gita According to Gandhi**; Navajiban, Ahmdabad, Oct.1954.

Message of the Gita; Compiled by R.K. Prabhu, June 1956, **Discourses on the Gita**; (Tr.) Valji Govindji Desai, April, 1960.

Desai, Narayan : **Bliss was it to be Young with Gandhi**; Bharatiya Vidya Bhavan, Bombay, 1988.

Dewan, Ram Prakash. : **Gandhi's Non-violence**; Dewan Publication, Lahore.

Dhenbar, U.N. : **Gandhi: A Practical Idealist**; Bharatiya Vidya Bhavan, Bombay, 1964.

Divatia, H.V. : **The Art of Life in the Bhagavad Gita**; Bharatiya Vidya Bhavan, Bombay, 1991.

Diwakar, R.R. : **Gandhi – A Practical Philosopher**; Bharatiya Vidya Bhavan, Bombay, 1964.

Diwakar, R.R. : **Gandhiji's Basic Ideas and Some Modern Problems**; Bharatiya Vidya Bhawan, Bombay, 1963.

— : **Mahayogi Sri Aurobindo**; Bharatiya Vidya Bhawan, Bombay, 1967.

Doke Joseph, J. : **M.K. Gandhi**; Publication, Division, 1967.

Dantwala, M.L. : **Gandhism Reconsidered**; Vora and Co, Bombay, 1944.

Fischer, Louis. : **The Life of Mahatma Gandhi**; (Vol.I & II), Granada, London, '982.

Gandhi, Manubahen. : **The End of an Epoch**; Navajivan Publishing House, Ahamedabad, 1962.

Gandhi, M.K. : **Complete Works of Mahatma Gandhi**; Publication Division, New Delhi, (90 Volumes).

— : **An Autobiography or The Story of Experiment with Truth**; Navajiban Publishing House, Ahmedabad, 1983.

— : **Cent Percent Swadesi**; Navajivan Publishing House, Ahmedabad, 1959.

— : **Satyagraha in South Africa**; 3rd Impression, Navajivan Publishing House, Ahmedabad, 1961.

— : **Hindu Dharma**; Orient Paperbacks, Delhi, 1993.

Gandhi, Rajmohan : **The Good Boatman**; Viking, New Delhi, 1995.

Ganguli, B.N. : **Gandhiji's Social Philosphy**; Vikas Publishing Hosue, Delhi, 1973.

George, S.K. : **Gandhiji's Challenge to Christianity**; Allen and Unwin, London.

Ghose, P.C. : **Mahatma Gandhi, As I Saw Him**; S. Chand & Co., 1968.

Ghose, Sudhir, **Ghandi's Emissary**; Rupa and Co., '1964.

Gokak, V.K. : **India and World Culture**; Vikas Publications, Delhi, '1972.

Gregg, R.B. : **A Discipline for Non-violence**; Navajivan Publishing Hosue, Ahmedabad, 1959.

Guha, A.C. : **Aurobindo and Yugantar**; Pndicherry, 1972.

Gupta, S.S. : **The Economic Philosophy of Mahatma Gandhi**; Ashok Publishing House, Delhi.

Hiriyana, M. : **Outlines of Indian Philosphy**; George Allen and Unwin (India) Pvt. Ltd., Bombay, 1973.

Iyengar, K.R.S. : **Sri Aurobindo : A Biography and a History**; Vols. I & II. Sri Aurobindo International Center of Education, Pondicherry, 1972.

— : **Indian Writing in English**; Sterling Publishers, New Delhi, 1995.

Kalekar. : **The Gospel of Swadesi**; Ganesan, Madras, 1922.

Kamal, K.L. & Mathur, P.C. : **Gandhi & Social Change**; University of Rajasthan, Jaipur.

Karunakaran, K.P. : **New Perspectives on Gandhi**; Indian Institute Advanced Studies, 1969.

Keen, Dhanjay. : **Mahatma Gandhi, Political Saint and Unarmed Prophet**; Indian Printing Works, 1973.

Kocha, R.A.S. : **The Big Bang and Bhagavad Gita**; Bharatiya Vidya Bhavan, Bombay, 1991.

Koshambi, D.D. : **The Culture and Civilization of Ancient India in Historical Outline**; Vikas Publishing Hosue, Delhi, 1982.

Kottaran, George. : **Ahimsa : Gautam to Gandhi**; Sterling Publishers, New Delhi, 1973.

Kripalini, J.B. : **Gandhi : His Life and Thought**; Publication Governemnt of India, '970.

Krushnananda, Swami. : **The Philosophy of the Bhagavadgita**; The Divine Life Society, Shivananda-nagar, Rishikesh, 1980.

Krishnamurti, G.G. : **Neo-Gandhism**; Nalanda Publication, Bombay, 1954.

Kytles, Calvin. : **Gandhi : Soldier of Non-violence**; Grolsset & Dunlap, New York, 1969.

Lal, B.H. : **Contemporary Indian Philosphy**; Motilal Banarasi Das, Delhi, 1989.

Langlay, G.H. : **Sri Aurobindo, Indian Poet, Philosopher and Mystic**; David Marlow Ltd., 1949.

Lester, Muriel. : **Ganhdi World Citizen**; Kitab Mahal, Allahabad, 1945.

Lohia, Rammanohar. : **Marx, Gandhi & Socialism**; Rammanohar Lohia Samata Vidyalaya Nyasa, Hyderabad, 1978.

Mahadevan, T.M. : **The Relevance of Mahatma Gandhi to the World**; Madras University, 1969.

Maheswar, Ed. : **Bhagavad Gita – In the Light of Sri Aurobindo**; Sri Aurobindo Ashram Press, Pondicherry.

Maitra, S.K. : **The Meeting of the East and the West in Sri Aurobindos Philosophy**; Sri Aurobindo Ashram, Pondicherry.

Majumdar, R.C., (Ed.). : **History and Culture of the Indian People**, Vol. I to XII; Bombay, 1988.

Marlow, A.N. (Ed.). : **Radhakrishnan and Anthology**; George Allen and Unwin Ltd. London, 1952.

Marx, Karl. & Angels, Fredrick. : **On Britain**; Moscow, 1953.

Marx, Karl. : **The Capital**; Vol. I, Moscow, 1954.

Mashruwala, K.G. : **Gandhi & Marx**; Navajivan Publishing House, Ahmedabad, 1960.

— : **Gandhiji's Philosophy of Life & Action**; Bharatiya Vidya Bhavan, Bombay, 1965.

Maurer, H. : **Great Soul**; Orient Longmans, 1969.

Mishra, Dr. Satyabadi. : **Central Philosophy of the Upanishads**; Santosh Publications, Cuttack, 1988.

Murty, K.S. & A, Vohra. : **Radha Krishnan, His life and ideas**; Ajanta, Delhi, 1989.

Nanda, B.R. : **Mahatma Gandhi**; Oxford University Press, Delhi, 1982.

Narayan, Shriman. : **Gandhi : The man & his thought**; Publications Divison, Gap of India, 1969.

Narrane, V.S. : **Modern Indian Thought**; Asia Publishing House, Bombay, 1964.

Nehru, J. : **Mahatma Gandhi**; Asia Publishing House, 1966.

Pande, Susmita. : **Medieval Bhakti Movement**; Meerut, 1989.

Pandit, M.P. : **Sri Aurobindo : A Survey**; Dipti Publications, Sri Aurobindo Ashram, Pondicherry, 1972.

Pandit, M.P. : **Talk on the Life Divine**, Vol.II; Dipti Publications, Sri Aurobindo Ashram, Pondicherry, 1988.

Pani, Binita. : **The Indian Scriptures and the Life Divine**; New Delhi, 1993.

Pani, Dr. R.N. : **Ingegral Education : Thought and Practice**; Ashish Publishing House, New Delhi, 1987.

Pani, S.P. : **Sri Aurobindo – A Study of His Thought in A Historical Perspective**; (Unpublished : Thesis for doctoral Degree). Utkal University, Bhubaneswar, 1985.

-- : **Sri Aurobindo - Life And Thought**; Himalaya Publishing House, Mumbai, 2007.

Patel, Raojibhai. : **Gandhiji sadhana**; Navajivan Publishing, Ahamadbad, 1939.

Prabhavananda, Swami. : **Spiritual Heritage of India**; Sri Ramakrishna Math, Madras, 1981.

Prabhupada. : **Srimad Bhagavad Gita**; Moulikarupare. Tr. Goura Govinda Swamy Bhakti Vedanta Bock Trust, Bhubaneswar, 1982.

Pradhan, B. : **The Soialist thought of Mahatma Gandhi**; G.D. Kapur & Sans., Delhi, 1948.

Prasad, Mahadeo. : **Social Philosophy of Mahatma Gandhi**; Viswavidyalaya Prakashan, Gorakhpur, 1959.

Prasad, Rajendra. : **At the Feet of Mahatma Gandhi**; Asia Publication, 1961.

Purani, A.B. : **The Life of Sri Aurobindo**; Madras, 1981.

— : **Some Aspects of His Vision**, Bharatiya Vidya Bhavan, Bombay, 1966.

Pyarelal. : **Gandhian Techniques in the modern World**; Navajivan, 1953.

— : **Mahatma Gandhi – the Last Phase**; Vol.II, Navajivan, 1958.

Radhakrishnan, S. : **Indian Philosophy**; Vol.I; Oxford University Press, 1991.

— : **The Bhagavad Gita**; (English), Oxford University Press, 1989.

— : **Eastern Religions and Western Thought**; Clarendon Press, Oxford, 1939.

— : **East and West in Religion**; George Allen and Unwin Ltd., London, 1954.

— : **The Recovery of Faith**; George Allen and Unwin Ltd., London, 1956.

— : **Religion and Culture**; Orient Paper backs Delhi, 1991.

— : **Indian Religion**; Orient Paper backs Delhi, 1992.

— : **Essays and Reflections on his life and Work**; Allen and Unwin; London, 1939.

Radhakrishnan, S. and J.H. Muirhead. (Ed.). : **Contemporary Indian Philosophy**; The Muirhead Library of Philosophy. George Allen and Unwin Ltd., London, 1952.

Radhakrishnan, S. and Moore Charles, A. (Ed.). : **A Soruce Book in Indian Philosophy**; Princeton University Press, 1957.

Radhakrishnan, S. and Raju, P.T. (Ed.). : **Concept of Man; A Study on Comparative Philosophy**; George Allen and Unwin Ltd., London, 1960.

Rajgopalchari, C. : **Gandhi's Teachinings and Philosophy**; Bhawan, 1967.

Raju, P.T. : **The idealistic Thought of India**; George Allen and Unwin Ltd., London, 1953.

Raju, P.T. and Others (Ed.). : **Contemporary Studies in Philosophy**; George Allen and Unwin Ltd., London, 1951.

Kamji, Dr. Marni Tata. : **The Concept of Personality in the Educatinal thought of Mahatma Gandhi**; NCERT, New Delhi, 1969.

Rao, P. Nagaraja. : **Contemporary Indian Philosophy**; Bharatiya Vidya Bhavan, Bombay, 1970.

Ray, Benay Gopal. : **Contemporary Indian Philosophers**; Kitalistan, Allahabad, 1957.

— : **Gandhian Ethics**; Navajivan Publishing House, Ahamadabad, 1958.

Reddy, V. Madhusudan. : **Sri Aurobindo's Philosophy of Evolution**; Institute of Human Study, Hyderabad, 1966.

Rishabhchand. : **Sri Aurobindo – His Life Unique**; Sri Aurobindo Ashram Press; Pondicherry, 1981.

Rolland, Romain. : **Mahatma Gandhi**; Publications Division, 1968.

Ronald Duncan. (Ed.). : **The Writings of Gandhi**; Oxford University Press, 1983.

Roy, Anil Baran. : **The World Crisis**; (Sri Aurobindo Vision of the Future) George Allen and Unwin Ltd., London, 1977.

Roy, Dilip Kumar Roy. : **Among the Great**; All India Books, Pondicherry, 1984.

Roy, Dilip Kumar. : **Six Illuminates of Modern India**; Bharatiya Vidya Bhavan, Bombay, 1982.

Saiyidain, K.G. : **Significance of Gandhi as a Man & Thinker**; Publication Division, 1970.

Saroja, G.V. : **Tilak and Shankar on Bhagavad Gita**; Sterling, New Delhi, 1985.

Sarma, B.S. : **Gandhi, as a Political Thinker**; Allahabad Press, 1956.

Sarkar, Sumit. : **Modern India**; 1885 – 1947; MacMillan, 1985.

Sastry, T.V. Kapali. : **Collected Works**; Vol.I; Dipti Publications, Sri Aurobindo Ashram, Pondicherry, 1977.

Schilpp, P.A. (Ed.). : **The Philosophy of Sarvepalli Radhakrishnan**; Tudor Publishing Company, New York, 1952.

Seal, Anil. : **Emergence of Indian Nationalism**; Cambridge University Press, 1974.

Sharma, Arvind, (Comp.). : **New Essays in the Bhagavad Gita**; Books and Books, New Delhi, 1987.

Sharma, D.S. : **The Upanishads : An Anthology**; Bharatiya Vidya Bhavan, Bombay, 1964.

Sharma, R.N. : **The Philosophy of Sri Aurobindo**; Kedarnath Rama Nath, Meerut, 1977.

Sheean, Vincent. : **Mahatma Gandhi, A Great Life in Brief**; Publication Division, New Delhi, 1982.

Shridharani, Krishnalal. : **The Mahatma and the World**; John Day Company, New York, 1939.

Shukla, C.S. : **Gandhiji as We Know Him**; Vohra and Co. Bombay, 1949.

Singhal, D.P. : **India & World Civilization**; Vol.I; Rupa & Co. Delhi, 1972.

Singh, Savannah. (Ed.). : **S. Radhakrishnan**; (Commemoration Volume), Leader Press, Allahabad, 1953.

Singh, Yogendra. : **Modernisation of Indian Tradition**; Thomson Press (India) Ltd., Faridabad, 1977.

Sinha, M.P. : **Contemporary Relevance of Gandhi**; Nachiketa Publication, Bombay, 1970.

Sircar, D.C. : **Studies in the Religions Life of Ancient and Medieval India**; Motilal Banarasi Dass, New Delhi, 1971.

Sitaramaya, B. Pattabhi. : **Gandhi & Gandhism** Vol.I & II; Kitabistan, Allahabad, 1943.

Sri Auro bindo, Complete works published as : **Sri Aurobindo's Birth Centenary Library** (S.A.B.C.L.) in 30 Volumes; Sri Aurobindo Ashram, Pondicherry, 1972.

Works of Sri Aurobindo published as **Sri Aurobindo International Center of Education Collection**; (S.A.I.C.E.) Sri Aurobindo Ashram, Pondicheery, 1959.

Srivastava, R.S. : **Sri Aurobindo and the Thesis of Evalution**; Chowkhamba Sanskrit Series Office, Varanasi, 1968.

Tagore, R.N. : **Mahatma Gandhi**; Viswabharati, 1963.

Tendulkar, D.G. : **Gandhiji – His Life and Work**; Karnataka Ptg, Bombay, 1944.

– : **Mahatma – The Life of Mohandas Karam Chand Gandhi**; Vithalbhai Jhaveai – (8 volumes), Bombay, 1951.

Tripathy, Amales. : **The Extremist Challenge**; Orient Longman, 1967.

Underwood, A.C. : **Contemporary Thought of India**; Williams and Norgats Ltd., London, 1930.

Verma, V.P. : **Political Philosophy of Mahatma Gandhi and Sarvodaya**; Lakshmi Narayan Agarwal, Agra, Modern Indian Political Thought, Lakshmi Narayan Agarwal, Agra, 1980.

Vivekananda, Swami. : **The Complete Works** (in ten volumes) Vol. I; Mayavati Memorial edition – Advaita Ashrama, Calcutta, 1989.

V.T. Patil, (Ed.) : **Studies on Gandhi**; Sterling Publishers Private Ltd., New Delhi, 1989.

JOURNALS

Bhattacharya, P.K. (Ed.). : **The Bulletin of Sri Aurobindo Intenational Center of Education**; Sri Aurobindo Ashram, Pondicherry.

Parekh, Jayantilal, (Ed.). : **Journal of Sri Aurobindo Archieves and Research**; Sri Aurobindo Ashram, Pondicherry, (Relevant Issues).

Pandit, M.P, (Ed.). : **The Advent**; Sri Aurobindo Ashram, Pondicherry, (Relevant Issues).

Rangarajan, S. (Ed.). : **The Call Beyond**; Sri Aurobindo Ashram, Delhi Branch, Delhi, (Relevant Issues).

Ray, Dr. B.C. (Ed.). : **Journal of Historical and Social Analysis**; Bhubaneswar, (Relevant Issues).

Sethna, K.D. (Ed.) : **The Mother India**; Sri Aurobindo Ashram, **Pondicherry**; (Relevant Issues).

Swami, Krishnananda, (Ed.). : **An Apostle of Indians Spiritual Culture**; (Souvenir), Divine Life Society Publication, Sivananda Nagar. 1976, (Relevant Issues).

INDEX

C

D

E

F

G

G

I

J

K

Q

R

S

T

U

V

W

Y

Z

• • •